Laurence Sterne
in the Twentieth Century

LAURENCE STERNE

in the Twentieth Century

An Essay and a Bibliography
of Sternean Studies
1900-1965

by

LODWICK HARTLEY

The University of North Carolina Press · *Chapel Hill*

Preface

The present annotated list of studies is designed to do for Sterne what Louis A. Landa and James Edwin Tobin's *Jonathan Swift: A List of Critical Studies Published from 1895 to 1945*, James L. Clifford's *Johnsonian Studies*, Anthony E. Brown's *Boswellian Studies*, and my own *William Cowper: The Continuing Revaluation* have attempted for their respective subjects. I have borrowed a title from an article by the late Professor Wilbur L. Cross that appeared in the *Yale Review* in 1926 on the simple theory that its relevance has increased over the four decades since it was first used. My other borrowings through the years from the most important twentieth-century authority on Sterne have been more significant and extensive.

Since my own interest in the subject has ranged over more than a quarter of a century, my list is the result of accumulation and accretion. This fact, of course, lends it no particular virtue. It merely argues that the habit has been persistent.

When Henri Fluchère's exhaustive study of the biography and of *Tristram Shandy* appeared in 1961, I was inclined to feel that the publication of my own list had been rendered unnecessary by the lengthy and remarkably detailed bibliography for the whole range of Sterne scholarship that is appended to the volume. An attempt to use this significant tool, however, convinced me that it was often unwieldy and confusing and that a better organized and more discriminating list for twentieth-century studies could still perform a valuable service, especially for the student who had not yet become thoroughly familiar with the field and toward whom a book of this sort should chiefly be directed. Moreover, I felt that important additions could be made and even that a salutary weeding-out process could be performed.

In the main, I have followed the format of other similar works in the field—most specifically in the use of consecutively numbered references with the inclusion of cross-references whenever they seemed necessary or desirable. If some confusion exists in M. Fluchère's bibliography, my own has not entirely escaped the same fault. The matter of classification has many times been vexing. Because there has been a persistent tendency for scholars and critics to write about all aspects of Sterne at once, especially in the mixing of biography and criticism, the keeping of strict categories for many items has been well nigh impossible. I have hoped, however, to escape some of the inconsistencies by cross references and ultimately by an index so that items of a mixed nature arbitrarily assigned to one category might not be lost to a searcher looking for them in another. For some items I have resorted to multiple listings.

My departure from the usual format has been, as it was in the Cowper volume, in extensive annotation, which I have intended to indicate significantly and economically the contents of the items included or the tenor of opinion expressed in them. To do the latter I have at times resorted to direct quotation—especially when the material in the item listed is so general as to make only a particular point of view significant. For books I have indicated what I have considered to be the most important reviews, sometimes double-listing such reviews or at least cross-referencing them when in themselves they have virtually constituted an independent critical contribution. Here, as elsewhere, I make no boast that I have been entirely consistent.

In addition to providing a practical and clear guide to the studies included, the intent of the annotation is to achieve a readable record of the scholarship, as well as of the tides of opinion and taste in regard to the subject. From this point of view, an introductory essay is rendered less necessary than it might otherwise be. I have elected, nevertheless, to write such an essay, not principally to summarize the individual items (though in some instances I have found it necessary to do so at some length and at the risk of some repetition), but rather to provide a setting for the scholarship reflected in the annotated list and to suggest in narrative form the development and the changes in critical opinion. Again, this effort is directed toward the reader who is less familiar with the field than the specialist would certainly be. If important scholars and significant studies go unmentioned, they are, I hope, properly and adequately noticed in the bibliography.

I have appended a "Chapter of Conclusions" in a lighter vein not because I wish to discount the proliferation of serious and frequently brilliant efforts to understand Sterne but because finally one must believe (to paraphrase T. S. Eliot's remark about poetry) that he can be enjoyed before he is understood. After all, the best and wisest conclusion about biographical and critical studies of Sterne is that there should be no conclusion.

Since orthodox footnoting of the introductory essay would have entailed a double system of annotation that might have caused more confusion than enlightenment, I have simply referred by superscript numbers to items appearing in the attached bibliography. Other sources are indicated as plainly as possible without resort to further apparatus.

In any attempt of this sort, the people to whom one is indebted are too numerous to catalogue in a limited space. I am especially grateful to a number of long-suffering colleagues and to several important Sternean scholars whose contributions are, I hope, adequately noticed.

Lodwick Hartley
North Carolina State University

Preface to the Second Printing

―――――――――

"It is too much to write books and find heads to understand them," Sterne wrote only a few weeks before his death on March 18, 1768. On the bicentenary of this untimely event, the author's plaintiveness is likely to sound charmingly quaint. Certainly, if this little volume proves anything, it is that the number of "heads" engaged in understanding Sterne has increased at an astonishing, if not a frightening, rate. Indeed, interest in the novelist and enthusiasm for reinterpreting him to a new age have never seemed higher.

In the year and a half since the first printing of this volume, so many books, dissertations, articles, and notes have appeared that a reprinting could scarcely dare to omit taking note of them—especially since they reflect so well the temper and climate of Sternean scholarship at the bicentenary. As early as 1936 Dame Una Pope-Hennessy remarked that "in America Sterne has been taken seriously." Although the assumption that the British regarded him otherwise or that they have not contributed enthusiastically and importantly to the understanding of him would have no validity now (if, indeed, it ever did), the activity of American scholars might still seem to a British observer as something only a little short of frenetic. So widespread has been the interest in American universities that hardly a major institution has failed either to turn out a dissertation on Sterne in the past two decades or to have one presently in progress. A number of these have been published either as monographs or as articles, single or multiple.

In an addenda I have attempted to include as many as possible of the recently published and abstracted items—together, of course, with a few earlier ones inadvertently omitted from the original printing.

Aside from adding items, I have made as careful a revision as possible in the direction of correcting errors. For aid in this essential undertaking I want to thank a number of friends and reviewers, including Professors Hilbert H. Campbell, Hans G. Heymann, William V. Holtz, and William Bowman Piper. I am further grateful for the editorial assistance of The University of North Carolina Press and also for that of my colleague, Professor John Easley, and of departmental secretaries, especially Mrs. Kathryn Hardee and Mrs. Sylvia Gurkin.

Lodwick Hartley
Raleigh, North Carolina
18 March 1968

Contents

Sterne's Life and Works

I

The Biographical Problems
and
Twentieth-Century Biographers

_____

If Laurence Sterne presents more than an ordinary problem to biographers, the reason is inherent in the nature both of the man and his work. Like many another humorist and wit, he created for himself a role that not only obscured the facts of his life to his own time and after, but also stimulated the extension of the fiction by myth-makers ever on the lookout for a peg on which to hang a story.

The urge to interpret, often in lieu of other biographical functions, is a constant in biographical writing. But the limits of interpretation can naturally be more confidently defined in subjects for whom ample factual documentation is accessible and reliable than when the evidence is scantier. Among Sterne's contemporaries, Samuel Richardson and Henry Fielding offer relatively little difficulty. Unlike them, Sterne had to wait for almost a century before a genuine approach could be made toward sorting out the legend from the actuality; and the job has not yet been—nor is it likely to be—completely achieved.

Traditionally, the biographer has found that he has in a sense had to take into account not one but several Sternes. First, there is the objective Sterne—"the man, Sterne" (in Dr. Johnson's blunt phrase), as he was known to his contempo-

raries and as this knowledge can be documented in opinion
and comment. Then there is—and far more elusive, of course
—the "subjective" Sterne who permeates or seems to permeate
Tristram Shandy, A Sentimental Journey, the *Sermons*, and the
Journal to Eliza. Naturally, these two Sternes are not the same,
and yet they are so intricately involved as often to seem so.
To complicate rather than to clarify the picture, there is also
the Sterne of the letters, which thanks to the criminal prudence
of the Reverend John Botham who burned many of them, and
the unscrupulousness of Lydia Sterne, who mutilated them by
her editing, will never provide completely reliable evidence.
And then there is finally the Sterne of the local and other
legends—an unclerical figure, indeed, who is openly disliked
by his parishioners, who argues with his ecclesiastical uncle
over a favorite mistress, who is caught by his wife while he
is in bed with a maid, who delays on his way to church in
order to shoot birds, and so on. The task of extracting the
"real" Sterne is not entirely dissimilar to one of the better
known labors of Heracles.

It should, therefore, not be surprising that although the
factual basis for the writing of Sterne's biography is now somewhat more reliable than it ever has been—thanks largely to Professor Wilbur L. Cross—the real contribution of twentieth-
century scholarship after the first three decades resides in a
change of attitude toward the man resulting from a new understanding of his nature and purpose as evidenced in his literary
product rather than from the discovery of any large amount of
new material.

It may be that the most significant biography of Sterne is
one that was never written. This was the projected work by
the politician, rake, and libertarian, John Wilkes—who was re-
quested to undertake it by Mrs. Sterne in conjunction with her
daughter, Lydia, and who was to be assisted both by Lydia,
with the responsibility of providing her father's correspondence
and some original drawings for the work, and by Sterne's eccentric friend, John Hall-Stevenson. Saintsbury has remarked
on the "refusal" of Wilkes and Hall-Stevenson to go ahead

with the task: ". . . they knew, better than anybody, the matter with which they would have to deal; and they knew as well as anybody, that their hands would scarcely be likely to make any handling of it the better for his memory in the public eye." The best that can be said for the scheme is that it was "Shandaic." It was doubtless fortunate that the project was not pursued; but the bad auguries that the idea invoked, in spite of its never having been implemented, were to haunt Sterne biography for some time to come. Lydia's independent issuance in 1775 of the hodge-podge *Letters of the Late Reverend Laurence Sterne*, together with (among other things) Sterne's own *Memoirs of His Life and Family*, began the incredible botching of the evidence that even the best of contemporary scholarship has not been able to untangle.

The late Professor Cross has told the story of subsequent biographical attempts ably and interestingly both in his introduction to his edition of the *Life* of Percy Fitzgerald[216] and in the introductions to the three editions of his own *Life and Times.*[211] Other material has been provided by Alan B. Howes in *Yorick and the Critics.*[803] Only the most important details need be repeated here.

In brief, anything like adequate biographical treatment had to wait until after the middle of the nineteenth century when the Reverend Whitwell Elwin competently and judicially summarized all that was known about Sterne in the *London Quarterly Review* for April, 1854.[335]

It is true that Sir Walter Scott had written a "prefatory memoir" for the Ballantyne edition of Sterne's works in 1823,[1003] but this account is notable more for its brilliant play on the paradox of the great plagiarist who was at the same time a great original genius than it was for substantive biographical material. Moreover, the French scholar, Charles Athanase Walckenaer, had made a far more scholarly attempt to reconstruct from primary materials an account of Sterne for the *Biographie Universelle* of 1825.[1006] In spite of these two treatments, however, by 1840 it could have seemed that Dr. Johnson's pronouncement, "Nothing odd will do long," had been justified; for at this time Isaac D'Israeli observed that of the three humorists once marked for immortality only "Cervantes is immortal—Rabelais and Sterne have passed away to the curious." (Yet even while he was making this statement, D'Israeli was contributing to the resuscitation of Sterne by printing five unpublished letters of the novelist to Kitty Fourmantelle).

If Thackeray's famous or infamous lecture of 1851 based (understandably but egregiously) on faulty information and published in *The English Humorists* in 1853 was designed to bury Sterne, its effect was actually to galvanize him and in time, though its effects were deleterious enough to Sterne, to become far more damaging to the reputation of the lecturer than to that of his target.[1004] Other than Elwin's almost immediate effort to put facts in their proper relationship and light, the lecture stimulated the youthful Percy Fitzgerald to a defense in a pioneering biography of a decade later. New letters and other materials had fallen into Fitzgerald's hands. All these he used to counter the image of the old "scamp" glibly sketched by Thackeray. So enthusiastically did he pursue the defense that he seemed, at least to some, to have overstated the case. "In consequence of [his] strongly reactionary attitude," Professor Cross remarked, "he slipped easily over difficult passages in Sterne's life, excusing weaknesses and vices and insisting upon virtues." And, the commentator continues, subsequent biographers like Bagehot, Gosse, Traill, and Sherer, as well as others, "but repeated him in the main." In this group, however, cannot be included Sir Sidney Lee, whose independent scholarship makes his account of Sterne in the *Dictionary of National Biography* of 1885-1891 (and subsequent reprintings) one of the most reliable and respectable of nineteenth-century biographical essays.[230]

Before Fitzgerald brought out his revised edition in 1896, he had been able to see the manuscript of the *Journal to Eliza* in the possession of Thomas Washbourne Gibbs at Bath. This new material brought about a revision of the portrait of Sterne that left him somewhat less than the "sainthood" to which (in the opinion of Cross) Fitzgerald had headed him. But even the new edition was "a long, bad book," falling far short of what a genuinely scholarly biography should be.

Of this fact Cross was fully cognizant when he reprinted the biography in 1904 with a significant preface listing the shortcomings of Fitzgerald and with equally important annotations of the text in correction of numerous errors in fact and in inference. The reprinting of what now seems to be an amateurish biographical effort would not have been an auspicious introduction of Sterne to the twentieth century had not the editorial work of Cross inspired him to a biography of his own, containing much new material and employing notably sound methods to achieve what in successive editions in 1909, 1925, and 1929 has become—though with shortcomings that have for some time needed amendment—the standard and the indispensable biography.

The 1909 edition, at the outset a major achievement and widely recognized as such, was followed closely in England by two other biographies: one by Walter Sichel in 1910[253] and another by Lewis Melville in 1911.[232] Unfortunately, in the light of the earlier biography, both are negligible. Sichel, it is true, modestly calls his book a "study" rather than a biography; and his pleasant style and his occasionally perceptive comments keep his work from being completely valueless. Melville, relying on copious quotations from the letters to do his work for him and often somewhat ostentatiously displaying his background research, is scarcely more successful.

Apart from Cross, in fact, Sterne's twentieth-century biographers have chiefly been interpreters, relying on materials already accessible and seeking new clues mainly in what Sterne wrote. The latter procedure is plainly not new, for it had been a necessary part of all the previous biographical effort. Because of the enigma of Sterne himself, the challenge has always been intriguing, even when the results of attempts to meet it have not been wholly acceptable or admirable.

It should be expected that Sterne could not escape the kind of psychoanalysis popularized by Freud in the twenties and

the thirties. In 1925, Dr. Arie de Froe[342] tested out his subject
according to the several instincts that he called the "dynamic
forces of the soul," finding the instinct of sex to be strong and
that of "escape" to be weak. The study uses the evidence of
the novels as well as of biographical data; but the biographical
sources are unfortunately not the best. Sterne's "sex complex"
De Froe considered to be "perverse," since the subject never
seemed to progress beyond "the courtship stage" in his relationship with women and since he seemed not to have indulged
in the sex act after the first years of his unhappy marriage,
thereafter giving it up as unsatisfactory. On the imaginative
plane, however, Sterne was found to show an extraordinary
obsession with sexuality, manifesting itself in the phallic symbols and the obscene jests of the novels. The conclusion is
that Sterne's life was "the tragedy of a Human Soul" impris-
oned or fettered by sexual cravings and struggling to get free,
at the same time lamenting from the depths of the "Unconscious Self," like the famous starling in *A Sentimental Journey,*
"I can't get out, I can't get out."

Belonging as it does to a mid-region between biography
and criticism, De Froe's study has been handled gingerly by
most scholars. Watkins found in it chiefly "Teutonic obfusca-
tion" and Cazamian complained that the final result was an
emptiness caused by the attempt to fit too laboriously all the
materials into the professional psychological framework suggested by McDougall's *Outline of Psychology.* Other dissenting opinions are recorded in the bibliography following.

The relatively short and "popular" biographies (also com-
bining interpretation and literary criticism in varying degrees)
have developed out of another kind of impulse. Because Sterne
has been a source of spontaneous delight, there has been a
feeling that something of his appeal is lost when his story is
told in two volumes of sober fact and analysis (as some of
the British reviewers remarked about the Cross biography).
The defense of such biographical studies as those of Hartley,[223]
Quennell,[245] and Yoseloff[264] is that they attempt to reduce the
materials to the normal demands and interests of the lay reader

rather than to those of the scholar—the latter of whom will understandably be satisfied only with the patient accumulation of facts and the careful weighing of evidence that can be achieved best in the long biography and who will usually reject out of hand any attempt to treat the subject with anything short of complete seriousness.

Though it is not an independent biographical treatment, James A. Work's biographical introduction to his edition of *Tristram Shandy*[142] is one of the most useful of the summaries. It deserves mention for this reason.

Since 1925 new materials have turned up infrequently. Only rarely have works appeared like Professor Lewis Perry Curtis's *The Politicks of Laurence Sterne* (1929), illuminating a segment of the subject's life with significant additions of primary materials.[213] Canon Ollard's discovery of relevant information in the visitation reports of two archbishops of York has been important in providing first-hand comment on Sterne's activities as a parish priest, especially since the evidence tends to counter gossip concerning his casual attitude toward his duties.[238] On the other hand, Professor James M. Kuist in 1964 discovered in the British Museum a document that tends to support this gossip and to add other stories about Sterne's amorous pursuits as a young Yorkshire vicar—the latter tending to contradict the assumption of De Froe and others about the limitations of his sexuality. The document in question is a brief series of notes made by Joseph Hunter, the nineteenth-century antiquarian and literary historian, from conversations around 1807 with Richard Greenwood, a seventy-nine-year-old Yorkshireman who maintained that he had been a servant in the household of the Sternes at Sutton on the Forest for three years prior to 1745.[227] Though the account as recorded tends to counter at several points the well-known testimony of John Croft in *The Whitefoord Papers*, in the main it strengthens Croft's allegations about Sterne's incontinence. New factual details are suggested, the most interesting of which is the possibility of the birth and death in infancy of a male child hitherto unmentioned.

Even in the absence of significant new sources, it has been possible—as we have already seen—to take a new tack or to make a new attack. Since the mid-century such an effort has been made on a major scale by Miss Margaret R. B. Shaw— long a vigorous and controversial member of the community of Sterne scholarship. Her *Laurence Sterne: The Making of a Humorist, 1713-1762*, published in 1957, was announced as a study "of the different forces that went into the making of [Sterne's] humour."[252] In her treatment of such forces, Miss Shaw has continued an attack on many of the inferences and assumptions of outstanding American scholars like Cross and Curtis that she began a generation ago in reviews and letters to the *Times Literary Supplement*, at the same time elaborating on her own theories about the authenticity of primary materials such as journals and letters. A second volume is promised.

Another kind of limited biographical study is that of Willard Connely in *Laurence Sterne as Yorick* (1958).[208] Taking up just a little before Miss Shaw's volume leaves off, Connely is interested only in the last nine years of his subject's life—the "writing years." Observing that the intimates of Swift and Pope were the leading literary lights of their own time, the biographer points out that Sterne was not befriended by his writing contemporaries in England. (Garrick was no exception, since the doors that he opened for Sterne in London were not actually literary doors.) His literary friendships were made in Paris. In London it was left to Sterne himself—"tireless, undeviating, unabashed"—to proclaim the great merits of his own works and conduct his own "public relations." With such a thesis, the biographer presents mainly the novelist's social life in England and France with richly detailed background material. The contribution of Connely's readable study is one of emphasis rather than of novelty.

In a multipurpose volume published in Paris in 1961, Henri Fluchère, as the result of a long devotion to the subject and as a labor of love, has intelligently summed up the whole body of accumulated biographical evidence and has made a conscientious examination of many of the problems—notably those relating to the evidence of the correspondence.[218] In so doing, he has effectually bridged the gap between the final edition of the biography by Cross and the subsequent scholarship. For its suggestions and insights, as well as for its careful and balanced review of existing materials, it is of value.

Work toward a new biographical treatment is now being undertaken by Professor Arthur Hill Cash, whose recent discovery of some minor unpublished letters is recorded elsewhere.[701]

II

Tristram Shandy
and the Critics

For reasons that should already be apparent, one does not easily abandon the discussion of biography when one moves to the literary production of the subject, though the most recent attitude toward Sterne is inclined to insist that, at least in order to arrive at any new and fruitful evaluation of the works, a dichotomy must be made.

There can be little argument that *Tristram Shandy* is one of the most important eighteenth-century English novels, as well as one of the most fascinating ones. Yet it was in Sterne's own day and has continued to be "more read than understood." Because from its seemingly eccentric and chaotic structure it has not been easy to comprehend and because it is not suited to every taste, its appeal has never been universal. Stuart P. Sherman once remarked, with truth finally sacrificed for a witticism, that "Sterne is not an author for all times or for all ages or for all sorts of people. He is for those who are ripe and perhaps on the verge of being overripe."[412]

When the first volumes appeared in 1760, Horace Walpole asserted promptly that the novel was "a very insipid and tedious performance." Richardson thought that it contained more to blame than to praise. Dr. Johnson refused to consider it dull, but he did think that it was immoral. These opinions were to be repeated in different forms throughout the rest of the eighteenth century, through the nineteenth century, and even into the twentieth. In a literary history of 1902, the German scholar Edward Engel remarked: ". . . we read . . . a good deal of [*Tristram Shandy*] with increasing impatience."[336] In the 1920's when Professor Cross at Yale was still engaged in contributing significantly to Sternean scholarship, a colleague, William Lyon Phelps, could assert that he found the book 'infernally dull'"[386] —a statement that spurred the famous bibliophile A. Edward Newton to a spirited rejoinder.[579] Peter Quennell, one of the most competent of the popular biographers, has given his own opinion that *Tristram Shandy* "taken as a whole, is probably one of the least readable of works to which critics of the past have decided to allot an important place on our bookshelves."[245] Elizabeth Drew in a recent textbook on the novel (1963) warns that the modern reader is "in for a good deal of tedium" in a work in which the author's stories tend to be overlong and coarse without being very funny. "Many of his double meanings are obsolete," she observes, "and a pun that must be explained in a footnote ceases to amuse."[533]

Nevertheless, one can still find critics who enjoy *Tristram Shandy,* as it has always been enjoyed, for its purely spontaneous qualities: its surprising wit, its seemingly naive sentimentality, its gay disorder. The novelist Elizabeth Bowen, for example, has expressed the enthusiasm for such qualities that even the most sophisticated reader can develop. "*Tristram Shandy,*" she writes, "is dementedly natural in its course; surrealist in its association of images. One does not attempt to 'follow' [it]; one consigns oneself, dizzily, to it."[516] And Thomas Wolfe (in a letter to F. Scott Fitzgerald on July 26, 1927) thought it "indubitably a great book . . . because it *boils* and *pours*" and because of "the *unselected* quality of its selection."[618]

The literary reputation of the novel and its critical history have not been neglected. The author of the leading article in the *Times Literary Supplement* for April 9, 1949, has suggested that it appeared in a "period of interregnum for the novel," pointing out that, though *Rasselas* had come out the year be-

fore, in 1760 *Pamela* had been on the bookstalls for twenty
years and *Tom Jones* for eleven. It was five years before *The
Castle of Otranto* and six before *The Vicar of Wakefield.*
"*Tristram Shandy* was the pride and discovery of the penetrating, then it was a rage, then a vogue and at last it settled
down to being a best seller." Though this last kind of generalization may not be adequate at all points—particularly in failing
to take into account the fact that not all the volumes were
equally popular—it is nevertheless accurate enough in the main.

There were at the outset, of course, baffled readers, bored
readers, and indignant readers; but, as Sterne himself observed,
even those who condemned the book bought it—and that was
what was important to the author. Professor Howes has suggested that the breadth of its popularity was in no small measure attributable to the fact that Sterne had given the book
many "handles" and that it ultimately fascinated more than it
merely puzzled.[803]

Its virtues and its vices, its beauties and its blemishes, as
distinguished by Sterne's contemporaries, became the commonplaces of future criticism. Its virtues included, of course, its
wit, its good humor, its good sense, its "just satire." Among
its vices were its "indecency," its chaotic structure, its typographical tricks. These qualities, superficially abstracted, became the stock in trade of numerous imitators and forgers
(chief among whom were William Combe, John Hall-Stevenson, and Richard Griffith) who flourished from the seventeen
sixties through the eighties.

Reaction that led to the condemnation of Sterne as a plagiarist and otherwise an immoralist began setting in toward the
end of the century, after Ferriar's publication of his work on
Sterne's literary borrowing and with the rise of Evangelicalism
as a popular religious movement.

In the main, the major figures of the Romantic period
treated Sterne favorably. Though Scott was not unaware of certain weaknesses, his general treatment of the novelist was
sympathetic.[1003] Hazlitt recognized as one of Sterne's great
gifts his conversational style—the kind a writer in one of the

great periods of the familiar essay might well admire.[1001] Coleridge, under the general Romantic doctrine that genius is its own law, properly regarded the "digressive spirit" of *Tristram Shandy* as in itself a kind of form.[1000] De Quincey and Carlyle were pleased with the blending of the pathetic and the comic; and Charles Lamb readily accepted Sterne as a classic.

The "loud angry noise" of dissent did not come until the mid-century. It may, indeed, have been loud "because [the critics] could not ignore Sterne, angry because they could not reconcile his talents with his morals."[350] This dilemma, plainly precipitated by Thackeray and corroborated by such important voices as those of Charlotte Brontë and Anthony Trollope, became so persistent that Dr. Saintsbury could remark as late as 1912: "It has become a commonplace and almost a necessity to make up for praising Sterne's genius by damning his character."[135] If Thackeray, as it has been seen, had had his opinion effectively challenged well before the end of the century, the stigma nevertheless remained for Sterne.

It may not be entirely accurate to say that the Bloomsbury writers promoted the first significant counter-reaction of the twentieth century—though Dr. F. R. Leavis and others have tended to give Virginia Woolf and E. M. Forster credit or discredit for much of it. But undoubtedly the weight of the new opinion of Sterne in such an important group should not be discounted.

In general, in the early decades of the twentieth century critical opinion as it is found in literary journals and in literary histories offers (with a few notable exceptions) little more than a wearisome repetition of what had been said for more than a century. Sir Herbert Read was right when he complained in 1927 that most Sternean comment was "lacking in interest or freshness."[399]

The generalizations applied to Sterne are too varied to be fully summarized, but it is obvious that he was frequently treated as a "wit and artist" but no moralist, a "fantastic sentimentalist and a disingenuous idealist," an ethical heretic with an equal amount of heresy in another direction—for had he not "destroyed" the "novel form"?

In C. E. Vaughan's article on Sterne in the *Cambridge History of English Literature* in 1913, the charges of "pruriency" and "insincerity" were still current.[425] In 1924 and 1925 reprints, Sir Arthur Quiller-Couch's 1896 essay on Sterne still had a wide audience. The noted critic, though admitting that Sterne is worth listening to without prejudice, nevertheless thought him "indecent" and "a convicted thief" [*i.e.*, plagiarist].[396] And in 1925 Stephen Gwynn continued to echo the lecture of Thackeray in his statement that "pruriency pervades everything," even though Gwynn was willing to admit (somewhat illogically though it may be) that Sterne offends against taste rather than against morals.[349] The fledgling critic Cyril Connolly, writing a review-essay in 1927 (reprinted in 1945), charged that Sterne's "habit of luxuriating in emotion" turned his "sympathy to self-congratulation" and set "a smirk on all his tenderness," constituting the "terrible flaw" tainting the finest of Sterne's effects and causing the word "sentimental" to lose caste early. "It is that latent insincerity," Connolly continued in what should now be detected as a familiar vein, ". . . that has . . . turned nearly every biographer into an apologist."[319] Dr. Leavis's sharp footnote of 1948[362] charging "irresponsible (and nasty) trifling" should be evidence enough of the persistence of the kind of subjective reaction that Sterne had long elicited.

The avoidance of the "monolithic" view of Sterne—that is, of the assumption that the writer and the book are one and the same—has only within the past few decades been regarded as a requisite for any new and rewarding study of the works. In concluding the introduction to his edition of *Tristram Shandy* in 1940, Professor James A. Work stated what has long been the standard opinion: ". . . the book and [Sterne] are indivisible, indistinguishable."[142] In a review published in 1949,[329] Professor Wayne C. Booth expressed what might be considered the manifesto of the new attitude as follows: "*Tristram Shandy* begins to be comprehensible as a whole only when one accepts, without reservations related to Sterne's biography, that it is essentially a kind of 'dramatic' comedy and that the key to it is not Sterne but Tristram."

Whatever the resolution of the problem of these two extremes may be, in the mid-century critics have felt increasingly less necessity for the defense of Sterne's "character." In the introduction to an edition of *A Sentimental Journey* in 1928, Virginia Woolf pointed out that if her own period objected to Sterne it was on the basis of his sentimentality rather than his immorality.[159] And in the introduction to his edition of the *Letters* in 1935, Professor Lewis Perry Curtis remarked (actually giving new emphasis to what Elwin had at least partially suggested almost a century before) that Sterne's faults "once set down to the score of wickedness seem now little more than foibles."[177]

The strongest evidence of an important change in attitude, however, had been expressed in Sir Herbert Read's leading article in the *Times Literary Supplement* in 1927 (later republished in *The Sense of Glory*).[399] Sir Herbert's objective was to meet squarely the charges of impiety and lack of moral seriousness like that of Walter Bagehot, who in a review written in 1864 had summed up a widespread feeling that, though Sterne went into the church, his sermons contained "not a single Christian sentiment." Just before Sir Herbert wrote his essay, De Froe had concluded that Sterne had no religion and no God. Sir Leslie Stephen had not only allowed him no positive merits of character but also no moral, political, or philosophical interests. Saintsbury could find no real greatness in him as a humorist. And even Professor Cross had regarded him as incapable of "moods of high seriousness," calling him a "humorist pure and simple, and nothing else."

Countering in a measure all of these positions, Sir Herbert argued that "[Sterne] was in reality a writer with a purpose, a moral preceptor, a subtle intelligence that masked beneath his humor and licentiousness the kindly philanthropy of his age—the age of Shaftesbury and Hutcheson." In the sermon called "The Abuses of Conscience" (inserted in *Tristram Shandy*) he arrived at a definition of conscience as moral sensibility, achieving something like a virtuoso identification of the Good and the Beautiful. He received the foundation of his "originality" (as he himself told Suard) by daily reading in the Old Testament and the constant study of Locke. And his "sentimentality" (a favorite subject of attack since Thackeray had pictured him as perpetually "blubbering" in his study) was an outgrowth of Locke's theory of knowledge as a product of sensation and reflection and, therefore, should not be too quickly related to the degenerated modern definition of the word as denoting "extreme stages of emotional deliquescence." Although there might be passages in Sterne's two novels that could be regarded as sentimental in the modern sense of the word, Sterne saved himself "either by a perfect control of expression . . . or, more remarkably, by a sudden humorous recovery."

A more thoroughgoing and, ultimately, a sounder defense of Sterne is that of Walter B. C. Watkins in *Perilous Balance* (1939).[259] Superficially, Watkins asserts, Sterne seems to share a great many things with Swift and Johnson—"his lifelong disease, his love of society, partly as an escape from melancholy, his devotion to la bagatelle, his dependence on women, his essential loneliness—without any of their power of personality, any of their hidden depths." It is the "hidden depths" that Watkins sets out to plumb in an author who "deliberately cultivated illusion and gaiety in order to fence against the evils of the world."

Serious thought, the argument runs, should not be denied to the gay optimism of *Tristram Shandy* because it is more easily apparent in the bitter pessimism of *Gulliver's Travels*. Watkins follows Read in emphasizing Sterne's belief in the innate goodness of man, his conviction that the principal spirit of the universe is joy, and his purpose of brotherly love and benevolence. But the intention is rather to demonstrate that Sterne's intellectual worth has been undervalued than to make him out a moralist.

Again going somewhat further than Read, Watkins finds in Locke the "real basis" for Sterne's religious belief—a belief founded rather on the evidence of God in the emotions and senses than on any rational proof of the Deity. Sterne, not infrequently splicing Locke and the Bible, we are told, "found the truth of Christian religion revealed not only in God's word, but in himself:"

O great SENSORIUM of the world! [runs an illustrative passage cited from *A Sentimental Journey*] which vibrates if a hair of our head but fall upon the ground, in the remotest desert of thy creation.

The defense of Sterne's sentimentality is based upon an argument that, though his novels are at times openly and incontestably sentimental, most of the sentimental passages even in *A Sentimental Journey* (where Mrs. Woolf has cast serious doubts on the sincere tenderness of the author's heart) are poised delicately between irony and seriousness. One must understand (says Watkins) Sterne's fascination for equivocation: the borderline between the comic and the serious, tears and laughter, the real and the fantastic. He is akin to Shakespeare, the critic continues, in his deep sympathy for human beings and his hatred of cruelty in any form and is completely incapable of the malignity of the Augustan wits. (Whether Dr. John Burton and the Bishop of Gloucester would have agreed with the latter contention is a reasonable question).

The remainder of the defense involves the intellectual basis of Sterne's art and labors valiantly to disprove any idea that an empty-headed sentimentalist or a mere "scrap-book mind" (Professor Work's phrase) could have produced *Tristram Shandy* and *A Sentimental Journey*. The "inventor" of the "stream of consciousness method" (an adaptation of an another idea from Locke) becomes in Watkins's opinion a psychological novelist of such stature as to make Richardson look "painfully amateurish:"

No other English novelist has ever portrayed with such delicate skill the very nerve centers of the brain and spinal cord, the raising or lowering of blood pressure, the instinctive muscular reaction to mental and emotional agitation—in short, the intimate relation and interaction between body and mind. And no one until Proust has equalled him.

The essay has an ingenious explanation of Sterne's treatment of time and an illuminating discussion of Sterne's exquisite mastery of the dramatic technique.

In conclusion, Watkins insists that there is too close an integration of Sterne's art and his beliefs to consider him merely an artist or a humorist, finding in him "elements of real tragedy and an underlying seriousness which explain the profundity of his greatest comedy."

Preceding Watkins by only a few years was a more intricate and a more highly specialized study, that of Rudolph Maack called *Laurence Sterne im Lichte Seiner Zeit* (1936).[368] This monograph takes full cognizance of Sterne's many references to the fine arts and to writers on aesthetics and philosophy; of the fact that his associations in England included people like Garrick and Reynolds and in France, some of the most important of the *philosophes*; and of the writer's own experience as painter and musician. Parallels are made between the acting style of Garrick and the literary style of Sterne, as well as parallels from the paintings, music, and ballet of the period that tend to show Sterne's method as a culmination of tendencies in all the arts toward sensibility, naturalness, and complexity of feeling and tone.

The matter of the relation between humor and sentiment is, unsurprisingly, found to be at the center of Sterne's art, the complexity of which is interpreted (as Professor Joseph Warren Beach suggests in his important review) in Hegelian dialectic. Antithetical terms or contradictories like ideal and real, heart and head, body and soul, freedom and constraint, great and small, comic and serious, irony and pathos are to be found throughout; and most of these are resolved in some term or effect that is a synthesis of the opposites. The numerous tensions existing between these terms find resolution finally in a kind of *je ne sais quoi* or "literary magic," humor being the background most often referred to as the basis of the reconcilement of contradictories.

The studies of Read, Watkins, and Maack may be regarded as landmarks; moreover they have been (to change the figure) significantly seminal. In their standing against existing opinion and their denial of long established commonplaces they are of first importance. Nevertheless, the most vigorous reinterpretation of Sterne has waited for the decades after 1940, in which a more serious effort has been made than ever before to isolate the literary product from the biography.

In a valuable summary of current trends,[376] Professor A. D. McKillop has pointed out that the most recent scholarship has moved in two directions: first, the analysis of Sterne's rhetoric, style, technique, and structure; and, second, the analysis of his relation to the intellectual traditions, current ethics, and popular philosophy of his age. Even apart from Read and Watkins, many of these directions had, of course, been suggested long before. In the first decade of the century, for example, Paul Elmer More had found in aspects of *Tristram Shandy* "a philosophy, a new and distinct vision of the meaning of life, which makes Sterne something larger than a mere novelist," and had accorded him an important place in the humanistic tradition of Rabelais and Cervantes.[379] Louis Cazamian's assertion in 1929[364] regarding Sterne's sentimentalism as "a new resource exploited by a severe and intellectual art" was followed by the opinion of Edwin Muir in a fine essay of 1931[381] presenting Sterne's "operation [as] the operation of pure style . . . a style that creates the world contained in [his novels]." These were in themselves seminal ideas, texts for further study. Quite plainly before 1940 there were competent and perceptive people who refused to take Sterne for a mere "fantasist" and who were willing to consider his art seriously apart from his character and his morality. However, detailed development of particular aspects of his style and manner are, admittedly, recent.

A basic critical difficulty, as Professor J. M. Stedmond has indicated, has all along been apparent in the struggle to find some satisfactory definition or *genre* for *Tristram Shandy*.[605] The various "handles" that Sterne had given the novel have provided not only various avenues to enjoyment of the work but also considerable range for the imaginations of literary historians and critics who have deemed it useful or necessary to categorize it. Among other things, it has been called "a Yorkshire epic" [Read],[593] a "bourgeois saga" [Foster],[340] a "picaresque of the intellect" [Whibley],[431] a "gigantic personal essay" [Stevenson],[418] "half novel, half essay . . . without unity of mood and exhibiting more caprice than plan" [Calder-Marshall],[523] "less novel than a sort of literary *revue*" [Osgood],[385] "less novel than a philosophical treatise or a lyric poem, rather a *mixtum compositum* of these and many other ingredients" [Dibelius],[532] Locke's essay "in a novelized form" [Cross],[322] "an idiosyncratic ode to an epoch which has just discovered reason, the machine and the infinite possibilities . . . of a man's worldly prospects" [Geismar],[545] an "anatomy" (that is, a kind of prose fiction traditionally known as the Menippean or Varonian satire) [Frye],[543] "a treatise on communication" [Traugott],[611] "a completed novel" (that is, not a fragment) [Booth],[512] "an exactly executed historical novel" [Baird].[502] Although these attempts at classification and definition have been set down more or less at random to indicate diversity rather than anything else, some kind of evolution may be suggested toward the tendency to regard the novel as a serious work possessing more unity than ordinarily meets the eye.

Structural studies of the novel have become so numerous, in fact, that whatever unwillingness twentieth-century readers may still have against accepting the idea of such closely knit structure as some scholars insist upon, they must at least concede that, in spite of his disclaimers of several sorts, Sterne had a reasonably firm idea of what he was doing, that he was not simply practicing a form of automatic writing, and that it is an oversimplification to insist that Sterne deliberately broke down the existing structure of the novel out of dissatisfaction with the work of his predecessors and contemporaries.

Professor Booth[513] has argued convincingly that, though a reader coming upon *Tristram Shandy* in the general milieu of Richardson and Fielding might naturally look upon it as being "strikingly new and revolutionary," it was actually well grounded in three established traditions: (1) the comic novel

(*Charlotte Summers, the Unfortunate Paris Girl* [c. 1750], for example, employing a dialogue between the "I" and a "Reader" with whom one can fairly easily identify but more often between the "I" and a "ridiculous, hypothetical reader" who is a comic character in the book); (2) the type of essay written by Montaigne, with the central character claiming "to paint himself," giving a running account of the writing as it is written and thus a picture of himself as a writer, and claiming that he writes what comes immediately into his mind; (3) the kind of satire that Swift and Arbuthnot had developed earlier in the eighteenth century. The relevance of the tradition of the "self-conscious" or "dramatic" narrator to the achievement of Sterne has been developed by Booth and others; and considerable attention has been given to Sterne's relationship to the mainstream of the humanistic tradition as it is found in Rabelais, Cervantes, and the great Elizabethans, as well as to the tradition of "learned wit" as it was apparent closer to Sterne's own time in the *Memoirs of Martinus Scriblerus, A Tale of a Tub*, and the *Peri Bathous*. Professor D. W. Jefferson has made a particular contribution in relating the major and more consistent elements of Sterne's comedy to this wit and has thus provided a broad unifying basis both for the form and content of *Tristram Shandy*.[562]

Sterne's own suggestion that he was writing not the usual kind of "history" found in antecedent and contemporary fiction but "a history-book of what passes in a man's own mind," together with his frequent allusions to Lockean psychology, has made the relationship of Locke and Sterne of persistent interest—though the earliest readers of the novelist, as Professor Howes has observed, curiously chose not to notice it. The statement of Cross that *Tristram Shandy* is "organized throughout on Locke's doctrine of the Association of Ideas" has long served as a standard assumption, supported by Professor Kenneth MacLean's important study of the Lockean influence on English literature in 1936[369] and John Laird's conclusion in 1946[567] that Shandean philosophy was "an elaborate application of Locke's methods," accurately applied and sometimes even improved upon. To the observation of Cross that *Tristram Shandy* was Locke's essay "in novelized form," MacLean had added that Locke had given Sterne "an entirely new principle of literary composition."

This position was significantly challenged and modified in the area of the conception of time by Professor Watkins, who took the position that Sterne's only direct debt to Locke is the simple theory of duration. The real Sternean conception of time, he argued, is that it is relatively dependent on the imagination and the point of individual consciousness—a means for "the man whose days were numbered" to triumph over time. Thus Sterne's complex concept embodies not merely the linear notion of Locke's duration but what Sterne calls Expansion, the Ideas and Length of which "are turned every way, and so make Figure and Breadth and Thickness"—achieving that extra dimension that "cubistic painters have striven for in vain" and leading to fictional uses of time like those of such contemporary novelists as Proust, Mann, and Virginia Woolf.

Ernest Tuveson[424] has argued that Locke was more of a reformer of Western thought than a scientist or a philosopher, liberating this thought from a smothering heritage of stultifying logic, and that it was on this basis that he appealed to Sterne, whose images "present with great exactitude the intellectual world of his time." Sterne, like Locke (Tuveson observes), attacks the traditional view of the independence of the mind, realizing that "the body thinks" and is an integral part of "one garment" with the mind. If Swift's scatology seems to warn us to be on guard against our physical side, Sterne calls for us to be "natural"—a state that is co-operation, not strife, between reason and sense.

There have also been other re-examinations of and challenges to assumptions about Locke's influence. D. R. Elloway, for example, has pointed out that none of the instances of associationism in *Tristram Shandy* cited by Cross in an article in the *Yale Review* in 1925 actually illustrated Locke's principle;[611] and Professor Cash has argued that Locke's associationism is better regarded as a subsidiary device than an organizing principle in the novel.[525] The organic stream of consciousness, he explains, was engendered in the atmosphere of Locke's empiricism, and the psychology of the train of ideas accompanying that empiricism accounts for the mind of Tristram and the "digressive" method.

Mrs. Alice G. Fredman, in a study of the relationship of *Tristram Shandy* and Diderot's *Jacques le Fataliste*, attempts a simple summary:

> The fundamental association of ideas helps to make [Sterne's] characters consistent and gives rise to his digressive method. By carrying over digressions from one book to another, Sterne links his novel together in a fluid but intellectually logical pattern. This is particularly successful for flashbacks and for the gradual development of a subject through a kind of musical or thematic construction. When the structural unity breaks down, he can still fall back on the familiar associations and digressions of characters and narrator.[858]

Moving in the same area, and beyond, is John Traugott's *Tristram Shandy's World: Sterne's Philosophical Rhetoric* (1954),[611] which has stimulated both interest and controversy. Sterne, according to Professor Traugott, is primarily interested in the problem of communication between isolated minds. Locke's answer to the problem was that such communication could come only through clearly determinate ideas and exactly determined language. In Sterne's world the characters do not hold exactly determined ideas; yet they communicate by private rhetoric apprehended through the context of human situations. "Locke's is a rational system for comparing ideas and determining language. Sterne's is something else, but by developing the confusion or absurdity in Locke's rational system Sterne has created a dramatic engine which controls situation and character." Thus he ultimately comes close to Hume's doctrine of sympathy.

"Though Locke disparages rhetoric as a deceptive art, wit as trivial, and the passions as distorters of truth," Professor Monk summarizes in a sympathetic review, "Sterne creates a believable world using rhetoric as his method, wit as his in-

strument, and the passions as ever-present forces shaping the
motives of the characters." In fact, Traugott asserted, Sterne
was "a rhetorician and not a 'novelist,'" with a view that "writing, properly managed . . . is warfare with the reader."

Important dissenting reviews have appeared from Mac-
Lean, Booth, and Elloway, all of whom feel that in various
ways Professor Traugott has misread (or failed to read) both
Locke and Sterne. Booth objects strongly to the "monolithic"
treatment of Sterne, as well as to the conception of *Tristram
Shandy* as "a treatise on communication" or as a work
of "philosophical rhetoric" in which Tristram-Sterne attempts
to persuade the reader through "dramatic" means to accept a
particular "conceptual world." The whole idea of "philosophical rhetoric," Booth contends, is vague; and the writer's own
rhetoric in developing the idea is so difficult as to be unclear.
MacLean, on the other hand, though arguing that the first half
of Traugott's book gives evidence of inaccurate reading of
Locke, feels that the second and "better half" presents the true
purpose of the writer of *Tristram Shandy,* which was to employ
the means of rhetoric toward their psychological end. "Sterne
did not cease to be a preacher when he became (if he ever
did) novelist," MacLean comments, accepting Traugott's argument. He is a rhetor, as are both Tristram and Walter Shandy,
the latter of whom becomes as a rhetor "the true man of feeling."

Rejecting both Lockean psychology and rhetorical analysis
as the "law" of the Shandean world, Sigurd Burckhardt[522] has
suggested in their places the law of gravity—in Sterne's definition "a mysterious carriage of the body to cover the defects of
the mind" or, in simpler statement, "things fall." He suggests
that Sterne's "irony," like Swift's, embodies the "final joke . . .
that he is not joking." Burckhardt feels that Sterne's "vast
system of indirections, circuitous approaches—of parables driv-
en to the point of hyperbole" argues that the language can
never communicate directly, but can "by indirections find directions out." In an article appearing in the same year as Burckhardt's, Robert J. Griffin renews the consideration of the ways

in which Tristram responds to Locke's ideas on communication
as reflected in the uses, abuses, and imperfections of words,
concluding that Sterne "was not overly dismayed by Locke's
treatment of (linguistic) communication," proof being available in Sterne's "constant confident play on or with words."[551]

A. D. McKillop has succinctly summed up the most recent
thinking about verbal and non-verbal communication in the
novel as follows: "Language interposes itself between man and
man. The brothers [Shandy] never reach an understanding on
intellectual terms. . . . Yet they can meet on the plane of human
sympathy, with gesture and physical circumstances effecting
what words cannot. . . ."[375]

After all, the important consideration may be that, though
Sterne both agrees and disagrees with Locke's philosophy, he
values it chiefly because, instead of attempting to explain "the
miracle of sensation," Locke leaves it in the hands of God,
placing the world of "riddles and mysteries" beyond the explanation of even the "clearest and most exalted of understanding." From such a position, Professor Drew[533] in one of the
clearest of the brief treatments of Sterne asserts what she considers to be the essential relationship of the novelist and the
philosopher:

Tristram Shandy is really Sterne's Essay Concerning Human
Understanding, and it poses the question whether our beliefs in
a rational world of controlled cause and effect, or free will, or
steady human identity, are perhaps fantasies contradicted continually by the facts.

The assumption that Sterne was the first "stream-of-consciousness" novelist and that he invented the Proustian method
of exploring memory has found frequent expression—a fact (it
may be argued) determined to some extent both by the absence of a firm definition of the term and by a failure to examine Sterne's method closely enough. It has, of course, been
easy to argue that Tristram Shandy was far ahead of its time,
that there are at least superficial affinities between Sterne and
the twentieth-century stream-of-consciousness novelists, and
that the appreciation of Tristram Shandy has been definitely

enhanced in a period accustomed to Joyce, Kafka, and Proust. Robert Curtis Brown,[817] for example, points out easily discernible affinities between Virginia Woolf and Sterne, feeling that both modeled structures on the "operative character of consciousness" and both believed that "the only true reality exists in the inner flow of thought," to be sought at "the moment of being."

Traugott, on the other hand, directly opposes those who wish to see the novel as an adumbration of the method of the "interior monologue." "I suggest that there is nothing unconscious about Tristram," he writes. "It is not [his] psyche that is in question, but his opinion." Robert Humphrey,[357] who has made one of the most extensive recent investigations of the subject, agrees that Sterne's work does not belong to the stream-of-consciousness genre "because his concerns are not serious in representing psychic content for its own sake and as a means of achieving essences of characterization." That is, he does not use the inner psychic life of emotional associations in himself or others, nor does he report such life. "He never uses the present to *interpret* the past," Professor Drew has observed; and he makes no exploration of unfamiliar areas of the mind. "All his digressions and expansions do," she continues, "is to emphasize the simultaneity in the mind of the present with the memory of the past, and the coexistence of competing memories clamoring for expression."

The surface impression of eccentric disorganization in the novel has served, as we have seen, as an increasingly lively challenge to an attempt to evolve a theory of unity for it, not only through patterns of structure and rhetoric but also through those of concept and philosophy as well. A dozen or more firmly fixed dates in a background of King William's Wars and a theory of Sterne's application of Locke's ideas about duration, for example, led Theodore Baird to call *Tristram Shandy* "an exactly executed historical novel."[502] Professor Booth[513] has found the secret of coherence to be "the dramatized narrator," and he has argued interestingly that instead of being a fragment, *Tristram Shandy* is actually complete—Volume IX representing "the completion of a plan, however rough, that was present in [Sterne's] mind from the beginning." William Bowman Piper,[585] elaborating upon Booth, sees Tristram as the tragicomical memorialist of the Shandys ("like Ossian or Melville's Ishmael, the last survivor of a sorrowful story") whose death as a childless man effectually and effectively ends his account. Northrop Frye and others find the principle of unity in "the sense of literature as a process."[544] In *Tristram Shandy*, the argument runs, "we are not being led into a story, but into the process of writing a story: we wonder not what is coming next, but what the author will think of next." One may also conclude simply that the unity of the novel resides in the fact that it takes place in the mind of Tristram. As Professor Booth has put it, "[*Tristram Shandy*] gives us a consistent over-all portrait of the inconsistent mind of man."

Professor Putney has observed that up to Chapter xx of Volume VI "the misadventures of Tristram's life provide the skeleton on which the digressions are hung, and his is the mind so lost in the flux of thought, as explained by Locke's theory of the association of ideas, that each mischance he suffers leads into tangential mazes." The alteration in the design in Volume VI for the interpolation of Uncle Toby's mimic wars and his love affair with the Widow Wadman tends to obscure the structural unity. Nevertheless, Sterne maintains the unity of Tristram's character as narrator and thus also the tone of comic irony that he had previously established.[660]

Since there is no forward-moving line, Mendilow observes from another viewpoint, digressions are not possible.[574] Digressions are really episodes; and since the novel has neither beginning, middle, nor end, it would be complete whenever it stopped. Sterne, the argument continues, was misled into using "line" in reference to the narrative. Rather did he work in stipples on a broad canvas "so that the picture grows not part by part but as a whole, into an indivisible unity out of the multitude of scattered strokes of brush distributed in no fixed order." This theory plainly offers a possible reconciliation of the "hodge-podge" theory of the novel's structure and the argument that it is a completed novel with a firmly established plan. Others have argued that the digressions themselves constitute a comic method and are a matter of "controlled artistry," a means of achieving order by making disorder.[584]

To a certain extent, shifting opinions and evaluations of the novelist both as artist and man represent a kaleidoscopic rather than a linear pattern. Almost like the book, in which all action can exist at once, divergent opinions have been able to exist simultaneously. Yet a definite process of evolution may be discerned in the twentieth-century evaluation of Sterne as man and author—from "foul satyr," to "mischievous faun," to joyous humanist and moralist, to subtle rhetorician and philosopher largely on the side of the angels.

To recognize Sterne as one who gave "enthusiastic support to all good fellows"[416] or to conclude that his comedy was concerned "with amiable, if slightly eccentric, men of good will"[419] may not be to assume an attitude peculiar to the twentieth century. On the other hand, to insist that his comedy tends "to become almost an act of faith in human nature" comes closer to being a typical contemporary view.

In the most elaborate and comprehensive mid-century study of *Tristram Shandy,* Henri Fluchère concludes that Sterne's cheerfulness is based not so much on a Rousseauistic belief in natural good as in a sort of *pantegruélisme* founded on an unshakable faith in human nature, and that through the comic mode of Shandyism the certainty of good in the whole of life is attested and apprehended.[540] (Further discussion of the debate concerning Sterne's "sentimentality" is reserved for later treatment).

In general, when the attempt is now made to evaluate the book in the background of the thought of Sterne's time, varyingly spacious claims are made for Sterne as a thinker, as well as for the acceptance of meaningfully serious concepts as unifying principles of his great book. D. W. Jefferson, as we have already seen, finding that in form and thematic pattern *Tristram Shandy* is easily perceived as being in the well-established tradition of "learned wit," observes a unifying principle

in the theme of "the comic clash between the world of learn-
ing and that of human affairs."[562]

From another point of view, Professor McKillop writes:

> [*Tristram Shandy*] is about the relation of the little to the great
> world. Whereas the current physico-theology emphasized simplicity
> and regularity, Sterne professes to find a just representation of the
> altered scheme endlessly intricate and perplexing.

He continues in his interpretation of Sterne's method of composition:

> Reality is not simply built up out of units; it is contained in
> the given unit. The individual experience somehow images in little
> and simultaneously a moral order and a cosmic order, the world
> of conscience and consciousness and the world of microscope and
> telescope.[375]

Professor Dorothy Van Ghent had previously suggested that
Sterne with a new structural principle based on the operative
character of consciousness had created a world in the form of
a mind conceived in the figure of such elemental units of
energy as Leibnitz's monads that have "mirrors but no windows," the mirroring capacity of which makes each unit a
microcosm of the universe.[614]

Professor Drew assumes what is perhaps more easily recog-
nizable and less recondite grounds when she observes from
the pervasive "sexual tinge of the book," emphasized by its
beginning with a joke about conception and ending with one
about impotence, that *Tristram Shandy* is about "the paradoxi-
cal creativeness and helplessness of man." Between the two
sexual jokes that form the framework, she remarks, is "a riot
of creative fantasy about the comic and pathetic frustrations
of the writing of books and the living of lives."

Since Sterne has proved adaptable to various patterns of
thought, the attempt to relate him to the popular twentieth-
century philosophy of Existentialism should surprise no one.
Fully cognizant of perils in fitting a fashionable philosophy on
an established work of literature of another era, especially if
that philosophy wears such an elastic garment as Existential-

ism does, Ernest H. Lockridge[365] achieves another reinterpretation of Sterne in the context of Albert Camus's early essay *The Myth of Sisyphus,* in which the philosophy of the Absurd is expressed by a writer who claims to be a literary man rather than a philosopher. In Sterne, Lockridge discerns two attitudes toward life: first, the "humorously pessimistic" view of the world as governed by chance and not by reason, an ever ridiculous chain of cause and effect, the explanation of which cannot help sounding absurd—this is *Tristram Shandy;* and, second, especially in *A Sentimental Journey,* the attitude that the world is full of things and experiences to be enjoyed if one knows how to enjoy them in the "little span of life" that one has. (To Sterne, as to the Existentialists, the prime reality is Death; and the flight from Death through the realization of life is a pervasive theme). It is by keeping these two polar concepts in mind—"the dubious value of the world, contrasted with the preciousness of human life within that world"—that we can see the vision of Sterne and the philosophy of Camus beginning to coincide.

To Camus, Lockridge explains, it is not that the universe or the world is absurd so much as that the Absurd is a human feeling arising out of man's longing for clarity in an irrational universe. Thus the Absurd exists only in man. This, Lockridge argues, is why Sterne thought the schoolmen, and his father, so ridiculous in their systems. And when the systems of Walter Shandy come into collision with the world, "the jolt is both hilarious and a little sad." In its basic premise that reason cannot penetrate existence, as well as in its inherent "vision of the Absurd," the comedy of Sterne comes close to tragedy.

The conclusion is that Sterne should not in any sense be treated as a "thesis novelist." Rather should he be regarded as one who "with a great openness of mind, in the very act of writing . . . wills his whole existence."

The broad spectrum of interpretative possibilities that we have just reviewed (not to mention other possibilities suggested in the attached annotated bibliography) may be regarded as being both intriguing and disconcerting. Critical comment has at times been astute and brilliant. On some occasions, however, it has been repetitious and on others over-elaborate. Some criticism has been ingenious when it has not actually been illuminating. In short (though such an extremity is clearly not demanded), it may even be possible to conclude that much of the most enthusiastic reinterpretation has gone into the creation of a novelist who never really existed or that Sterne has been made into a novelist's novelist or a scholar's novelist removed from the normal capacities for comprehension possessed by the lay reader.

In quite a different category has been the substantive sort of contribution made by Louis Landa in 1963 through his investigation of the background of the Homunculus, Sterne's "Little Gentleman" and the focal point of the novelist's exploration of the various "systems" involving him.[568] The discussion of the ways in which Sterne's description of the homunculus accurately reflects contemporary embryological speculation—as well as the discussion of numerous aspects, both serious and witty, of the running debate between the *animalculists* and the *ovists*—provides delightful and highly valuable annotation to a most significant portion of *Tristram Shandy*.

Another somewhat more basic consideration—that of textual criticism—deserves brief concluding mention. The vexing bibliographical problems of *Tristram Shandy* have long been recognized. After the appearance of the final edition of the Cross biography, the main attempts to solve them have been made by Professors Curtis[10] and Yoklavich.[28] Since the bibliographical difficulties are what they are, since the manuscript of the novel is not extant, and since Sterne gave little evidence of being interested in correcting or revising later editions of his work, it is not entirely curious that, in spite of numerous reprints in the nineteenth and early twentieth centuries, no editor thought it worth while to do more than reproduce the text by an anonymous editor in the first collected edition of 1780, twelve years from Sterne's death and longer from the time of his reading proof.

The first scholar to address himself seriously to the prob-

lems of the text was Professor James A. Work in his edition
of 1940.[142] As one might well expect, Work found the differences between this text and the text that Sterne himself had
corrected for the press to be substantive and numerous—with
evidence of marring of style, dulling of wit, and alteration of
sense. Since later editions differ from the first London edition
only in correcting some errors while introducing new ones and
in effecting some changes in the conventions of style, spelling,
and punctuation, Professor Work's decision to print the first
edition of each of the nine volumes was sound. In doing so,
the editor preserved Sterne's peculiar variety of oral rather
than syntactical punctuation (faithfully preserving the various
"orders" of dashes and other devices of what Professor Monk
has called "aesthetically functional" punctuation), as well as
his spelling even when inconsistent, making only a few silent
corrections of obvious errors and of inconsistencies in the use
of italics in the last three volumes. Since its publication, the
Work text has generally been regarded as standard.

Nevertheless, other texts based on the first London edition are now available. The best of these are by Monk,[145]
McKillop,[148] and Watt.[149] Monk makes no attempt to regular-
ize inconsistencies, dissenting from Work on the regularization
of italics. Watt pursues the same policy. McKillop makes
modernizations in spelling. Watt has made the most elaborate
collation to date of the first edition of all nine volumes, the
second edition of Vol. I [II], the so-called London collected
edition of 1780, the three-volume edition "London Printed for
D. Lynch," and the Dublin collected edition. A list of variants
toward an ultimate critical text is appended.

III

Sentimentalist or Jester?
—A Sentimental Journey

The French critic Émile Montégut once observed humorously that Rabelais, Sir Thomas Browne, Robert Burton, and "I don't know how many old physicians and theologians" collaborated in the making of *Tristram Shandy*, but that *A Sentimental Journey* belongs to Sterne and nobody else. It is, of course, possible to say that Sterne wrote only one book and that this book includes everything that he wrote: sermons, letters, journals, novels. Moreover, he wrote *A Sentimental Journey* not once but twice, the first version being included in *Tristram Shandy* as Book VII. Yet there are, as Montégut suggested, clearly defined differences between the long novel and the short one. There have consequently been wide differences in appeal. If Peter Quennell, for example, can think that *Tristram Shandy* is at times one of the least readable of English masterpieces, he assures us that *A Sentimental Journey* is one of the most readable. This kind of opinion has been current from the time of the publication of both works.

Superficially, at least, the shorter book has few of the qualities about which the "common reader," rightly or wrongly, has found occasion to complain in *Tristram Shandy*. Most of the stylistic tricks, the complexity of structure, the elaborate and sometimes stale bawdiness are not in evidence.

In point of view, the *Journey* is simpler. Whereas in *Tris-*

tram Shandy, as William Bowman Piper points out in a doctoral thesis,[388] the hero continually tries to tell Sir, Madam,
and other generalized social figures about his family's past in
a manner that can be both frustrating and puzzling, in *A Sentimental Journey* Yorick in his study is simply writing a selection
of his social adventures in France. In short, the kind of complexity of style and language that seemed to make *Tristram
Shandy* at the outset untranslatable into French, German, and
Italian, did not exist as an obstacle to the translation of *A
Sentimental Journey,* which quickly became one of the most
widely read of English books on the Continent and one of the
most important influences on Continental literature.

If in *Tristram Shandy,* Sterne set out to write a new kind
of novel, in *A Sentimental Journey* he ostensibly intended to
write a new kind of travel book. As such, it may properly be
considered in the context of the travel literature written up to
and including his own time—and most contemporaneously in
the context of the allegedly ill-natured account of his fellow
novelist, Tobias Smollett.[658] Professor Cross early observed
(following Joseph Texte and others) that Sterne was one of
the first "impressionists," that his impressions all come from
scenes and incidents on the way, and that there are no mean-
ingless digressions on things in general.[152] Thus in one respect
A Sentimental Journey, subjective though it is, may also be regarded as "the most objective of books."

For this reason, it has been a constant challenge to illustra-
tors—of whom Rowlandson, Stothard, and Leloir have been the
best known. (Among the earliest illustrations, John Winterich
has, incidentally, reminded us of the existence of three copies
of a 1795 edition in New York in which the drawings by an
anonymous artist may be considered too erotic for public display).[167] That the general appeal has remained to twentieth-
century artists can be documented by items included in this
bibliography.

Professor Cazamian's remarks about the book are made with
this distinguished French scholar's usual astuteness:

The *Sentimental Journey* is of a much more concentrated and sober form, of a purer line, than *Tristram Shandy*; and it cannot be said that the matter has become poorer, for the impressions and the episodes of this sojourn in France allow a reflection that is always alert to indulge in a constant meditation upon life. The manners and character of the French occupy the foreground; and Sterne, certainly, has not seen all, or understood all he saw; his liberty of judgment is only relative; but it is remarkable, and his psychological interpretation is often of a penetrating accuracy.[364]

Nevertheless, though Sterne was traveling in France and though accurate concrete details of scenes and incidents are in evidence, Virginia Woolf remarked that "the road was often through his own mind and his chief adventures were . . . the emotions of his heart," the assertion of the good of which (she adds) constituted the novel's chief fault.[159]

Sir Herbert Read, as we have already indicated, warned in 1927 that the word "sentimental" must not be used with its common connotation when applied to Sterne. That this warning was justified is to some extent demonstrated by the fact that Francis Bickley in his preface to *A Sentimental Journey* in 1922 had continued to advance the view that the word indicates "abnormal sensitiveness and reaction to emotional stimuli."[155] In 1925, it is true, Edith Birkhead had shown considerably more perspicacity in the opinion that to Sterne "sentimental" involved "a pleasant philandering with emotions," whereas to Richardson it meant "sententious."[307] Though in 1928 and 1932 Virginia Woolf stressed the fact that Sterne's sentimentalism was tied up with his constant play for "our good opinion of his heart," she perceived that *A Sentimental Journey* evolved a "philosophy of pleasure" which removed the word "sentimental" from its usual relationships.[159] Sir Herbert regarded it as indicating a refinement of feeling, always set off and balanced by humor, leaving "the soul calm and serene [because] it is grounded in [the] elemental facts of the human organism."[160] Watkins's treatment of Sterne's sentimentality, like Read's, has been discussed elsewhere. Adopting an attitude toward the manifestations of sentimentality similar to Watkins's, Quennell, in his critical biography,[246] has more recently called the little book "the work of a humanist in the truest sense of the word, who makes his 'true dimensions' the capacity and mind of man, who loves life, welcomes experience, and has not yet lost all his faith in the infinite possibilities of common human nature." In *A Critical History of English Literature* (1960) David Daiches, with less expansiveness, regards "sentimentality" as simply a self-conscious responsiveness, at once humorous and moral, to the slightest emotional stimulus.[324] And finally, Ernest H. Lockridge in the light of his parallel reading of Sterne and Camus concludes that it is the "deep feeling for all the possibilities of life itself which accounts for, and helps define Sterne's 'sentiment.'" He continues by defining "sentiment" and "sentimentality" as "an intense apprehension of life, an intense feeling for everything we can encompass" in the small amount of time allotted to us.[365] There have been, of course, other definitions, as well as various etymological studies[338] involving not only Sterne's use of the word but also the question of his precedence in its use and the influence of his use of it on its succeeding history. Nevertheless the definitions cited are sufficient to suggest the range of the meanings given the term itself as well as the range of the attitudes toward Sterne's achievement that can be based on these definitions.

In spite of the occurrence well into the twentieth century of unflattering opinions about Sterne's emotional annotations to his work, Ernest Nevin Dilworth[329] both oversimplified and overstated the case when he asserted in 1948 that "from Thackeray down to the present our tutors have whipped us into believing that Sterne, when he is not being dirty, spends his skill in imploring us, with a stupid lack of humor, to admire the tenderness of his heart." If the statement quite neatly telescopes the attitudes of Thackeray and Virginia Woolf, it not only is unfair to the total position of the latter but it also fails to take into account many instances of changes in attitude toward Sterne's sentimentality at least after 1925.

In addition to the evidence already cited for the ameliorative changes in definitions of the terms involved, one may point to such important observations as Cazamian's in 1929[364] that in Sterne there is the "absolute victory of sentiment," achieved through art and artifice and "a complete mastery of emotion by the devices employed," making sentimentalism a new resource and liberating it from ethics; or that of Charles G. Osgood in 1935[385] (also from a literary history widely used as a college text) who noted that while Sterne was feeding the world sentimentality he was simultaneously laughing at it. Norman Collins also remarked in 1933 that, though Sterne was "the founder of sentimental fiction," he was not himself "a true sentimentalist."[318]

In an important article in 1940, Professor Rufus D. S. Putney insisted that the distinguishing qualities of *A Sentimental Journey* are to be attributed neither to disease nor to the affair with Mrs. Draper, further contending that the little book was a mockery of the sentimentalism that Sterne had made to order in the *Journal to Eliza*—in fact, that it was "a hoax by which [he] persuaded his contemporaries that the humor he wanted to write was the pathos they wished to read."[659] In a later article in 1949 (necessarily discussed here though it is chronologically out of place), Putney argued that to regard Sterne as a sentimentalist in the usual sense is "to ignore the hard core of comic irony that made him critical of the emotional vagaries of his own life and of his imagined characters," much of his reputation for excessive sensibility having come from "a misunderstanding of *A Sentimental Journey* fostered by uncritical dependence on the four letters supposed to have been written to Elizabeth Lumley before she became Mrs. Sterne and on the *Journal to Eliza*."[660] Putney further contended, regarding not only the *Journey* but the whole of Sterne's literary production, that, though Sterne often wept to demonstrate the soundness of his heart, he had no faith in the "moral efficacy of tears." Unlike George Meredith he had an insatiable love of laughter and a belief in its worth, but like Meredith he had confidence in "the value and healthiness of comedy."

With essentially the same point of view, a biographer observed in 1943 that, in spite of the fact that the *Journal to*

Eliza had at times been regarded as "a unique exhibition of sentimentality in the raw, uninhibited and unrevised," such a judgment could hardly be substantiated by the evidence:

> Sterne himself plainly intimated almost at the outset that he was intent upon creating another love legend, at least in the tradition of Swift and Stella if not that of Abelard and Heloise. . . . Both the *Journal* and the *Journey* must be regarded as conscious literary productions, the main difference being in the degree and kind of artistry.[223]

This attitude toward Sterne had not been infrequently expressed. In fact, it can be found to some extent in most of the twentieth-century reaction to Thackeray's picture of the "blubbering" Sterne. Thus to assume as Dilworth did so late as 1948 that the novelist had consistently been regarded as the "prince of sentimentalists" indulging in "lachrymose divagations"—or to state in 1957, as Miss Margaret Shaw does almost frenetically in another context, that "the main pack of critics is still in full cry against this author"—is suggestive of setting up a straw man.

Dilworth, of course, had elected to elaborate upon the extreme opposite view. Picking up sentimental passages wherever he could find them—not simply in *A Sentimental Journey* but also in *Tristram Shandy* and the *Letters*—he concludes that they are all jests:

> To the sentimentalist of yesterday, today, and tomorrow, as to the plain honest man, something is sacred; to Sterne everything is words, the immaterial substance out of which appear the clothes, the rattle, and the handspring of the jester.[329]

If Cross felt that Sterne's emotions were "always sincere," Dilworth boldly holds that they are never sincere. Although Dilworth's monograph has been praised for its vigor, its value as entertainment, and its service as an antidote to highly sentimental interpretations, its total position has not found universal acceptance.

Even though it may be demonstrable that Sterne persistently parodied and satirized the sentimental fashion of his day—as reviewers have observed—one must also account for the part that he played in setting that fashion.[329] Moreover, to deny a constant ambivalence in Sterne is to deny one of his most apparent qualities. There is nothing to keep us from believing that he could not delight in the very things that he ridiculed; moreover, the kindliness of his satire often transmutes it into something tantalizingly like sentimentality—if not the real article.

Perhaps the most vigorous rebuttal came in the middle article in the *Times Literary Supplement* for April 9, 1949, in which the reviewer sums up his position as follows:

> To represent Sterne as a satirist is to suppose in him a moral sense which he did not possess; and to say that he believed only in the calculating side of human nature is to pretend that he was logical when he was merely commonsensical, and consistent when he was the reverse. Reality for Sterne was neither reason nor feeling but the opposition of the two. The humorous and poignant consequences of this conflict, and the pleasure of self-awareness, probably have a greater share in the enjoyment of Sterne than satirical amusement.[350]

In a recent doctoral dissertation, Arthur Hill Cash has returned to the view of Sterne as humorist initiated by Jean Paul Richter and followed by Coleridge, Scherer, and Read—arguing that Sterne saw as laughable the clash of man's fleshly lusts with his high ideals.[652] Thus he sees *A Sentimental Journey* as a comedy of moral problems with Sterne's "ethical rationalism" (as expressed in the Sermons) as its underlying assumption. His further development of this idea is the subject of a monograph just off the press.[652a]

In complement to Cash's study, Gardner D. Stout, Jr., sees the book as a "comic Pilgrim's Progress" for an "Age of Sensibility," contending that the "sentimental" and the "comic" handles of the work can be reconciled as comprehensive aspects "of a unified comic version of human existence."[663]

Lockridge's interpretation in the light of Camus's treatment of the philosophy of the Absurd (with emphasis on the "quiet intensity" of the book) tends to give a new dignity to the classic and to provide it with a new relevance to contemporary life and thought.

Because few of the previous reprints of *A Sentimental Journey* had been made with careful attention to the text, Sir Herbert Read's edition of 1929[160] made an effort to achieve a better reading than that of extant texts by using the second edition of 1768 as a basis, with punctuation of the first volume brought into accord with the MS in the British Museum. A new textual study has been completed by Gardner D. Stout, Jr., who has edited the text as doctoral dissertation.[662] His forthcoming edition will reprint from the first edition (London, 1768), with textual apparatus analyzing the relationship between extant manuscripts in the British Museum and in the Pierpont Morgan Library, together with notes recording all variants between the manuscripts themselves and between the manuscripts and the first edition. An extensive introduction will deal with background materials.

IV

The Province of the Letters

The letters of Sterne, as Professor Curtis has remarked, have "in a small way become a classic . . . and stand next to *Tristram Shandy* and the *Sentimental Journey* in order of excellence." Editions preceding and succeeding Lydia de Medalle's three small volumes of 1775 attest their popularity at the end of the eighteenth century.[177] Their acceptance fluctuated with the tides of Sterne's reputation in the nineteenth century; and they have received, like the rest of Sterne's work, adequate editorial and critical attention only in the twentieth.

The reviewer of Lydia's collection in the *Monthly Review* (LIII [1775], 403-413) indicated as a basic reason for the appeal of the letters that they enabled one "to see in the recesses of private life, the man who so conspicuously shone in the capacity of an author." Here is the standard index to the eternal appeal of the intimate life of the famous. Because Sterne still manages to maintain a kind of contemporaneity, even the uncritical reader of our time can delight in sharing these intimacies. The value of the letters to the biography requires no argument.

Nevertheless, judging as we must from the relatively small number of letters that have come down to us (through no real fault of Sterne's own, we might add), we are forced to rank Sterne somewhat behind the great letter writers of a century in which the art of letter writing was very highly developed indeed. Thomas Gray, possessing astonishing erudition and yet ability to write colloquially with wit and affectionate warmth; Horace Walpole, brilliant, witty, humorous, acutely knowledgeable in politics, current affairs, literature, architecture, painting; William Cowper, with quiet integrity and seemingly complete lack of self-consciousness, with classical elegance and simplicity of style, and with an ineffable personal charm—all of these excel Sterne as letter writers, so much so in fact that the best contemporary book on the English letter writers, though pointing out elements of his appeal, makes short shrift of him.[708]

Like almost everything else that Sterne wrote, the letters seem for the most part intensely personal. As Professor Curtis and others have observed, they "deal less with events of the great world than with details sufficient unto the day." With political events, with social conditions, even with the great victories of 1759 (in spite of Uncle Toby's interest in military affairs of an earlier date), they are not concerned. If Sterne's letters show diffidence to the kinds of political events that make Walpole's correspondence so valuable to us, they also have little to do with the trivialities of domestic daily living that Cowper can set down with such charming accuracy. Coleridge and Lamb spoke of Cowper's "divine chit-chat." Sterne was a master of chit-chat, too, though his may require a different adjective.

Ultimately, like almost everything else that he wrote, his letters must be considered as a part of his total literary product —not separate from it. Indeed, they are sometimes indistinguishable from it. Since they, therefore, preserve their unique appeal, evaluative comparisons with other letter writers become somewhat irrelevant. One may easily see that, except for a number of letters purely utilitarian in purpose, they assume the same devices, rhetorical and otherwise, and achieve the same effects as his other prose. His advice to Lydia to write simply and naturally if she wished to achieve the best in epistolary art is also applicable—albeit in a special way—to his own product. If he applied the generalization "Great wits jump" to his method in the longer works, it can also be ap-

plied to the letters—which are, as their writer takes occasion
to make them, digressive, spontaneous, intimate, nonsensical,
sentimental. And the "self-conscious narrator" is still in evidence—as the discovery of the *Letter Book* makes even more
plain than it might have been otherwise. Sterne never got
around to doing what Pope did in surreptitiously bringing out
a volume of his own letters; nor was he self-conscious in the
same way as Horace Walpole, who seemed to select his corre-
spondents so that the resulting letters would be of the broadest
interest to posterity. But as his final directions to Lydia indicate, he had written most of his letters with the feeling that
they would one day be printed.

The fact that so few of them are extant—compared with
the sometimes overwhelming bulk of letters by Johnson, Boswell, Walpole, and Cowper—is ironic. Members of Boswell's
family who wished to conceal their kinsman's indiscretions hid
his papers in cabinets or in croquet boxes, to which by happy
chance the twentieth century has had access as an incompara-
ble treasure trove. On the other hand, bundles of Sterne's
papers and letters were (in Curtis's phrase) "piously destroyed" in an ill-conceived attempt to protect the family. On
one occasion Lydia wrote to her cousin, Mrs. Elizabeth Montagu, that her uncle Botham in London had "burnt what he
did not think proper to communicate to us." Burned also, or
otherwise destroyed, must have been numberless letters at Cox-
wold and in garrets in York. As a result, Sterne's letters always
have been, and doubtless will continue to be, rare. Curtis's
comment in the preface to his edition of the letters is significantly brief:

The principal sources of Sterne's autograph letters . . . are few
in number. Seven letters and the manuscript of the *Journal to Eliza*
are found in the British Museum; twenty-three in addition to the
fourteen contained in Sterne's *Letter Book* are found in the Morgan
Library.

The remaining few letters that have turned up since 1945 are
recorded in the bibliography.

The best criticism of the letters is that of Professor Curtis—

and most justly so, considering his performance in the labor
necessary to achieve a firm basis for criticism: that is, the task
of establishing the best possible text.

In this job he tackled one of the most complex of all
eighteenth-century editorial puzzles. The reason for the complexity lies both in the absence of holograph sources in particular and in the unscholarly attitude of most of the eighteenth-
and early nineteenth-century editors toward their materials
in general. Instead of attempting to print as exactly as possible
what their subjects actually wrote, many editors seemed more
interested in producing what their subjects might or should
have written, having in mind rather the effect of the whole as
a literary work or as a favorable portrait of the writer than
its truthfulness to the facts.

When the minor poet, William Hayley, for example, under-
took a biography of William Cowper which was designed to
incorporate the correspondence as an important part, he did
not hesitate to mutilate and suppress letters—deleting single
words, sentences, phrases, paragraphs, in addition to making
numerous substitutions—chiefly at the request of his sponsor
and Cowper's cousin, Lady Hesketh, who insisted that references to certain family relationships, to the poet's madness,
and to what she considered to be his religious excesses should
not appear. When Hayley wrote, "I suppressed even *more*
than I printed," he was stating what was, unfortunately, widely acceptable editorial license. No modern edition of Cowper's
letters has yet appeared to repair all the damage thus accomplished.

In the case of Sterne's literary remains, the situation
was far worse, for in her editing of her father's correspondence
Lydia Sterne de Medalle not only suppressed proper names,
created errors in dates, and revised and embellished according
to either her vanity or her pious intentions, but she also went
so far as to invite and perhaps even to perpetrate forgeries.
Her suggestion to John Wilkes that he might write a few letters
in imitation of her father's style as substitutes for the correspondence that he had burned is properly shocking. As M.

Fluchère has observed, one certainly has reason to mistrust everything that she did—and particularly to suspect as forgeries the famous letters that Sterne presumably wrote to her mother when she was his fiancée.[218]

As if matters were not bad enough in Lydia's publication of 1775, other problems are raised by editions that preceded and followed it in 1775, 1779, and 1788. Here, too, the question of textual corruption is complicated by that of forgeries— with William Combe, best known as the author of the *Tours of Dr. Syntax*—emerging as the favorite candidate for the title of chief perpetrator. One does not wonder at Fluchère's pronouncement: "La situation devant laquelle nous nous trouvons est inextricable."

Although two editions of the letters after the middle of the nineteenth century had some validity—that of Dr. James P. Brown in 1873 and that of Dr. George Saintsbury as a part of his edition of the *Works* in 1894—a new and more painstaking approach was necessary. This was initiated by Cross, who in the introduction to his edition of the letters in 1904, has described the difficulties encountered in arriving at his text, working as he did from materials that he took over from Fitzgerald.[171] To these materials he was able to add substantially. He was also able to make other important additions in the process of writing and revising his own biography of Sterne, the most significant of which came through the discovery of the *Letter Book*. Lewis Melville[172] and R. Brimley Johnson[176] did little toward the solution of the main problem; and the volume of the letters in the Oxford edition of the *Works* (1926), containing fifty-five doubtful letters in a total of 184, can hardly be said to represent a discriminating editorial job.[101]

The major achievement in contemporary editing of the letters is Professor Lewis Perry Curtis's volume of 1935.[177] Making a thorough re-examination of the sources and the evidence, Curtis printed the most complete and the most elaborate annotated edition now extant—including 236 letters of carefully argued authenticity, the *Journal to Eliza* inserted in the chronological order of the entries, and a number of letters relative to

Sterne and his family, as well as the *Memoirs* that Sterne left to his daughter.

In addition to a valuable preface in which he provides an annotated list of the principal printed sources and outlines the editorial problems involved in arriving at his text, Curtis contributed in the same year an illuminating article on the forgeries, examining forty-seven doubtful letters and demonstrating why he rejected them.[703]

By no means, however, are all questions of authenticity answered—particularly since the evidence is what it is. Fluchère has conveniently summarized the most important issues in Chapter XXV of his recent *Laurence Sterne,* using some materials that he had previously published in a periodical article and a review.[218]

Debate with Cross and Curtis has been joined at several points by Miss Margaret R. B. Shaw.[712] The contention, turning mainly on the authenticity of the letters to Elizabeth Lumley (Mrs. Sterne) in 1740, actually began (as I have previously suggested) in 1929 when Miss Shaw brought out the *Second Journal to Eliza,* an edition of a collection of correspondence originally published in 1779 as *Letters supposed to have been written by Yorick to Eliza* and later claimed for William Combe.[179] In a warmly argued introduction Miss Shaw adduced a wealth of stylistic evidence to prove (particularly by a comparison of Combe's style and Sterne's) that the letters were not forgeries. In a review in the same year, Professor Cross dissented sharply, contending that Miss Shaw had "lightly cast aside" external evidence. Cross furthermore categorically denied the validity of the stylistic proof, finding the collection "very dull, quite out of harmony with the temperaments of Sterne and Mrs. Draper." Even in view of this dissent, Miss Edith Morley, a highly respected authority in eighteenth-century literature, at first found it hard to reject Miss Shaw's evidence—though she was later inclined to modify her opinion when Curtis's edition of the *Letters* appeared. Curtis made no mention of the *Second Journal,* and Fluchère's survey of the scholarship relegates it to a footnote or two.

The matter of the *Second Journal,* at least, may be regarded as closed for the time being. But Miss Shaw's letter to the *Times Literary Supplement* in 1935[711] and the first volume of her 1957 biographical study indicate that she still has ideas of her own contrary to those of Cross and Curtis on a number of matters. Curtis, she contends, "fails to distinguish between first-hand evidence and hearsay," and in so doing demonstrates bias against Sterne. Although she cites some instances of his "rushing to form conclusions," her case is by no means fully established.[252]

In her second volume she has promised to develop more extensively the question of the "sensibility" of her subject, to give full treatment to the "last, sad stages" of his life as he reveals it in the *Journal to Eliza,* and to answer the critics who objected to her ascription of the journal.

V

Mr. Yorick in the Pulpit:
The Sermons

There can be no question about the popularity of the *Sermons* during Sterne's lifetime. Sometimes, in fact, they seem to have been more popular even than *Tristram Shandy*. The list of some five hundred subscribers to the two volumes of 1760 contained the names of the dukes of Devonshire, Portland, and Marlborough, not to mention such names of social and literary importance as Garrick, Hogarth, the Earl of Chesterfield, and famous old Lord Bathurst, the friend of Swift and Pope. Six years later an additional brace of volumes included a dazzling group of subscribers whose friendship Sterne had won in France, including Baron d'Holbach, Diderot, Crébillon *fils*, and Voltaire.

Back in England, William Cowper, who read the early volumes before his first great religious and mental crisis, expressed the feeling that Sterne was "a great master of the pathetic" and that no writer was "better qualified to make proselytes to the cause of virtue than he." Thomas Gray asserted that they were in a style "most proper for the pulpit" and that they showed "a strong imagination and a sensible heart"—though he did feel that one could see Sterne "tottering on the verge of laughter and ready to throw his periwig in the face of the audience." No one need be surprised that Dr. Johnson found them not so much the "cup of Salvation" as "merely the froth from the surface." A reviewer like Owen Ruffhead in the *Monthly Review* professed to being scandalized by the fact that the name of the jester Yorick was prefixed to the volume. But other reviewers, and the public at large, greeted the volumes admiringly.

At the end of the century, however, and in the opening decade of the next, interest in the sermons tended to decline with the deteriorating respect for the character of their author as a divine. From this decline they have never revived in popular interest.

If they were not read by laymen, they were also apparently not read with any care by the critics and scholars of the nineteenth century who continued to pass judgment on them. Commenting on the contradictory opinions expressed by H. D. Traill and George Saintsbury on the two sets of sermons, Cross remarks: "Professor Saintsbury evidently read the first set, and Traill evidently read the second set.—That accounts for the charming disagreement."[180]

In an era like ours in which sermons are no longer widely read as they were in the eighteenth century, lack of popular interest is easy to understand. It may be, on the other hand, that scholarly neglect (as Dr. Lansing Hammond has remarked)[751] is a little more difficult to explain. Nevertheless, if the sermons have not received the careful study that they have deserved, their worth as literature and their importance for their relationship to Sterne's more enduring literary contribution have not gone unnoticed.

Cross early pointed out the ways in which the "Charity Sermon" of 1727, the earliest published by the thirty-three-year-old prebend, adumbrates the later work of the novelist in its use of whimsy, unorthodox punctuation, digression, anecdote, and paraphrase of an old writer, in addition to sentimentality that seems to lead directly to *A Sentimental Journey*. And notice has naturally been taken of the particular qualities of "Abuses of Conscience Considered," also at first published separately and later skillfully incorporated into *Tristram Shandy*: the taking of a text that immediately undergoes a surprised sort of "Shandean" rejection, a description of the kinds of men who are deceived by their consciences, a thrust or two at the Roman Catholic Church, and a conclusion with a pathetic picture of a poor wretch undergoing the tortures of the Inquisition—of which much was made in the novel. The general dramatic qualities of Sterne's homiletics have also been fairly obvious: the choice of the concrete rather than the abstract in materials, the use of the kind of Biblical narrative that offered possibilities of contrast in character, the effective use of dialogue, the vivid etching of *mise en scène*—all in keeping with Sterne's constant feeling that the pulpit and the stage were cousins-german. Also observed have been the rhetorical devices through which Sterne delighted alternately in shocking his audience and in moving it to tears.

However, the Cross edition of the *Sermons* in the *Works* of 1904 and the two volumes without annotation in the Shakespeare Head edition of the *Works* in 1926-27 are the only twentieth-century editions. Moreover, the introductions to the Cross volumes, along with the biographer's comments in the *Life and Times,* constituted the only substantial critical comment for almost the first half of the century.

Dr. Hammond's study of 1948[751] has done much to correct the record. In an exhaustive search into the sources of the sermons with a careful examination of the passages that show indebtedness, Hammond developed two hypotheses: first, that the sermons published during Sterne's lifetime (Vols. I-IV) were actually his later and most finished compositions and that the posthumously published ones (Vols. V-VIII) were written earlier; and, second, that all but one of the forty-five printed sermons had been committed to paper in some form before 1751. Since he finds that only the posthumously published sermons betray conspicuous instances of verbatim copying and that the sermons published under Sterne's own supervision show creative use of source materials, he argues that the usual blanket charges of plagiarism lose much of their relevance. Because he feels that many of the sermons were written before 1751, he sees the appearance of "Shandyism"

much earlier than it is usually assumed; thus he argues that
Shandyism was not a sudden and drastic stylistic change com-
ing into simultaneous being with Sterne's conception of "the
Homunculus," but the result of a steady development clearly
manifested at least a decade before the opening chapters of
Tristram Shandy were written.

Cross had written in the introduction to his edition of the
Sermons of 1904:

> Without denying in the least evil and disorder in the world,
> Sterne yet implicity believed in the essential goodness of human
> nature and in the wise and just ways of Providence. He preached
> a sort of common sense philosophy, which, if it had nothing to do
> with Christian dogma, never contradicted them.[180]

In more recent years Fluchère has commented:

> Ce qui donc lui tient à coeur bien plus que Dieu, c'est encore
> l'homme, et sa fonction de pasteur lui semble bien remplie, si par
> l'amour des hommes il incite à l'amour de Dieu, et par l'amour de
> Dieu à celui des hommes.[218]

In a new study of Johnson as a moralist, Robert Voitle expresses an opinion at which it has not been difficult to arrive
when Sterne is viewed in the shadow of Ursa Major himself
and in the total background of the moral philosophy of the
century:

> No one is likely to think of Sterne as a moralist, even when he
> speaks from the pulpit, but on such optimistic estimates of humanity
> as his was based the cult of feeling—what might be termed a
> pseudo-ethic of virtue—which sanctioned the pleasurable pastime
> of emoting for emotion's sake, on the pretext that emotion is all
> that matters in morality and that good emotions are so efficacious
> that actions and their results need not be regarded at all.[752]

This last kind of judgment Hammond does not counter directly. But his convictions about the sermons are far more assuring
than most previous opinions in regard to Sterne's essential
Christianity and his basic sincerity:

> . . . it is neither accurate nor just to dismiss the sermons as
> "mere moral essays." Sterne was a Christian clergyman and the
> doctrine he preached is not unworthy of that high calling. . . . Like

[many twentieth-century preachers] he was content to refer to, rather than expound, the great truths of Christianity; but his acceptance of those truths is clear.

Moreover, from the evidence of the way in which the sermons were composed, Hammond feels that the case for Sterne's conscientiousness and sincerity in the performance of his duties as a priest can be better understood and defended than ever before.

Hammond's book is important for the insights that it gives us into Sterne's method and thought, as well as for the appendix of sources. Fluchère applauds it as having fixed once for all the manner of Sterne's activity as a preacher. But Miss Margaret Shaw has not been so certain. In fact, she has questioned seriously Hammond's two groupings—"imitative and platitudinous" and "original and Shandean"—as well as the entire procedure of dating the individual sermons. On a much broader basis, she objects to what she considers to be the limitations of Hammond's source-hunting, contending that he has not gone far enough back in time to determine the real roots of Yorick's theology in the humanistic tradition.

An answer to Miss Shaw's challenge and an elaboration of a portion of her own position are to be found in a recent examination of the "Abuses of Conscience," deemed by Cross as an example of Sterne's most logical thinking and by Sir Herbert Read as a central document in his role as "moral preceptor." A study of this sermon in the light of its background and in relation to its significance to the whole of Sterne's thought has led Arthur H. Cash to erect another case against those critics who have decried Sterne's lack of philosophy.[750] Far from indicating that Sterne was non-Christian or merely superficially Christian in his pulpit, the sermon reveals (in Cash's view) that he had assimilated the most liberal and enlightened tradition of Christian philosophy—chiefly that of the Christian Platonists who discovered a divinity in man allowing him to approach his Maker with dignity rather than in primitive dread. Completely denying the kind of generalization just cited from Voitle, Case concludes that Sterne is a "moral realist" and that as such he develops a "*Moral* theory [that is] more imaginative than his orthodox religion and more complex as a philosophy."

Plainly, a radical development in thinking about Sterne as priest and preacher has taken place. This comes understandably in a century of great religious change in which in many areas the ethical values of religion are considered to be far more important than the doctrinal. At such a time Sterne's Christianity is, at least, not so readily called into question as it has formerly been.

The new interest in Sterne as a rhetorician already discussed has also brought about a rereading of the sermons as "exercises in style." From this reading Professor Traugott, seconded by Professor MacLean (as we have seen), concludes that Sterne the novelist never gave up the devices of Sterne the preacher. With this point of view, Fluchère has in the main agreed; moreover, he has provided one of the most useful summaries of the stylistic and thematic qualities of the sermons as they later apply to *Tristram Shandy.*

VI

On Two Continents:
The Literary Reputation and Influence

Early twentieth-century scholarship in some respects showed a more lively interest in Sterne's impact on the Continent than it did on his reputation at home. This fact is demonstrated by the gap of over half a century between Harvey Waterman Thayer's comprehensive study in 1905 of Sterne's reputation in Germany[804] and Allan B. Howe's definitive book in 1958 on the reputation in England up to 1868.[803] Actually, the popularity and influence on the Continent were different from and at times even greater than they were in England. "The spoilt child in England," Professor Ernest Baker has remarked, "was furnished with the power of a literary authority in Germany and in France."[304]

The reputation and influence in England had, of course, not gone entirely unnoticed before Howes. Frederick Behrmann's 1936 index to imitations of Sterne in England[811] had provided evidence of his immense vogue. In the same year Archibald B. Shepperson had made a critical discussion of the imitations and burlesques.[834] Prior to both, Professor J. M. S. Tomkins[837] and others had generalized about the nature of Sterne's influence in his great revelation to his age regarding the significance of the small and fleeting, as well as about the novelist's importance in teaching his century "to feel." Concerning the imitations, Robert D. Mayo has recently remarked that the long parade of imitations in the miscellanies for more than forty years (that is, roughly from 1785 to 1815) is "one of the dreariest chapters in magazine history."[825]

Though Sterne may have helped teach his century "to feel," he was by no means alone in doing so. The influence of Rousseau and others must be taken into account. And in other respects than in sensibility his literary influence should not be overestimated. Even a Scottish "man of feeling" like Henry MacKenzie (as Professor Harold William Thompson has noted)[836] borrowed from Sterne without admitting that he did so and without fully approving of him. Though he won the admiration of such important Romanticists as Coleridge and Hazlitt and though he may have had some influence on Byron, his impact on the major literary production of the period from 1790 to 1830 was by no means so important as it was on the literature of the first half of the nineteenth century on the Continent.

In the emerging nation of the United States, interest in Sterne was considerable. Americans of the first rank like Benjamin Franklin and Thomas Jefferson, as well as less important writers and statesmen like William Wirt and James Iredell, were among those who admired him. Moreover, he had the distinction of influencing "the first native American novel," William Hill Brown's *The Power of Sympathy* (1789), and "the second comedy by a native American to be performed on the professional stage and the first so performed to be printed," William Dunlap's *The Fathers; or American Shandyism* (1788-89).[818] Professor Herbert R. Brown[800] has discussed the late eighteenth-century interest in Sterne as it centered about the *Massachusett's Magazine* (1789-96); and, along with Professor Tremaine McDowell, he has treated Sterne's influence on such novelists of sensibility as Mrs. Morton, Mrs. Susannah Rowson, and Mrs. Hannah Webster Foster.[816] McDowell called the English novelist "demonstrably the most powerful of the influences which produced sensibility in America."[826]

Beyond these studies there has yet been no extended effort to treat the reputation and influence of Sterne in America.

Among the relationships in the literature of mid- and later nineteenth-century England, Bulwer-Lytton's use of Sterne's methods in a series of novels beginning with *The Caxtons*,[820] the relationship of Sterne and George Borrow,[821] and Sterne's influence on Dickens, Thackeray, Marryat, Carlyle, and other Victorians have been discussed by design or at random in articles and monographs.

The novelist's influence on and affinities with a number of important twentieth-century writers like George Moore, Joseph Conrad, James Joyce, Virginia Woolf, and Henry Green have been frequently noticed.

Though the popularity of Sterne's works in France (particularly *A Sentimental Journey*) is beyond question, Professor Charles Sears Baldwin warned in 1902 that the novelist's actual literary influence could be exaggerated.[842] Brushing off as unconvincing many previous attributions of influence, Baldwin found only one book, Xavier de Maistre's *Voyage autour de ma Chambre* (1794) as summing up "the influence of Sterne's best form [that of the *Journey*] on French literature" and, in addition, one imitation of *Tristram Shandy*, Diderot's *Jacques le Fataliste*, that was actually entitled to be called such. He did admit a "score of passages here and there, reminiscent possibly of [Sterne's] sentimentality"—including parts of Victor Hugo's youthful *Bug Jargal*, Charles Nodier's *Histoire de Roi de Bohême*, and Théophile Gautier's *Fortunio*. A good deal more evidence in Sterne's favor was adduced in Francis Brown Barton's dissertation of 1911.[843]

The brilliant social success achieved by the novelist on his visits to Paris was, of course, an indication rather of the admiration held for him as a wit and a famous man than as an author, especially since the number of people in France capable of appreciating his total literary output was somewhat limited. Since he was a lion rather than a lion hunter, he did not achieve the success of his compatriot James Boswell—lion hunter *par excellence*—in snaring the two most important men in French letters, Rousseau and Voltaire. But the literary figures that he did capture—d'Holbach, Crébillon *fils,* and Diderot, for example—were of a very high intellectual and social level, indeed. If not every intelligent Frenchman who could read English could cope with *Tristram Shandy,* far fewer difficulties were offered by A *Sentimental Journey.* It is, therefore, not surprising that the popularity of this little volume was widespread. And Sterne became in France, as well as elsewhere (in the words of Joseph Texte) "a prophet of the new religion of the *self*" brought into fashion by Rousseau.[895]

Sterne's relationship with Diderot has understandably been the subject of a number of critical treatments. Most of these have been ably evaluated and summed up by Mrs. Alice Green Fredman,[858] whose *Diderot and Sterne* (1955) is an informative chapter on Sterne's most important French connection. For this reason it deserves more than a casual attention.

When the French Encyclopedist and the Yorkshire parson met in Paris in 1762, they were both forty-nine years old. Furthermore, each had established a reputation as a man of sensibility who enjoyed indulging in buffoonery and who believed in jettisoning inhibitions where "feeling" was involved. Not only in temperament but also in reading background, Diderot was eminently capable (as few other Frenchmen were) of penetrating beyond the eccentric surface of *Tristram Shandy.* Diderot knew both Rabelais and Cervantes as well as Sterne did; and he had an undoubtedly deeper comprehension of John Locke, for whom both men had a well-advertised enthusiasm.

On his side, Sterne was plainly no mere country parson from an obscure "living" in the north of England. Whatever provinciality he might previously have been accused of had been lost in the glow of his sensational success as a novelist in London. But what was even more important was his considerable knowledge of French literature, especially that of the precursors and the authors of the Enlightenment. Thus the fact that Sterne was admirably equipped to match wits with and win the friendship of the important *philosophe* should be self-evident.

The friendship that developed so inevitably lasted until Sterne died six years after the first meeting. Nevertheless, the contacts of the two men, except through correspondence, were relatively few; and this marriage of true minds can hardly be said to be famous in literary history. In at least one of his novels, *Jacques le Fataliste,* Diderot—as previously suggested— cemented the connection by admitting plagiarism from *Tristram Shandy* and *A Sentimental Journey.* Yet until Mrs. Fredman published her study, the relationship had been regarded as a decidedly minor part in the lives of both men. It still may be so regarded. At the same time, one must admit that the study of this friendship does much toward illuminating the whole meaning of Sterne to his age.

Mrs. Fredman's book has two basic purposes. The first is to demonstrate how Sterne and Diderot were attempting either consciously or subconsciously to break away from certain aspects of the neo-classical manner, ultimately arriving at modes of literary expression that foreshadowed Romanticism. The second purpose is to defend Diderot from a broad charge of plagiarism. In the pursuit of her thesis, Mrs. Fredman has been able to show where both writers stand in relation to their literary and philosophical milieu and, concomitantly, to indicate clearly how both led the way to new ideas and to new ways of literary expression.

As French as Sterne frequently seems and as significant as his popularity was in France, he appealed more forcibly to Germany. "Germany, indeed," as Walter Sichel remarked in 1910, "proved the foster-mother of Sterne's genius. Societies were founded in his name, which still flourish."[253] Lessing said that he would have sacrificed ten years of his own life if he could have prolonged that of Sterne. Goethe made Sterne "a companion," delighting in and imitating Sterne's whimsy in "his most intimate personal correspondence, showing his delight at being free from the conventional shackles of logic and pedantry."[880] Heine did not hesitate to claim kinship with Sterne, expressing the opinion that he was a greater artist than Fielding and reserving the term "poetic" for him because he "opens a window" on "the hidden reserves of the soul."[897]

Though, as usual, *A Sentimental Journey* became the most immediate influence, *Tristram Shandy* was also important. Sterne's influence on the sentimental novel in Germany has been treated by Lawrence Marsden Price in a chapter in his *English Literature in Germany* of 1953[881] and more exhaustively by Peter Michelson in a monograph of 1962.[878] Among the imitations of the *Journey,* Thümmel's ten-volume *Reise in die mittäglichen Provinzen von Frankreich* (1791-1805) is generally considered to be the most original and entertaining.[896] As a writer of the "sentimental period," Jean Paul [Richter], whose inner life seemed to be rich to overflowing, who loved the grotesque and bizarre, who disliked formalism and was fascinated by the irrationalities of life, found Sterne a ready influence.[890] (Wieland, who was also influenced by Sterne, called Jean Paul the German Yorick and the German Rabelais). Jean Paul's novels, quite plainly like Sterne's, abound in lengthy digressions and footnotes, overgrown prefaces, and appendices—most of which have little connection with the main topic. It is not difficult to understand why studies of his relationship with Sterne have been numerous.

Professors René Wellek and Austin Warren have observed that through *Tristram Shandy* Sterne became the "founder" of a line of novels using the romantic-ironic mode of epic narration (in which the role of the narrator is deliberately magnified and the written character of the book is emphasized), including not only the novels of Jean Paul, but also those of Tieck in German, Veltman and Gogol in Russia, and extending up to such works of fiction in the contemporary era as Gide's *Les Faux-Monnayeurs* and Huxley's *Point Counter Point.*[902] It has also been noted that Wilhelm Raabe of Brunswick (1831-1910) found some of his stylistic ideals in Sterne's use of the romantic-ironic method and his interruption of his tales with didactic digressions and seemingly pointless interpolations.[854]

Dr. Gertrude J. Hallamore has made the most exhaustive

study of Sterne's influence on German intellectual history of two generations from the *Aufklärung* to the *Romantik*,[861] giving corroboration to Joseph Texte's early generalization that the philosophy of Sterne was "the most brilliant invention of eighteenth-century anglomania," as well as to Professor Thayer's summation of the total appeal of Sterne to his German public:

> He stood as a figure of benignant humanity, of lavish sympathy with every earthly affliction, he became a guide and mentor, an awakener, and consoler, and probably more than all, a sanction for emotional expression.

The influence of Sterne in Italy may be dated from the completion of the translation of *A Sentimental Journey* by the poet, Ugo Foscolo, in 1813. As it did in Germany, the little book influenced a whole generation of Romantic and sentimental writers. Giovanni Rabizzani[885] has written the most comprehensive treatment of the nature and extent of the influence.

The impact of Sterne in Russia was not less important. Alexander Radischev (1744-1802) read Sterne in German; and the influence of *A Sentimental Journey* is apparent in his *Voyage from St. Petersburg to Moscow* (1790), in which he attacked serfdom and exposed the inhuman treatment of peasants, together with the corruption of police and minor officials. This influence has been treated at some length by D. M. Lang.[870]

By 1800 both of Sterne's works of fiction had been translated into Russian, and a volume called *The Beauties of Sterne* appeared in Moscow in 1801. From this point Sterne's popularity began to rise and imitations appeared to such a degree that Shakhovskoi was prompted to bring out a satire on the resulting sentimentalism under the title of *The New Sterne*. The great imitator of the new school of pre-Romantic sentimentalism was Nicholas Karamazin (1766-1826), who filled his *Letters of a Russian Traveler* with references to and quotations from Sterne and who in *Poor Liza,* a tale of love and suicide, achieved an attitude of refined pity not unlike Sterne's.

When sentimentalism declined in nineteenth-century Rus-
sia—as Franklin Dolier Reeve has observed in a review of
Sterne's popularity and influence with special reference to
Gogol—Pushkin and Gogol "picked up that half of Sterne Kara-
mazin had left out: the humor, the common sense, the literary
gamesmanship itself."[887] Moreover, the young Tolstoy, as Peter
Rudy has recently revealed, was influenced by *A Sentimental
Journey* and the *Sermons*.[889]

In addition to studies of Sterne's influence upon writers in
Germany, France, Italy, and Russia, studies have been made
of the influence of Sterne on Dutch writers[872] and on Johannes
Ewals, the great Danish lyric poet.[848]

Though the available studies are capable of giving a comprehensive view of Sterne's reputation and influence on the
European continent, a number of these studies are in languages
other than English and no one of them makes an extensive
comparative study of the interrelationships of this influence.
Such a study in English might make a valuable contribution.

VII

A Chapter of Conclusions

―――――――――

A *Sentimental Journey* remains one of the small gems of English fiction—admired now not so much as it was in the eighteenth and nineteenth centuries for its sensibility as for its subtle humor and for the exquisite perfection of its prose style. As for *Tristram Shandy*, critics who have for a long time had the habit of calling either *Tom Jones* or *Clarissa* the "greatest English novel" have not been quite so extravagant with their evaluations of Sterne's masterwork. Yet for all their elements of appeal and of greatness, the novels of Richardson and Fielding are more likely to appear to twentieth-century readers as "period pieces" than *Tristram Shandy* is. In an age when the experimental in all art forms is a hallmark of modernity, the work of Sterne finds a congenial atmosphere. The novelist was in at least one sense almost two centuries ahead of his time. The fact that most of his numerous followers failed to understand the essence of his art and thus tended to imitate chiefly the most superficial things in it stands as an interesting and curious kind of proof. When Virginia Woolf in the late twenties said that Sterne was "singularly of our age," she gave authoritative critical recognition of his belonging to the twentieth century. Earlier it had still been possible to talk about the novelist's quaint "hodge-podge" structure, his "saurian jokes" and his "crude antediluvian fun." For some decades now there has been no really serious challenge to Mrs. Woolf's judgment.

Writing in the *New Republic* of August 7, 1965, the British novelist and critic, John Wain, comments that James Joyce's distrust of a linear conception of time is at present shared by more people, consciously or unconsciously, than it was when Joyce was writing. Wain continues with some broad generalizations about eighteenth- and nineteenth-century fiction to the effect that the narrative unilinear view of experience underlying such fiction is an abstraction, resulting from "standing back and reasoning about experience, sorting out its thick knotty texture into manageable threads." There is at present, he contends, a reluctance to stand back and ratiocinate. Thus the "traditionally written novel" is in trouble. Wain goes on to support the thesis of Professor Marshall McLuhan, who in *The Gutenberg Galaxy* apparently contended that the invention of movable type shifted the sensibility of man to a unilinear plane and that the consequences were felt "in every area of life." So far as fiction was concerned, the contention seems to have run, "people began to read silently and passively as consumers."

Whatever reliance one may place on such generalizations as they relate to eighteenth-century fiction as a whole, one may see that they have little relevance to Sterne's narrative method or effect. Certainly in regard to *Tristram Shandy*, the reader is allowed to read neither passively nor (in a special way) silently.

It has been recognized for a long time that *Tristram Shandy* is in one sense a long monologue or, in another, a dialogue between the narrator and a complex of readers or hearers—being in the latter sense both like and unlike the later nineteenth-century dramatic monologue in which a "hearer" is developed often as an effectively realized character. The basic elements of this device are not peculiar to Sterne. Fielding and other contemporaries used it extensively. But no other writer of fiction in the century was able to engage and, further, to exploit the reader in the same way that Sterne does. It is no secret that a large part of the suspense and, therefore, the attraction of the novel lies in our wondering not merely what the narrator is going to do next but also into what role he is going to trick the reader—whose sex, status, and point of view are changeable at the narrator's whim. Thus the device of the shifting putative reader or hearer becomes a kind of game that the author-narrator (it is often difficult to tell which is which) plays with the one who actually has the novel in his hands.

In the space of four chapters (vii-x) in Book I, it may be quickly seen, this putative reader or hearer is addressed as "your worship," "Sir," "my Lord," and "madam." In a single chapter of Book IV (xvii), the range is considerably greater: from "dear Sir" to "madam" to "your reverences and your worships" back to "Sir." Numerous times the reader must assume the part of "madam" not to mention that of the more familial and intimate "dear girl" or "Jenny." Less frequently he is merely "gentle reader" or "Sir Critick" or "you gentry with the great beards"; or he may be asked to assume the role of a real person like "my dear Garrick." Most frequently he is "your worship" or "your worships," or "my brethren," or "your reverences and worships." In some of these parts he must sense (and in time does sense instinctively) the deprecation that is subtly limned and in which he is just as subtly involved. In this connection, Sterne's statement in III, xx, "As for the great wigs, upon which I may be thought to have spoken my mind too freely . . . I write not for them" can strike one as being highly ironical. Indeed, the reader may find himself breaking silence and exclaiming to the narrator, "Then you write not *for,* but *to* them." If it is always possible to put *Tristram Shandy* down, it is not possible to read it without some definite sort of engagement.

The ways indicated above are, of course, not the only ones through which the reader is entrapped and exploited. The multiple uses of a character like Uncle Toby, for example, to engage the reader's identity and empathy go rather far beyond the usual exploitation that the "dramatic" or self-conscious narrator, or any other kind of narrator for that matter, is expected to make of his audience. In no other work of fiction than in *Tristram Shandy* is the reader so often and so delightfully caught off guard—that is, if he is willing to commit himself to the game. Those who are not willing are simply those who for one reason or another do not like the book. They had better go their own way and leave *Tristram Shandy* alone. As in the instance of the "great wigs," Sterne writes not for them.

In a novel about the writing of a novel, the reader should not be surprised to be ushered frequently into the writer's study. But only in *Tristram Shandy* is the reader likely to find himself so suddenly and so intimately there:

> It is not half an hour ago, when (in the great hurry and precipitation of a poor devil's writing for daily bread) I threw a fair sheet, which I had just finished and carefully wrote out, slap into the fire, instead of a foul one.

The crinkled black ashes are still on the hearth in evidence!

Thus the game not only of *who* the reader is but also *where* he is is played against a background of people, ideas, and things that are themselves shifting but have for their moment (and after) a vivid conviction of reality.

It hardly needs to be said that as a narrator Tristram succeeds where his counterpart in real life most often fails miserably. Who can tolerate the person who in ordinary conversation is forever backing and filling, embroidering and elaborating, detailing and digressing in such a way as never to get his story told—or almost never? The secret is, again, the game —the subtle engagement.

But even to those who are willing to commit themselves, the charm does not always work. Eventually the reader may become wary. Finally he may tire. No one can argue sensibly that the novel is of a piece. The brilliance of the first four books shows some signs of wavering even as early as the third. And for all the choice materials of the fifth and sixth books— the circumstances around Bobby's death, the accidental circumcision of Tristram, Mr. Shandy's system of auxiliary verbs, the story of Le Fever—the Sternean manner (as others have noticed) at times becomes a kind of parody of itself. The announced digressive-progressive movement of the book is not always so progressive as it might be. The return to Uncle Toby's affair with the Widow Wadman in the two final books has been adjudged by some to be inconclusive and unsatisfactory but by others to offer a successful completion of what Tristram said he was going to do.

The rather recent contention, indeed, that the book is complete with the final chapter may suggest that criticism abhors a fragment in the same way that nature abhors a vacuum; and the argument may fail not because it is less than admirably pursued but because in a novel like *Tristram Shandy* it may seem irrelevant. Had not Tristram early threatened that he could go on turning out two volumes a year as long as he lived and could he not have done so had he lived? ("I have forty volumes to write and forty thousand things to say.") To what useful end can this kind of debate be taken?

The arguments for the unity of the book may also strike one as irrelevant. Still the idea that there is a palpable force holding the book together in spite of all its tendencies to fly apart is tantalizingly undeniable. The feeling of inward cohesion has a way of running in counterpoint to the outward evidence of chaos. It may be wise, when all the evidence is in, to conclude that the various arguments for the unity of the novel are useful chiefly to balance a less perceptive and less thoughtful judgment of disorder and that a settlement for an ineffable combination of plan and caprice is about as much as we can do. One may, of course, fall back ultimately on the simplicity of statement in a critic like Coleridge, whose well demonstrated skill and profundity might have been expected to allow him to come up with a better principle of unity if there was one: "Hence the digressive spirit is not mere wantonness but in fact the very form and vehicle of [Rabelais's and Sterne's] genius. The connection, such as was needed, is given by the continuity of the characters."

After all, the true genius of *Tristram Shandy* is (in a sense at least obliquely suggested by Coleridge) not so much in its unity as in its flexibility. The remarkable thing about most of the contemporary attempts to find principles of unity in structure, rhetoric, theme, or philosophic background is that such a variety of arguments is admissible—even when some of them tend to be contradictory. And if the novel can be variously interpreted in terms of the physico-theological, the Neo-Platonic, the Newtonian, the Lockean, the Hutchensonian, the Shaftesburian, the Humean thought of the eighteenth century, and even the Hegelian dialectic of the nineteenth, it can also be interpreted according to the Freudian psycho-analytical, the Camusian Existential, or perhaps even the Dalian Surrealistic "systems" of the twentieth.

The irony is that the critic who attempts to impose any kind of system on *Tristram Shandy* immediately assumes the role of Tristram's father. (This is one of the traps that Sterne himself has laid). And the critic should not be astonished if the normative reader tends to react somewhat in the role of Mr. Shandy's less systematic brother: "You puzzle me to death, cried my uncle *Toby*."

As a healthful corrective to any tendency to make an excessively academic critical treatment of the novel, one may well keep its domestic and local origins in mind. It began—and to a degree remains—as what Sir Herbert Read has called a Yorkshire epic. It is also in part an obstetrical romance. (Does not recent investigation indicate that Sterne knew the midwifery of his time at least as well as he knew Lockean psychology?) Dr. Slop, Didius, Kysarcius, Kunastrokius, Phutatorious are all disguises for real Yorkshire people—most of them involved with Sterne in the politics of the Shire or in the quarrels around the chapter house of the York Cathedral. The satire here is as sharply personal (though perhaps on a slightly different plane) as that to be found in Pope's portraits of Atticus and Sporus—a fact, incidentally, that is too often forgotten when Sterne's satire is adjudged to be closer to Swift's than to Pope's.

However, if the matter simply ended here, *Tristram Shandy* might well have gone the way of the ill-fated *Political Romance*. All the minor satirical portraits are, of course, overshadowed by those of that most remarkable Yorkshire family, the Shandys, who are just as limited geographically and ethnically as the characters in a novel by Jane Austen. They achieve their universality, in at least one way shared by the creations of Miss Austen, simply by coming vividly alive.

In this regard the testimony of a distinguished novelist and short story writer is interesting if it does nothing else than reassert the continued validity of reading *Tristram Shandy* in terms of the direct communication of the printed page to the reader. "That novel," Katherine Anne Porter has written, "contains more living breathing people you can see and hear, whose garments have texture between your finger and thumb, whose flesh is knit firmly to their bones, who walk about their affairs with audible footsteps, than any other one novel in the world." The Shandys, she goes on, "all live in one house with floor boards under their bootsoles, a roof over their heads, the fire burning and giving off real smoke, cooking smells coming from the kitchen, real weather outside and air blowing through the windows. [Miss Porter leaves out a real sash that unexpectedly falls and a real door hinge that chronically squeaks; but no matter!] When Dr. Slop cuts his thumb real blood issues from it, and everybody has a navel and his proper distribution of his vital organs."

This may all sound like the obvious. Is not the least one can say for great fiction that it creates believable people? Yet there is need for frequent repetition of such a statement chiefly because from the outset critical efforts toward evaluation of the novel have, whether for a worse or a better final judgment, been adulterated by moral, aesthetic, and philosophical issues tangential to the main business.

But however successful Sterne may have been in creating believable characters, what he was able to do with the novel as a form has a significance all its own.

The fact that he has been acclaimed a great force for Romanticism may be more important to the literary historian than it is to the contemporary critic or reader. If he was such a force, it was not because he "liberated" the novel as a form but chiefly because he seemed to elevate Feeling above Reason. And though *Tristram Shandy* played its part in spreading Sterne's influence in this respect, the most immediately effective agent (as we have already seen) was *A Sentimental Journey*. The evidence of this influence is abundant and undeniable. The true nature of Sterne's own sentimentality and sensibility is another matter. Could he possibly have tricked a generation or two of German, French, Italian, English, and American sentimental novelists into another one of his traps? The answer is far from simple. If the novelist could use and exploit a single reader, he could presumably do the same thing for many readers. It is not difficult to see that Sterne was just as fond of educing feeling as he was of giving expression to it—very likely more so. In everything that he did—his novels, his sermons, his letters—he gives constant indication of keen relish in his ability to play upon his audience, to mold, shape, and control its reactions not entirely unlike the way in which a masterful conductor "plays" an orchestra. But are we to assume that he was always the jester, that he was never capable of real feeling? "Every thing in this world, said my father, is big with jest,—and has wit in it, and instruction, too,—if we can but find it out." This is Tristram's report of what Walter Shandy observed. It cannot be taken as an easy generalization of the novelist's own attitude. It answers the basic question neither one way nor the other.

One may not be able, it is true, to dismiss altogether considerations of Sterne's morality or his "sincerity" as irrelevancies in the consideration of his art, but the question of what he did to the form of the novel is of far more importance to the twentieth century. If in *Tristram Shandy* he did not "destroy" the structural conventions that had grown up before he began writing, he did not passively accept them. And if his innovations were not actually so original as they may have seemed to be, the form that he arrived at was (beyond question) different. However he may have used, dramatized, and burlesqued ideas from Locke's *Essay concerning Human Understanding*, however much he may have been influenced by the tradition of the familiar essay as it had come down from Montaigne, or that of the satires of "learned wit," or that of the self-conscious narrator in antecedent fiction, he neverthe-

less evolved an architectonic all his own—far too subtle for
his imitators to follow effectively and subtle enough to keep
fluid our own efforts to define it. His ability to discover as
early as he did that he did not have to conform to an artificial
and restrictive "unilinear view of experience" in fiction enabled
him to strike a blow for individualism and freedom worthy of
any Romanticist. And if *Tristram Shandy* did not have the
kind of immediate influence upon the form and content of the
English novel as such a revolutionary volume, let us say, as
Lyrical Ballads had on English poetry, it may have been for
no other reason than that for its own time the novel was so
ineluctably *sui generis.*

Sterne himself did not fail to recognize this fact. On February 9, 1768, only a little more than a month before he died,
the novelist wrote a letter of thanks to Dr. John Eustace of
Wilmington, North Carolina. This gentleman had sent Sterne
"a piece of shandean statuary" in the form of a curious walking
stick formerly owned by a Colonial governor of North Carolina named Arthur Dobbs.

"Your walking stick is in no sense more *shandaic* than in
that of its having *more handles than one,*" Sterne wrote. "—The
parallel breaks only in this, that in using the stick everyone
will take the handle which suits his convenience. In *Tristram
Shandy,* the handle is taken which suits their passions, their
ignorance or sensibility. . . . It is too much to write books and
find heads to understand them."

The weariness of the writer and his pathetic need for appreciation and affection are evident; but also, as we proceed, is
his graciousness: "I am very proud, sir, to have a man like
you, on my side from the beginning." And there is more than
a spark of pride and confidence in the feeling that the "people
of genius" in England are, after all, on his side and that the
reception of his novel in France, Italy, and Germany has been
gratifying.

What any book needs, Sterne goes on to say, is a sympa-
thetic reader: ". . . a true feeler always brings half the entertainment along with him. His own ideas are only call'd forth

by what he reads, and the vibrations within, so entirely corre-
spond with those excited, 'tis like reading *himself* and not the
book." Not everyone can appreciate humor, Sterne asserts
"—'tis the gift of God."

The various "handles" that Sterne had admittedly given his
book had too frequently led to misunderstanding and condemnation rather than to appreciation. And except for the
support of people of sufficient "genius," Sterne can find reason
for feeling that he has been victimized by his own cleverness,
his own ambiguities, his own ambivalences, his own "negative
capability." Being something like all things to all people may
be a virtue in a work of art, but it is not always tolerated in
the human being, the artist. And when the work of art and
the artist are not dissociated, the real burden of the intolerance
seems to fall on the latter. This was and has been a basic
problem of criticism from the time that the first two volumes
of *Tristram Shandy* appeared in the bookshop of John Hinxman
in York (late in December, 1759) almost to the present.

The attempt to make this dissociation and to allow the work
of art to stand on its own has been one of the major achieve-
ments of twentieth-century criticism of Sterne. The various
"handles" have been used to probe the secrets of his acknowl-
edged genius, not to oversentimentalize or to denigrate his character, his mind, or his literary product. The fact that all the
investigation has failed to solve the final mystery and that his
genius still remains elusive and undefined should add not so
much to our despair as to Sterne's credit.

The narrator of *Tristram Shandy* believes that in order
properly to set forth his life and opinions he must consider all
possible systems of thinking (educational, physiological, cos-
mological, domestic) focalized by that fascinating and complex
"Little Gentleman," the Homunculus. Through such a narrator
Sterne has woven an intricate web leading to the kind of picture of the human situation (elaborately involved in impulses,
obsessions, sensations, associations, "hobby-horses") that may
better be apprehended than understood. Thus, as Sterne him-

self suggested, the most confident approach to understanding may be that of the "true feeler"—that particular type of "man of feeling" who, willing to enter the game, "always brings half of the entertainment with him" and trusts to the author and God Almighty for the rest.

Bibliography
of Sternean Studies, 1900-1965

Abbreviations

AB	*American Bookman*
Archiv	*Archiv für das Studium der neueren Sprachen und Literaturen*
AUMLA	*Journal of the Australasian Universities Language and Literature Association*
BNYPL	*Bulletin of the New York Public Library*
CE	*College English*
Comp. Lit.	*Comparative Literature*
DA	*Dissertation Abstracts*
ELH	*Journal of English Literary History*
ES	*English Studies*
HLQ	*Huntington Library Quarterly*
JEGP	*Journal of English and Germanic Philology*
JHI	*Journal of the History of Ideas*
LGRP	*Literaturblatt für Germanische und Romanische Philologie*
MLN	*Modern Language Notes*
MLQ	*Modern Language Quarterly*
MLR	*Modern Language Review*
MP	*Modern Philology*
N & Q	*Notes and Queries*
NYHTB	*New York Herald Tribune Books*
PMLA	*Publications of the Modern Language Association of America*
PQ	*Philological Quarterly*
RAA	*Revue Anglo-Americaine*
RES	*Review of English Studies*
SAQ	*South Atlantic Quarterly*
SR	*Sewanee Review*
SRL	*Saturday Review of Literature*
TBR	*New York Times Book Review*
TLS	*London Times Literary Supplement*
UKCR	*University of Kansas City Review*
VQR	*Virginia Quarterly Review*
WHR	*Western Humanities Review*
YR	*Yale Review*
YWES	*Year's Work in English Studies*

I

Bibliographical Aids

Ashley Library (The). *A Catalogue of Printed Books, Manu-* [1]
scripts, and Autograph Letters, collected by Thomas
James Wise. London: Privately printed, 1925.

Bartholomew, A. T. [Bibliography for] "Sterne and the Novel [2]
of His Times" in *Cambridge History of English Literature.*
New York: G. P. Putnam's Sons; Cambridge: The University Press, 1913. X, 475-476.

Block, Andrew. *The English Novel, 1740-1850: A Catalogue.* [3]
London: Dawsons, 1961. P. 225.

British Museum General Catalogue of Printed Books. Photo- [4]
lithographic edition to 1955. London: British Museum,
1959-65. CCXXIX, 780-800.
  The most comprehensive single record of editions old
and modern.

Brown, T. J. "English Literary Autographs XXVII: Laurence [5]
Sterne, 1713-1768," *Book Collector,* VII (1958), 285.

Cordasco, Francesco. *Laurence Sterne: A List of Critical* [6]
Studies Published from 1896 to 1946. (Eighteenth Cen-
tury Bibliographical Pamphlets, No. 4) Brooklyn: Long
Island University Press, 1948.

Crane, Ronald S., *et al.,* eds. *English Literature, 1660-1800: A* [7]
Bibliography of Modern Studies. 4 vols. Princeton: Prince-
ton University Press, 1950-1962.
  Reprint of annual bibliographies in *PQ,* 1926-1960.

Cross, Wilbur L. *The Life and Times of Laurence Sterne.*   [8]
New Haven: Yale University Press, 1929.
Important bibliographical appendix. See 211.

Curtis, Lewis Perry. "Laurence Sterne" in *Cambridge Bibli-*   [9]
ography of English Literature, edited by F. W. Bateson.
New York: The Macmillan Company; Cambridge: The
University Press, 1941. II, 521-523.
See Green (16).

————. "The Printer of Sterne's 'Political Romance,'" *TLS,*   [10]
February 28, 1929, p. 163.
Considers evidence of a printer's ornament.

Devonshire, M. G. "Sterne" in *The English Novel in France,*   [11]
1830-1870. London: University of London Press, 1929.
Pp. 90-92.
Chief French translations are listed. Cf. 22 and 853.

Eaves, T. C. Duncan. "Graphic Illustration of the Principal   [11a]
English Novels of the Eighteenth Century." Unpublished
Ph.D. dissertation, Harvard University, 1944.
See 534.

Evans, Charles. *American Bibliography.* New York: Peter   [12]
Smith, 1942 (Reprint). IV-X.
For American editions prior to 1800.

A Facsimile Reproduction of a Unique Catalogue of Laurence   [13]
Sterne's Library. With a preface by Charles Whibley.
London: James Tregaskis; New York: Edgar H. Wells &
Company, 1930.
Catalogue of a sale beginning on August 23, 1768, by
J. Todd and H. Sotheran, booksellers in York.—Reviewed
by G. M. Troxell in *SRL,* VI (1930), 812; *Oxford Maga-*
zine, March 13, 1930, p. 620; *Library,* XV (1930), 390.

Fluchère, Henri. *Laurence Sterne de l'homme à l'oeuvre.*   [14]
Paris: Gallimard, 1961. Pp. 657-693.
Contains the most comprehensive of twentieth-century
bibliographies. See 218.

Fränzel, Walter. *Geschichte des Übersetzens im 18. Jahr-*   [15]
hundert. (Beiträge zur Kultur- und Universalgeschichte
25) Leipzig, 1914.
German translations of Sterne.

Green, Roger Lancelyn. "Laurence Sterne" in *Cambridge*   [16]
Bibliography of English Literature. Cambridge: The Uni-
versity Press, 1957. V (Supplement), 452-453.
  Brings Curtis (9) up to date.

Leary, Lewis, ed. *Contemporary Literary Scholarship.* New   [17]
York: Appleton-Century-Crofts, Inc., 1958. Pp. 100, 103,
277, 280, 284.
  Comments by James L. Clifford and Bradford A.
Booth on recent scholarship.

Oates, J. C. T. "Notes on the Bibliography of Sterne: I. *Let-*   [18]
ters from Eliza to Yorick, 1775; II. *Letters from Yorick to*
Eliza, 1775," *Transactions of the Cambridge Biblio-*
graphical Society, II (1955), 155-169.

———. "On Collecting Sterne," *Book Collector,* I (1952), 247-   [19]
258.
  Notes on a private collection of editions, translations,
and imitations.

"Points in 'Tristram Shandy,'" *TLS,* February 22, 1934, p. 132.   [20]
  Concerns the bibliographical description of the first
edition of *Tristram Shandy,* adding to the material of
Cross in the third edition of the *Life and Times* (211).
Cf. 28.

Reitzel, William. "Cobbett and Sterne," *TLS,* December 10,   [21]
1931, p. 1006.
  Queries an allegation made by William Cobbett in
Porcupine's Works (London, 1801), IV, 8on., that an edition of *A Sentimental Journey* coming from the bookshop
of Citizen Thomas Bradford of Philadelphia contained a
set of bawdy cuts explaining the "double entendre [*sic*]
and filthy innuendoes." See remarks of Winterich (167).

Rochedieu, C. A. *Bibliography of French Translations of En-*   [22]
glish Works, 1700-1800. Chicago: University of Chicago
Press, 1948.
  See 11.

Ryan, M. J. "An Edition of Sterne," *TLS,* September 16, 1926,   [23]
p. 616.
  A note and a query on the "first collective edition of
Sterne" as indicated in the *Dictionary of National Biog-*
raphy by Sir Sidney Lee (230).

Sellers, H. "A Sterne Problem," *TLS*, October 21, 1926, p. 722.   [24]
    Bibliographical problems involved with the copy of
Tristram Shandy in the Grenville Collection at the British
Museum. See comment by C. Wanklyn, *ibid.*, November
4, 1926, p. 770, and Yoklavich (28).

Stamm, Rudolph. *Englische Literatur.* (Wissenschaftliche   [25]
    Forschungsberichte Geisteswissenschaftliche Reihe. Her-
ausgegeben von Professor Karl Hönn, Band II) Bern: A.
Francke, 1957. Pp. 243-244.
    A compact annotated bibliography of recent scholar-
ship.

Straus, Ralph. *Robert Dodsley, Poet, Publisher, and Play-*   [26]
    wright. London: John Lane, 1910.
    Sterne's first publisher.

Tobin, James E. *Eighteenth Century Literature and Its Cul-*   [27]
    tural Background: A Bibliography. New York: Fordham
University Press, 1939. Pp. 160-161.
    A basic short list of editions and studies.

Yoklavich, John M. "Notes on the Early Editions of *Tristram*   [28]
    Shandy," *PMLA*, LXIII (1948), 508-519.
    Bibliographical evidence raising questions about the
early printings. Cf. 20, 24.

"Yorick at Yale," *Yale University Library Gazette*, XX (1946),   [29]
    51-52.
    New materials relating to Sterne.

    For additional bibliographical aids, see the following
items: 142, 145, 147, 148, 177, 183, 184, 185, 222, 223, 359,
397, 513, 804, 851, 863, 882, 883, 888. The reader is further
advised to consult *Abstracts of English Studies*, the *Annual
Bibliography of English Language and Literature* (published by the Modern Humanities Research Association
since 1920), the *Year's Work in English Studies* (published
by the English Association since 1921), and the annual
eighteenth-century bibliographies published in *PQ* (see 6
above) and *PMLA*.

II

*Editions and Selections**

A. Complete Works

Works and Life, edited by Wilbur L. Cross. 12 vols. (York   [100]
Edition: Sutton Issue) New York: J. F. Taylor & Company, 1904.
    Includes Fitzgerald's *Life* (216). Each volume con-
tains valuable introduction and commentary. Individual
works listed in entries 134, 152, 171, 178, 180, *q.v.*—Reviewed in *Bookman* (London), XXI (1905), 638. See 379.

Works. 7 vols. (Shakespeare Head Edition) Oxford: Basil   [101]
Blackwell; Boston and New York: Houghton Mifflin Company, 1926-27.
    Prints generally reliable text without introductions and
annotations. Individual works listed in 138, 157, 175, 182,
q.v.—Reviewed in leading article in *TLS,* May 26, 1927,
pp. 361-362 (399); see also "Hibernicus," *ibid.,* June 2,
1927, p. 392; L. P. Curtis, *ibid.,* June 23, 1927, p. 440;
M. R. B. Shaw, *ibid.,* July 21, 1927, p. 504. See also 319.

B. Selections

Sterne. Memoirs of Mr. Laurence Sterne. The Life and Opin-   [120]
*ions of Tristram Shandy. A Sentimental Journey. Selected
Sermons and Letters,* edited by Douglas Grant. (The
Reynard Library) London: Rupert Hart-Davis, 1950;
Cambridge, Mass.: Harvard University Press, 1951.
    A handsomely printed volume with a brief introduc-

---

* A representative rather than an exhaustive list is attempted. For minor
editions and miscellaneous printed items, the *British Museum Catalogue* of
Printed Books (4) should be consulted.

tion but without annotation.—"Laurence Sterne is the [Ancient] Mariner among novelists. He takes no notice of the public; he will not throw his message upon its impatient waters; but he collects from here and there a few to whom he will tell his tale . . . Our attitude toward him will always be a curious mixture of pity and affection, admiration and contempt." [Introduction]—Reviewed in *TLS*, March 2, 1951 (325). See also 317, 325, 588.

Selections are included in 156, 158, 166, 170a.

C. *Tristram Shandy*

The Life and Opinions of Tristram Shandy, Gentleman, and   [130]
A *Sentimental Journey*, [edited by A. W. Pollard.] (Library of English Classics) London and New York: Macmillan & Company, 1900.

The Life and Opinions of Tristram Shandy, Gentleman. Edi-   [131]
ted by Walter Jerrold. (The Temple Classics) London: J. M. Dent & Company, 1902.

———. (The World's Classics) London and New York: Ox-   [132]
ford University Press, H. Milford, 1903.
      Reprinted 1905, 1910, 1921, 1926, 1928, 1931, *etc.*

———. (The Unit Library, No. 32) London: Unit Library,   [133]
1903.

———. 4 vols. With an introduction by W. L. Cross. (*Works*   [134]
and Life. Vols. 3-6. York Edition. Sutton Issue) New York: J. F. Taylor and Company [1904].
      The introduction is still valuable. See 100.

———, edited by George Saintsbury. (Everyman's Library)   [135]
London: J. M. Dent; New York: E. P. Dutton, 1912.
      Reprinted in 1930, 1935, *etc.* The introduction provides brisk and highly valuable comment.

———. Introduction by W. L. Cross. New York: Liveright   [136]
Publishing Company, 1925.
      Reprinted in 1942.—"Sterne bequeathed himself to posterity in *Tristram Shandy*, wherein may be seen his image as in a mirror . . . the narrative . . . is in accordance with a carefully prepared design." See 134 above.

———. Illustrated by Rowland Wheelwright. London: Harrap; New York: Brentano, 1926. [137]

———. 3 vols. (*Works.* I-III. Shakespeare Head Edition) Oxford: Basil Blackwell, etc., [1927]. [138]
See 101.

———. With illustrations by John Austen and an introduction by J. B. Priestley. London: John Lane, The Bodley Head; New York: Dodd, Mead and Company, 1928. [139]
Introduction compares Virginia Woolf and Sterne to the advantage of the latter. Lists as Sterne's faults "his dirty little sniggers," "his catch-penny appeal to the reader's sensibilities," his "tricks" of "an eighteenth-century funny man."

——— and *A Sentimental Journey.* New York: The Modern Library [1928]. [140]
Reprinted in 1941. See 144.

———. With an introduction by Christopher Morley and illustrations by T. M. Cleland. New York: The Limited Editions Club, 1935. [141]
The introduction is a short, enthusiastic essay.

———, edited by James Aiken Work. (Odyssey Series in Literature) New York: Odyssey Press, 1940. [142]
The first carefully edited modern text has become standard. Reprints the first London edition of the nine volumes, with facsimiles of the title pages and of Hogarth's illustrations. A compact introduction of first importance, together with useful notes and bibliography.

———, edited by Peter Quennell. London: Lehman, 1948. [143]

———. Introduction by Bergen Evans. New York: The Modern Library, 1950. [144]
Useful standard comments.

———, edited with an introduction by Samuel Holt Monk. (Rinehart Editions) New York: Rinehart and Company, 1950. [145]
A brief but highly perceptive and valuable introduction.—"The spirit of the age makes itself felt in the optimistic view of the goodness and benevolence of the human

heart, as well as in the gently satiric tone which pervades *Tristram Shandy* and which reminds us of one of the basic convictions of the period: that illusion is unreality and that the private light of the individual mind is an uncertain guide to truth and conduct." This volume reproduces the text of the first London edition with some modernization in spelling. Cf. Work (142).

————. With an introduction by Maxwell Geismar. New   [146]
York: Pocket Books, 1957.
  Introduction adapted from *New Republic,* CXXXV (November 12, 1956), 21-22. See 545.

————, edited with an afterword by Gerald Weales. New   [147]
York: The New American Library of World Literature, 1962.
  Reprints the first London edition with modernized spelling and punctuation. Cf. Work (142) and Monk (145). Selected bibliography. The "Afterword" is a reprint of "Tristram Shandy's Anti-Book." (616).

————, edited, with critical and biographical material, by Alan   [148]
D. McKillop. New York: Harper & Brothers, 1962.
  Valuable biographical, critical, and bibliographical notes. Contains an important discussion of Sterne's indebtedness to the humanistic tradition of the Renaissance as well as to English empirical philosophy and compares the novelist with his great contemporaries in prose fiction. See 375. Carefully edited text. Cf. 142, 145, 149.

————. (A Laurel Edition) New York: Dell Publishing Com-   [148a]
pany, 1964.
  Representative of inexpensively printed popular editions without annotations. Also issued by Paper Books and Premier Books.

————, edited by Ian Watt. (Riverside Editions) Boston: [149]
Houghton Mifflin Company, 1965.
  Comprehensive introduction discussing biography, eighteenth-century background, the literary reputation, and critical problems, with appendices on military references and textual problems. Bibliography and notes. Text based on the first edition, collated with the second edition, the London collected edition of 1780, the three-volume "Lynch" edition, and the Dublin collected edition, with a list of variants. An edition of first importance. Cf. 142, 145, 148.

D. *A Sentimental Journey*

A Sentimental Journey. New York: Dodd, Mead & Company, [150]
1900.

———. With an introduction by L. F. Austin. London: Cas- [151]
sell's National Library, 1902.

———. With an introduction by W. L. Cross. (*Works and* [152]
Life. Vol. 7. York Edition. Sutton Issue) New York: J.
F. Taylor [1904].
See 100.

———. With biographical introduction by Hannaford Bennett. [153]
(John Long's Classics) London: John Long, 1905.

———. Illustrated by Everard Hopkins. London: Williams [153a]
and Norgate, 1910.

———. Illustrated by T. H. Robinson. London: Chatto and [153b]
Windus, 1912.

———. With *Pride and Prejudice* by Jane Austen. (The Har- [154]
vard Classics Shelf of Fiction) New York: P. F. Collier &
Son [1917].

———. With a preface by Francis Bickley. (Abbey Classics) [155]
London: Simkin Marshall, 1922.
Reviewed by Virginia Woolf (666).

———. With decorations by Norah McGuinness. [London, [155a]
etc.] Macmillan & Company [1926].

———, edited with an introduction by W. L. Cross. With se- [156]
lections from the journals, sermons and correspondence.
New York: Horace Liveright, 1926.
    In an introduction that is chiefly biographical, the edi-
tor rejects the psychological assessment of De Froe (342)
and characterizes *A Sentimental Journey* as "the most
sentimental book ever published."—Reviewed by J. C.
Metcalf, *VQR*, III (1927), 306-310.

———. (*Works. IV.* Shakespeare Head Edition) Oxford: Basil [157]
Blackwell, *etc.* [1927].
See 101.

—— *and The Journal to Eliza.* With an introduction by   [158]
George Saintsbury. (Everyman's Library) London and
Toronto: J. M. Dent & Sons; New York: E. P. Dutton &
Company [1927].
  Reprinted 1930.—Valuable introduction.

——. With an introduction by Virginia Woolf. (The World's   [159]
Classics) London: H. Milford, Oxford University Press
[1928].
  Important critical introduction. See *TLS*, January 10,
1929, p. 25 (829), and Woolf (667).

——, edited by Herbert Read. London: Scholartis Press,   [160]
1929.
  Valuable critical introduction. The text is based on
the second edition of 1768, with punctuation of the first
volume brought into accord with the MS in the British
Museum.—Reviewed by Augustine Birrell, *Nation-Athe-
naeum,* XLIV (1929), 22.

——. Illustrated by Valenti Angelo. New York: Dodd, Mead   [161]
& Company, 1929.

——. Illustrated by Mahlon Blaine. New York: Williams,   [162]
Belasco and Myers [1930].

—— in *An Eighteenth Century Miscellany,* edited by Louis   [163]
Kronenberger. New York: G. P. Putnam's Sons, 1936.
  Useful critical introduction.—". . . there has always
been the suggestion of cult about Sterne's warmest admirers."

——. With etchings by Denis Tegetmeier and introduction   [164]
by W. L. Cross. High Wycombe, England: Limited Editions Club, 1936.

——. Ornamented by Martin Travers. (The Abbey Classics,   [165]
IV) [London]: Simkin Marshall [?1937].

—— *together with The Journal to Eliza, Letters to Eliza.*   [166]
[Reading, Pa.]: The Spencer Press [1937].

——. Illustrated by Sylvain Sauvage. Foreword by John   [167]
Winterich. New York: The Heritage Press [1941].
  See Reitzel (21).

——— in *Great Short Novels,* edited by Edward Weeks. New   [168]
York: The Literary Guild of America, 1941.
    Introduction treats the novel as autobiographical:
"Laurence Sterne himself is the hero, and Eliza Draper
the heroine."

———, edited by John Cowper Powys. Illustrations by Brian   [169]
Robb. London: Macdonald, 1948.

———. With an introduction by Oliver Warner and illustra-   [170]
tions by Nigel Lambourne. London: Folio Society, 1949.

——— and *The Journal to Eliza.* Afterword by Monroe Engel.   [170a]
(Signet Classics) New York: New American Library of
World Literature, 1964.

See also 130 and 140 above.

E. Letters and Journals

Letters to His Most Intimate Friends, edited with an introduc-   [171]
tion by W. L. Cross. 2 vols. (*Works and Life.* Vols. 8 and
9. York Edition. Sutton Issue) New York: J. F. Taylor
& Company [1904].
    Contains—with Vol. 10 (178)—176 letters by Sterne
and one that may be spurious. See 100.

Life and Letters. By Lewis Melville. 2 vols. London: Stan-   [172]
ley Paul and Company, 1910.
    Contains 152 letters with excerpts from others. See
232, 714.

Laurence Sterne's Letter to the Rev. Mr. Blake. St. Louis: [173]
Privately printed, 1915.
    A letter in possession of William K. Bixby.

Life and Times. By Wilbur L. Cross. New Haven: Yale Uni-   [174]
versity Press, 1929.
    Fourteen letters from *Letter Book,* ten published for
the first time, plus one other unpublished letter. See 211.

Letters. 1 vol. (*Works.* V. Shakespeare Head Edition) Ox-   [175]
ford: Basil Blackwell, *etc.* [1926-27].
    184 letters, of which 129 are certainly by Sterne. See
101.

Letters. Selected with an introduction by R. Brimley John-   [176]
son. London: John Lane; Dodd, Mead, and Company,
1927, 1928.
    91 letters of which one may be spurious.—See review
article by Clark (702); also *New Statesman,* XXIX (1927),
820.

Letters, edited by Lewis Perry Curtis. Oxford: Clarendon   [177]
Press, 1935.
    The standard text. 222 letters attributed to Sterne, one
(#18) bearing his signature. Ten letters printed for the
first time. Includes "Memoirs of the Life and Family of
the Late Rev. Mr. Laurence Sterne" and letters relating to
Sterne and his family. Highly valuable annotation.—Reviewed in *TLS,* March 21, 1935, p. 173; corr. by M. R. B.
Shaw, *ibid.,* June 6, 1935, p. 364; by Edith Morley in
YWES, XVI (1935), 283-284; by M. R. B. Shaw in *Observer,* March 17, 1935; by W. King in *English Review,*
LX (1935), 748-749; by J. Sparrow in *Mercury,* XXXII
(May, 1935), 79-80; by C. E. Vulliamy in *Spectator,* CLIV
(1935), 492, 494; by L. Kronenberger in *TBR,* September
1, 1935, pp. 2, 5; by C. D. Abbott in *VQR,* XI (1935), 606-
609; by A. Brandl in *Deutsche Literaturzeitung* (Berlin),
LVII (1936), 64-67; by M. D. Zabel in *MP,* XXXIV
(1936), 101-102; by G. Kitchin in *MLR,* XXXII (1937),
99-101. See also 390, 703, 704, 705.

The Journal to Eliza and Various Letters by Laurence Sterne   [178]
and Elizabeth Draper. With an introduction by W. L.
Cross. (*Works and Life.* Vol. 10. York Edition. Sutton
Issue.) New York: J. R. Taylor & Company [1904].
    See 100, 171.

Second Journal to Eliza. Hitherto known as Letters supposed   [179]
to have been written by Yorick and Eliza, but now shown
to be a later version of the Journal to Eliza. Transcribed
from the copy in the British Museum and presented with
an introduction by Margaret R. B. Shaw, together with a
foreword by Charles Whibley. London: G. Bell and Sons,
1929.
    Reviewed in *TLS,* October 21, 1929, p. 867 (254); by
E. E. K. in *New Statesman,* XXXIV (November 9, 1929),
p. 7; by W. L. Cross, who rejects ascription, in *SRL,* December 21, 1929, p. 587; by Edith Morley in *YWES,* X

(1929), 280-281; in *Criterion*, IX (1930), 363-364. See
Birrell (205), Curtis (705), Fluchère (706), and Behrmann (811).

See also 120, 158, 166, 170a.

F. Sermons

The Sermons of Mr. Yorick. With an introduction by W. L. [180]
Cross. 2 vols. (*Works and Life.* Vols. 11 and 12. York
Edition. Sutton Issue) New York: J. F. Taylor & Com-
pany [1904].
See 100.

———. 2 vols. (*Works.* VI-VII. Shakespeare Head Edition) [181]
Oxford: Basil Blackwell, *etc.* [1927].
See 101.

G. Miscellaneous

A Political Romance < 1759 > . . . an exact reprint of the first [182]
edition. With an introduction by W. L. Cross. Boston:
The Club of Odd Volumes, 1914.
Reprinted from "a beautiful transcript of the Hailstone
volume made by Miss Elizabeth Hastings of London."

H. Anthologies

Alden, Raymond M., ed. *Readings in English Prose of the* [183]
Eighteenth Century. Boston: Houghton Mifflin Company,
1911. Pp. 480-501.
Selections from *Tristram Shandy* and *A Sentimental
Journey*.

Mendenhall, John C., ed. *English Literature,* 1650-1800. Chi- [184]
cago-Philadelphia-New York: J. B. Lippincott Company,
1940. Pp. 856-863.
Selections with introduction, bibliography, notes.

Pettit, Henry, ed. *A Collection of English Prose, 1660-1800.* [185]
New York: Harper & Brothers, 1962. Pp. 547-552.
[Introduction to] *A Sentimental Journey.* Bibliog-
raphy.

I. Translations

1. Collections

Tristram Shandy. Voyage sentimental. Lettres à Elisa, Ser-   [186]
mons . . . pages choisies par Charles Simond. (Les Prosa-
teurs illustrés français et étrangers, III) Paris: L. Michaud,
1908.

La Vie et les opinions de Tristram Shandy. Le Voyage senti-   [187]
mₑ ntal. Traduction par M. Frénais-de Bonnay; introduction, extraits et notes par Paul de Reul. (Les Cent chef-
d'oeuvres étrangers) Paris: la Renaissance du livre, 1931.

2. *Tristram Shandy*

La Vie et opinions de Tristram Shandy, gentilhomme. Tra-   [188]
duit de l'anglais par Charles Mauron. (Pavillons. Collection Amalthée) Paris: R. Laffont, 1946.
    Reprinted with a preface by Jean-Louis Curtis. Paris:
le Club Français du Livre, 1955 and 1961.

Das Leben und die Ansichten Tristram Shandys. Übersetzung   [189]
von Rudolph Kassner. Wiesbaden: Dieterich, 1946.

3. *A Sentimental Journey*

A Sentimental Journey through France and Italy, translated   [190]
from the English by Dragomir M. Janovic. Belgrade:
Shtamparija D. Gregorina, 1926. [In Serbian]

Voyage sentimental en France et en Italie. Traduction nou-   [191]
velle et notice ,de M. Emile Blémont. Illustrations de
Maurice Leloir. Paris: J. Tallandier, 1927. Reprint of
original edition of 1884.

Le Voyage Sentimental à travers la France et l'Italie. Trans-   [192]
lated and prefaced by Aurélien Digeon. (Collection
bilingue des Classiques anglais) Paris: Aubier, 1934.

Voyage sentimental en France et en Italie. Avec des figures   [193]
de Sylvain Sauvages, gravée sur bois par Pierre Bouchet.
Paris: Creuzevault, 1942.

Viaggio Sentimentale di Yorick lunga la Francia e l'Italia.   [194]
Tradotto di Didimo Chierico (Ugo Foscolo) a cura di
Adiano Seroni. [Milano]: Bompiani [1944].

Viaggio Sentimentale, a cura di Enrico Falqui (Scritti di [195] Didimo Chierico [Ugo Foscolo]). Roma: Colombo [1944].

Viaggio Sentimentale in Foscolo, Ugo, *Poesie e Prosa d'Arte.* [196] [Torino]: Unione tip.-editrice torinese [1948]; Firenze: F. Le Monnier, 1951.

4. Sermons

Yoricks Predigten. Übertragen von Joseph Grabisch. München- [197] en: G. Müller, 1921.

III

Biography
and Biographical Materials

Bensly, Edward. "Laurence Sterne's Daughter," *N & Q*,   [200]
CLXV (1933), 29.
  Notes on Lydia Sterne and her son, with a correction
on the latter, *ibid.*, p. 85.

———. "Laurence Sterne's Father-in-Law," *N & Q*, CLXV   [201]
(1933), 137.
  Cites Cross (211) in answer to query about the Rev.
Robert Lumley made in *ibid.*, p. 101.

———. "St. George's Hanover Square: Burial Ground," *N & Q*,   [202]
CLIX (1930), 84-85.
  Corrects Cross's *Life* (211) and G. W. Wright's reproduction (*N & Q*, CLVIII [1930], 410) of the two inscrip-
tions on Sterne. See 263.

———. "Sterne and Lord Aboyne," *N & Q*, XL (1926), 65-66.   [203]
  Argues against Lewis Melville's assumption in the *Life
and Letters*, I, 66-67 (232), that Sterne went abroad in the
autumn of 1741 as "bearleader to the young Earl."

Bill, Alfred Hoyt. *Alas, Poor Yorick.* Boston: Little, Brown   [204]
and Company, 1927.
  A novelized biography.—Reviewed by G. H. Gerould
in *SRL*, IV (October 29, 1927), 225; *New York Evening
Post,* November 26, 1927, p. 13.

Birrell, Augustine. "Yorick and Eliza," *Nation and Athenaeum,*   [205]
XLVI (December 7, 1929), 347-348.
  See Shaw (179) and Wright (262).

Brunskill, Elizabeth. *Eighteenth-Century Reading, Some*   [206]
Notes of the People Who Frequented the Library of York
Minster in the Eighteenth-Century, and on the Books
They Borrowed. York: York Georgian Society Occasional
Paper, No. 6, 1950.
See discussion by Paul Kaufman (226).

Bullock, H. "Sterne's Eliza," *N&Q*, CXCIX (1954), 474-475.   [207]
Identifies Eliza's half sister, Louisa, as the daughter of
Judith [Whitehall] Sclater and her second husband, Cap-
tain Samuel Hough. See Wright and Sclater, *Sterne's*
Eliza (262).

Connely, Willard. *Laurence Sterne as Yorick.* London: The   [208]
Bodley Head, 1958.
A biography chiefly concerned with Sterne's last nine
years, his "writing life." Uses Cross (211), Curtis (177),
and Hammond (751) freely. Paying little attention to
Sterne's works or considerations of his philosophy, this
"portrait" presents mainly the novelist's social life in England and in France, with elaborate inquiry into the background of Sterne's activities and contacts.—Reviewed in
Listener, LX (1958), 574-575; in *TLS*, May 23, 1958, p.
284.

Cross, Wilbur L. "About Laurence Sterne," *Atlantic Monthly*,   [209]
XCVI (July, 1905), 127-132.
Discusses Fitzgerald's biographical researches and
"much fresh information [that] has found its way into
print, or drifted in manuscript to the British Museum,"
notably Croft's anecdotes and the *Journal to Eliza* "discovered by a Mr. Gibbs of Bath among waste books and
papers." See 216.

———. "Laurence Sterne" in *Encyclopedia Americana.* New   [210]
York, Chicago, Washington: Americana Corporation, 1924.
XXV, 631-632.
See new entry under Howes, Alan B. (225).

———. *The Life and Times of Laurence Sterne.* New York: [211]
The Macmillan Company, 1909.

———. . . . *A new edition.* New Haven: Yale University Press,
1925. 2 vols.

————. . . . *Third edition, with alterations and additions.* New
Haven: Yale University Press; London: Oxford University
Press, 1929; New York: Russell and Russell, 1967.
   The 1925 edition is a thoroughgoing revision of the
1909 edition. It includes Sterne's Letter Book and a valuable bibliography of the published works. The 1929 edition adds material from Curtis (213). It is now the standard biography.—Reviewed in *Dial,* XLVII (1909), 22;
Athenaeum, September 18, 1909, p. 327; *Contemporary
Review,* XCVI (1909), 14-17; *Nation,* LXXXIX (1909),
346-349; *Spectator,* CIII (August 28, 1909), 310; *Forum,*
XCII (1909), 94; *Literary Digest,* XXXVIII (1909), 1070;
by S. L. Wolff in *Nation,* LXXXIX (1909), 346; *SR,* CVIII
(1909), 107; *North American Review,* CXC (1909), 557;
New York Times Saturday Review, XIV (July 24, 1909),
107; *AB,* XXX (1909), 253-256; *North American Review,*
CXCI (1910), 273-276; *AB,* LXII (1925), 330; by L. Woolf
in *Nation and Athenaeum,* XXXVIII (1926), 554; by J. M.
Turnbull in *RES,* II (1926), 356-360; *PQ,* V (1926), 370;
by Edith Birkhead in *MLR,* XXI (1926), 322-324; by J. B.
Priestley in *SRL,* February 20, 1926, pp. 567-570; by A.
Edward Newton in *YR,* XV (1926), 593-95; by Augustine
Birrell in *Nation and Athenaeum,* XLIV (1929), 22, 574;
by J. M. Turnbull in *RES,* VII (1931), 104-105; by O.
Hachtmann in *Deutsche Rundschau,* LVII (1931), 265.
See also 308, 363, 366, 386, 412, 434, 435.

Curtis, Lewis Perry. "The First Printer of *Tristram Shandy,*"   [212]
PMLA, XLVII (1932), 777-789.
   Mrs. Ann Ward of York printed the first two volumes.

————. *The Politicks of Laurence Sterne.* Oxford: Oxford Uni-   [213]
versity Press; London: H. Milford, 1929.
   Early political activity of Sterne in Yorkshire and his
relationship with his uncle, Dr. Jaques Sterne, the Dean of
York.—Reviewed by W. L. Cross in *Yale Review,* XIX
(1929), 181-182; in *TLS,* March 28, 1929, p. 253; by E. B.
in *Nation and Athenaeum,* XLV (1929), 164-166; *SRL,*
VI (September 14, 1929), 140.

————. "Sterne in Bond-Street," *TLS,* March 24, 1932, p. 217.   [214]
   Discusses the exact whereabouts of Sterne from January, 1767, to March, 1768, in Old Bond Street, and
queries the possible connection between Mrs. Mary Four-

mantel, the proprietress of the "silk-bag shop" at which
Sterne lived, and Catherine Fourmantel[le] with whom he
had an intrigue in 1759-60. See Yoseloff (264).

Evans, A. W. *Warburton and the Warburtonians: A Study in*   [215]
Some Eighteenth-Century Controversies. London: Oxford
University Press, 1932. Pp. 226-232.
The relationship of Sterne and the Bishop.

Fitzgerald, Percy. *The Life of Laurence Sterne.* Introduction   [216]
by W. L. Cross. 2 vols. (*The Works and Life of Laurence
Sterne.* York Edition. Sutton Issue) New York: J. F. Taylor and Company, 1904.
Reprints the 1896 edition. The introduction discusses
the biographical treatment of Sterne before Fitzgerald's
first edition of 1864 (designed as a counter portrait to
Thackeray's) and gives an account of the development of
the 1896 edition. See 100.

——. *The Life of Laurence Sterne.* London: Chatto and   [217]
Windus, 1906 [1905].
Third edition of the original two-volume work. See
above.

Fluchère, Henri. *Laurence Sterne, de l'homme à l'oeuvre:*   [218]
*Biographie critique et essai d'interpretation de Tristram
Shandy.* (Bibliothèque des idées) Paris: Gallimard, 1961.
Based on an extensive survey of antecedent scholarship, this work achieves what is at once a full and a
balanced biographical summary that does much to fill the
gap between Cross and contemporary scholarship. In addition, it includes a remarkable *omnium gatherum* of interpretation and criticism of *Tristram Shandy,* together
with a compendious but inconveniently organized bibliography. See also listing under *Tristram Shandy* (540).—
Reviewed in leading article in *TLS,* June 8, 1962, 421-
422; by G. Ross Roy in *Books Abroad,* XXXVI (1962),
284; *YWES,* XLII (1961), 209; by Norman Sanders in
MLR, LVIII (1963), 565-566; see *PQ,* XLI (1961), 627;
XLII (1962), 374; XLIII (1963), 388. See also 371, 372,
389.

——. "Sterne's Documents," *TLS,* February 12, 1925, p. 104.   [219]
An announcement of intent to bring out a new study
of Sterne. See 218.

Gallaway, W. F. "Boswell and Sterne," *Letters*, V (Novem-   [220]
ber, 1931), 21-25, 30.
    Supplements Pottle's article (242) and argues that the
omission of a mention of the meeting of Boswell and
Sterne in the *Life of Johnson* is not to be taken as evidence
that the two did not at some time encounter each other.
Cf. 249.

Hailey, Emma. "Charles Brietzcke's Diary 1761," *N&Q*, CC,   [221]
N.S. II (1955), 443.
    Contemporary reference to Sterne's sermon at the
Foundling Hospital.

Hartley, Lodwick. "Laurence Sterne" in *Cyclopedia of World* [222]
Authors, edited by Frank Magill and Dayton Kohler. New
York: Salem Press; Harper and Brothers, 1958. Pp. 1023-
26.
    Brief biographical and critical account with bibliog-
raphy.

———. *This Is Lorence: A Narrative of the Reverend Lau-*   [223]
rence Sterne. Chapel Hill: University of North Carolina
Press, 1943.
    An account of the leading events in the life of Sterne
with attention centered on the complexity of his character
and with intermingled comments on his writings.—Reviewed by Edward Wagenknecht in *TBR*, June 20, 1943,
p. 8; by S. C. Chew in the *Christian Science Monitor*, June
19, 1943, p. 10; by J. T. Frederick in *Book Week*, June 6,
1943, p. 2; by Katherine Anne Porter in the *Nation*, CLVII
(July 17, 1943), 72-73; by Desmond MacCarthy in [Lon-
don] *Sunday Times*, December 19, 1943, p. 6; W. B. C.
Watkins in *MLN*, LIX (1944), 363-364; J. A. Work in
JEGP, XLIII (1944), 479-481; J. M. S. Tompkins in *RES*,
XXI (1945), 79. See 391.

———. "Tristram and the Angels," *College English*, IX (1947), [224]
62-69.
    Reviews biographical interpretations of Sterne from
Coleridge and Thackeray to the present.

Howes, Alan B. "Laurence Sterne" in *Encyclopedia Ameri-*   [225]
cana. New York, Chicago, Washington: Americana Corporation, 1960. XXV, 631-632.
    Replaces article by Cross (210). Bibliography.

Kaufman, Paul. "Mr. Yorick and the Minster Library," [226]
N&Q, CCV, N.S. VII (1960), 308-310.
Sterne's borrowings from the library of the cathedral
as revealed in Elizabeth Brunskill's *18th Century Reading,*
(206).

———. "A True Image of Laurence Sterne," *BNYPL,* LXVI [226a]
(December, 1962), 653-656.
Identifies small bronze cast in the Library of York Minster as a statue of Sterne and challenges the identification
of "Portrait of a Young Gentleman," ascribed to Gains-
borough, in the City of Salford Art Gallery as being a like-
ness of the novelist.

Kuist, James M. "New Light on Sterne: An Old Man's Recol- [227]
lection of the Young Vicar," *PMLA,* LXXX (1965), 549-
553.
A brief set of notes (Brit. Mus. Additional MS. 24446
ff., 26-27) taken by Joseph Hunter, nineteenth-century
antiquarian and literary historian, from a conversation in
1807 with Richard Greenwood, an old Yorkshireman who
maintained that he was servant to Sterne at Sutton on the
Forest for three years prior to 1745. Both corroborates
and counters extant gossipy stories. Suggests a few new
facts, the chief being that a short-lived male child was
born to the Sternes. Cf. *The Whitefoord Papers,* edited
by W. A. S. Hewins (Oxford, 1898), pp. 225-232.

Kunitz, Stanley J., and Howard Haycraft. *British Authors be-* [228]
fore 1800. New York: The H. W. Wilson Company, 1952.
Pp. 494-496.
Brief biographical sketch with bibliography. "Sterne's
character is not an ingratiating one . . . but as a writer he
revolutionized the novel."

Lamborn, E. A. Greening. "Great Tew: A Link with Sterne." [229]
N&Q, CXCIII (1948), 512-515.
Information on the family of Eliza Draper's friend,
Hester Eleanora Light.

Lee, Sir Sidney. "Laurence Sterne" in *Dictionary of National* [230]
Biography. Oxford: Oxford University Press, 1921-22,
1937-38, 1949-50, 1959-60. XVIII, 1086-1108.
Article as originally issued in the edition of 1885-91 is
still of importance for biographical and bibliographical
materials.

Macdonald, John. *Memoirs of an Eighteenth-Century Foot-*   [231]
man, with an introduction by John Beresford. London:
G. Routledge & Sons [1927].
     The eyewitness account of the death of Sterne.

Melville, Lewis [pseud.] [Lewis Saul Benjamin]. *The Life*   [232]
and Letters of Laurence Sterne. 2 vols. London: Stanley
Paul and Company [1911].
     A readable but undistinguished biography that, ac-
cording to the author, was "more than half finished" when
Cross's biography appeared. The judgment of the review
in *TLS* that the work is "colourless, superficial, and incomplete" may seem harsh, but it is hard to refute.—Reviewed
in *TLS,* November 3, 1911, p. 420; *Saturday Review* (London), CXII (1911), 736; *TBR,* XVII (June 2, 1912), 336;
by J. W. Tupper in *Dial,* LIII (July 16, 1912), 51. See
714.

———. "Sterne and the Demoniacs," *AB,* XXX (1910), 640-647.   [233]
     The friendship of Sterne with Hall-Stevenson and
other of his company at Skelton Castle. Included as a
chapter in the *Life,* above.

———. "Sterne's Eliza," *Fortnightly Review,* XCIII (1910),   [234]
1137-1147.
     Contains material later included in *Some Eccentrics
and a Woman,* below, and in the *Life,* above.

———. "Sterne's Eliza" in *Some Eccentrics and a Woman.*   [235]
New York: James Potts and Company, 1911.
     A sketch of Eliza Draper, "largely from unpublished
letters."—See review in *Dial,* LI (1911), 538.

Montagu, Elizabeth Robinson. *Elizabeth Montagu, the Queen*   [236]
*of the Blue Stockings: Her Correspondence from 1720 to
1761,* edited by Emily J. Climenson. London: John Murray, 1906.
     Establishes relationship between Mrs. Sterne and Mrs.
Montagu. See continuation below.

———. "The Sternes and Their 'Cosin' Montagu" in *Mrs.*   [237]
*Montagu, "Queen of the Blues," Her Letters and Friend-
ships from 1762 to 1800,* edited by Reginald Blunt from
materials left to him by her great-grand niece Emily J.
Climenson. London: Constable and Company; Boston
and New York: Houghton Mifflin [1923]. I, 185-214.

Ollard, S. L. "Sterne as Parish Priest," *TLS*, May 25, 1933,   [238]
p. 364, and June 1, p. 380.
    Additional information about Sterne as a priest found
in the Returns of the Visitation of Archbishop Drummond
in 1764, giving evidence that "Sterne's parishes were certainly not neglected" but citing the "off-hand, jaunty" way
in which he treated "his curate's ordination to the priest-
hood." See below.

———. "Sterne as a Young Parish Priest," *TLS*, March 18,   [239]
1926, p. 217.
    Sterne's reply to a questionnaire sent out by Arch-
bishop Herring of York in preparation for his Primary
Visitation in May, 1743, found in the diocesan records at
Bishopthorpe, is used to counter gossip about his character
as a pastor contained in *The Whitefoord Papers*. See below (240) and Kuist (227).

———, and P. C. Walker, eds. *Archbishop Herring's Visita-*   [240]
tion Returns, 1743, III, 92-93, in *The Yorkshire Archae-*
ological Society's Record Series, LXXV [?1930].
    See Ollard (238, 239) above.

"The Politics of Sterne," *TLS*, March 28, 1929, p. 253.   [241]
    Observes errors in Curtis's *The Politicks of Laurence*
Sterne (213).

Pottle, Frederick A. "Bozzy and Yorick," *Blackwood's Maga-*   [242]
zine, CCXVII (1925), 297-313.
    An account of the relationship of the young Boswell to
Sterne, the literary lion, with quotations from Boswell's
"A Poetical Epistle to Doctor Sterne [,] Parson Yorick and
Tristram Shandy." See 220.

Pressly, I. P. "Laurence Sterne" in *A York Miscellany*. Lon-   [242a]
don: A. Brown, 1938. Pp. 188-209.
    Also contains an essay on Dr. John Burton (Sterne's
"Dr. Slop"), pp. 141-153.

Putney, Rufus D. S. " 'Alas, Poor Eliza,' " *MLR*, XLI (1946),   [243]
411-413.
    Argues that Mrs. James, not Eliza Draper, inspired
Sterne's epitaph of 1767.

———. "Sterne's Eliza," *TLS*, March 9, 1946, p. 115.   [244]
    Correcting a misstatement in Quennell's essay on

Sterne (246), Putney argues that the *Journal to Eliza* is semi-fictitious and that *A Sentimental Journey*, the sentimentality of which has been exaggerated, was not written when Sterne was desperately ill but when he had recovered and was in the gayest spirits. Cf. Shaw (179).

Quennell, Peter. "Laurence Sterne," *Horizon*, VIII (1943),   [245]
337-349, 419-433; X (1944), 36-57.
A colorful and vigorous biographical account reprinted in *Four Portraits*. See below.

———. "Sterne" in *Four Portraits: Boswell, Gibbon, Sterne,*   [246]
Wilkes. Reprint Society, 1945; published in the United States as *The Profane Virtues: Four Studies of the Eighteenth Century*. New York: The Viking Press, 1945. Pp. 139-194.
Reviewed by V. S. Pritchett, *New Statesman and Nation*, XXIX (1945), 375; *Time*, XLVI (July 16, 1945), 88; *Newsweek*, XXVI (October 8, 1945), 114; *Spectator*, CLXXIV (May 18, 1945), 456; *TLS*, May 26, 1945, p. 247. See Putney (244).

Read, Herbert. "Alas, Poor Yorick!" in *The Contrary Experi-*   [247]
ence: Autobiographies. New York: The Horizon Press, 1963. Pp. 324-333.
Sterne in his Yorkshire setting.

Reed, Myrtle. *Love Affairs of Literary Men*. New York: G.   [248]
P. Putnam Sons, 1907. Pp. 65-84.
"Laurence Sterne was a veritable 'Light o' Love' . . . and his biography is strewn with his various attachments."

Reid, W. Lewis. "Sterne and Johnson at 'The Cheshire   [249]
Cheese,'" *N&Q*, V (1906), 108.
Queries the possibility of Sterne's meeting Johnson at the famous tavern. Cf. 220, 242.

Sclater, William Lutley. "Letters Addressed by Eliza Draper   [250]
to the Strange Family, 1776-78," *N&Q*, CLXXXVI (1944), 201-204, 220-224; CLXXXVII (1944), 7-13, 27-33, 48-54.
Reprints letters in possession of Alexander Trotter of Teffont, Wilts, supplementing *Sterne's Eliza* (262).

Seligo, Irene. "Der muntere Yorick," *Frankfurter Zeitung*,   [251]
November 27, 1938, p. 6.

Commemorates the two hundred twenty-fifth birthday of Sterne.

Shaw, Margaret R. B. *Laurence Sterne: The Making of a*   [252]
Humorist, 1713-1762. London: Richards Press, 1957.

The first volume of a projected two-volume work sets out to examine "the different forces which went into the making of [Sterne's] humour" until he left England for France in 1762, considering the influences of his insecure boyhood and youth, his social and personal background, his education, his courtship and marriage, his brief excursion into politics—especially as all these aspects of his life are reflected in the first two volumes of the sermons and the first six volumes of *Tristram Shandy*. In addition, there is an account of the reception of the novel, as well as of Sterne's breakdown and flight to France. Revealing no access to an appreciable amount of new material, Miss Shaw takes issue on matters of interpretation with Cross, Curtis, and Hammond. Essentially a "defence," the book is spirited even when it becomes somewhat too combative. —Reviewed by Edith J. Morley in *YWES*, XXXVIII (1957), 196-197; in *TLS*, October 25, 1957, p. 642.

Sichel, Walter. *Sterne, A Study, To Which Is Added the*   [253]
Journal to Eliza. Philadelphia: J. B. Lippincott; London: Williams and Norgate, 1910.

A biographical and critical treatment with "an undercurrent of reproof" that gives it a backward rather than a forward-looking orientation. Adds some slight material to Cross: for example, a discussion of the relationship of Mrs. Montagu and Mrs. Sterne (from Emily J. Climenson, see 236), of the personality and character of Kitty "de Fourmantelle," and of the relationship between Sterne and Mrs. Vesey. Includes some unpublished letters and the whole text of the *Journal to Eliza,* the inclusion of which provides the best argument for the publication of the book.—Reviewed in *Living Age,* CCLXV (1910), 700-702 (reprinted from *Outlook*); *Current Literature,* XLIX (1910), 443-444; in *Athenaeum,* April 16, 1910, p. 451; by William S. Walsh in *New York Times Saturday Review,* XV (1910), 518; *TLS,* April 8, 1910, p. 122, *q.v.* See 321, 417, 428.

"Sterne, Eliza and Another," *TLS,* October 21, 1929, p. 867.   [254]
Review of Shaw's *Second Journal to Eliza* (179).—"We do not believe that even in the character of Eliza, Sterne

could have written some parts . . . of the journal. . . . We
are very nearly certain that . . . [not] any but Laurence
Sterne himself could have written most of Yorick's own
two-thirds of it."

St. Swithin [pseud.] "Anecdote of Laurence Sterne," *N&Q*,   [255]
    12th ser., VIII (1921), 129.
        Reprints an anecdote from *The Yorkshire Herald*. See
    comment of Edward Bensly, *ibid.*, p. 215, and reply in
    ibid., IX (1921), 55.

Thomas, Henry, and Dana Lee Thomas. "Laurence Sterne"   [256]
    in *Living Biographies of Famous Novelists*. Garden City,
    N.Y.: Garden City Publishing Company, [1943]. Pp. 79-
    90.
        A typical popular biographical account, enthusiastic
    but valueless.

Tyler, Dorothy. "A Lodging in the Bayswater Road," *Atlantic*   [257]
    Monthly, CLV (1935), 321-324.
        A "sentimental journey" to Sterne's grave with a de-
    scription of its contemporary setting in the parish of St.
    George's, Hanover Square.

Watkins, W. B. C. "Laurence Sterne" in *Collier's Encyclope-*   [258]
    dia. New York-Toronto, 1950 [1960], XVII, 675-676.
        A biographical entry chiefly interesting for critical
    comments. Sterne seemed outside the main tradition of
    the novel until contemporary stream of consciousness
    novelists like Joyce and others made us aware of his
    "subtle, if seldom profound, psychological penetration."
    See also Watkins's articles on *Tristram Shandy* and *A*
    Sentimental Journey, ibid.

————. "Yorick Revisited" in *Perilous Balance: The Tragic*   [259]
    Genius of Swift, Johnson, and Sterne Princeton: Prince-
    ton University Press, 1939. Pp. 99-156. (Also Cambridge,
    Mass.: Walker-de Berry, 1960.)
        Argues that to understand Sterne one must remember
    that he was acutely self-conscious and that he was all his
    life a sick man. "Sterne deliberately cultivated illusion
    and gaiety in order to fence against the evils of this
    world," choosing the role of Yorick rather than that of
    Hamlet. This study counters Bagehot's (303) and De
    Froe's (342) contentions about Sterne's lack of religion,

Sir Leslie Stephen's refusal to allow him positive merits of character, Saintsbury's (404) statement that he was not really a great humorist, and Cross's idea that he was incapable of "moods of high seriousness," approving Sir Herbert Read's general position on Sterne's intellectual seriousness (399). Considers Sterne's "stream of consciousness" technique and his relationship as a psychological novelist to Proust.—Reviewed by Alexander Cowie in *SRL*, XXI (January 20, 1940), 17; by C. Bradford in *Saturday Review* (London), XLVIII (1940), 428-429; by H. Williams, in *RES*, XVII (1941), 125; by F. A. Pottle, *MLN*, LVI (1941), 394-395; see *N&Q*, CLXXXV (August 28, 1943), 148.

Woolf, Virginia. "Eliza and Sterne," *TLS*, December 14, [260] 1922, p. 839. Reprinted in *Granite and Rainbow*, London: Hogarth Press, 1958, pp. 176-180.

A review-article based on Wright and Sclater's *Sterne's Eliza* (262).—"If we must censure Eliza, it is not for being in love with Sterne, but for not being in love with him."

———. "Sterne's Ghost" in *The Moment*. New York: Har- [261] court, Brace and Company, 1948. Pp. 43-49.

A charming little essay about how the supposed ghost of Sterne affected Eliza Mathews, who lived in the room where *Tristram Shandy* was written in the house of Mrs. Simpson, Stonegate, Yorks.

Wright, Arnold, and William Lutley Sclater. *Sterne's Eliza,* [262] *Some Account of Her Life in India: with Her Letters Written between 1757 and 1774.* London: William Heinemann, 1922.

Places the affair with Sterne in the proper perspective as a brief episode in the life of a young woman of twenty-four who met a famous author; emphasizes the possibility of interest in Eliza for her own sake as the author of letters that skillfully reflect epoch-making events in India, as well as interesting aspects of Anglo-Indian life. See 179.—Reviewed by V. Woolf in *TLS*, December 14, 1922, p. 839 (260), above.

Wright, G. W. "St. George's Hanover Square Burial-Ground," [263] *N&Q*, CLVIII (1930), 410-411.

Reproduces inscription of Sterne's headstone. See
Bensley, *ibid.*, CLIX (1930), 84-85 (202), and Tyler
(257).

Yoseloff, Thomas. *A Fellow of Infinite Jest.* New York: Pren-   [264]
tice-Hall, 1945.
An enthusiastic appreciation, often inaccurate factual-
ly and inferentially.—Reviewed by R. Ellis Roberts in
SRL, XXVIII (October 27, 1945), 13-14; by W. B. C.
Watkins in *TBR*, March 10, 1946, p. 29; by H. K. Russell
in *MLN*, LXI (1946), 430; *TLS*, March 27, 1948, p. 182;
Observer, April 18, 1948, p. 3.

See also 303, 308, 326, 335, 342, 352, 358, 359, 363, 366, 387,
390, 394, 405, 412, 704, 953, 960.

IV

Criticism

A. General

"Alas, Poor Yorick," *TLS*, June 8, 1962, 421-422.   [300]
A leading article occasioned by the publication of Fluchère's *Sterne* (218). Admitting that he has been daunted by the 325,000 words [*sic*] of the book and that he has resorted to scanning, the reviewer gives a routine account of Sterne's sentimentality, his narrative structure, and his bawdiness. He allows Fluchère credit for some vividness in the biographical section and for some insights in the critical section but denies him credit for anything new in either field.

Allen, B. Sprague. "The Dates of *Sentimental* and Its Deriva-   [301]
tives," *PMLA*, XLVIII (1933), 303-307.
Cites Horace Walpole's use of *sentimentally* in 1746 before Mrs. Balfour's use of *sentimental* in a letter to Richardson in 1749; other uses cited in reference to *NED* entry, *q.v.* See Birkhead (307), Erämetsä (338), Curtis (705).

Allen, Walter. *The English Novel: A Short Critical History.*   [302]
New York: E. P. Dutton and Company, 1955. Pp. 72-78.
Counters Dr. Leavis's contention that *Tristram Shandy* is an "irresponsible (and nasty) trifling," arguing that the book is a novel and nothing else and that Sterne discovered in the delights of sensibility "a whole continent of experience which other eighteenth-century writers invaded with alacrity." Finds influence of Sterne in the work of such twentieth-century humorists as Clarence Day and James Thurber. See Leavis (362).

Allott, Miriam. *Novelists on the Novel.* New York: Columbia   [302a]
University Press; London: Routledge and K. Paul, 1959.
Pp. 168-169 and *passim.*
"Sterne's art was not finally freed from its age; its re-
bellion, after all, takes place within that age's system of
values."

Bagehot, Walter. *Literary Studies,* edited by R. H. Hutton.   [303]
London: J. M. Dent and Sons, 1916. II, 282-325.
Reprints Bagehot's review of John Camden Hotten's
Thackeray the Humorist and the Man of Letters and
Fitzgerald's *Life of Sterne* from *National Review,* April,
1864. One of the famous *loci classici* of mid-Victorian
criticism of Sterne.

Baker, Ernest A. *The History of the English Novel.* London: [304]
H. F. and G. Witherby, 1924; New York: Barnes and
Noble, 1950. IV, 240-276; V, *passim*; VII, 107, 197; IX,
190; X, 23-24.
In the important main entry (IV) Sterne is treated as
a wholesome corrective and complement to Richardson,
giving sensibility not only pathos but humor. Closer to
Smollett than to Fielding, Sterne "opposed sentiment to
reason, sensation to reflection, and with his impressionism
revived that joy in the passing show which the graver
spectator of the human drama runs the risk of letting slip."
Influences and imitations, particularly on the sentimental
novel (V), possible influence on Marryat and influence
on Bulwer-Lytton (VII), influence on George Moore
(IX), and similarities in narrative method between Sterne
and Conrad (X) are also treated.

Baugh, Albert, *et al. A Literary History of England.* New   [305]
York and London: Appleton-Century-Crofts, 1948. Pp.
1022-1026.
The method of *Tristram Shandy* is comparable to that
of a newspaper comic strip, where one must husband material, deal with minutiae, and get nowhere. Sterne uses
facile ease, spirit, and "knowledge of the heart . . . as materials for comedy, if not for grotesque farce." The over-
tones are "rich and amusing, if not logically arranged."
Sterne's stylistic and typographical tricks would have been
classed by Addison as "false wit"; and his "recurrent gross-
ness" is not easy to tolerate; but his prurience is "comic
rather than corrupting." [George Sherburn]

Bernbaum, Ernest. *Guide through the Romantic Movement.* [305a]
New York: Ronald Press, 1949. Pp. 15-16.
Brief treatment of Sterne as a "pre-romantic" who was
"the very genius of incoherence and sensibility" and who
thought that "each novelist should be a law unto himself."

"Bicentenary of Laurence Sterne," *Edinburgh Review,* [306]
CCXVIII (October, 1913), 355-367.
Reviews the *Works,* edited by Cross (100) in an admirably balanced and highly perceptive critical essay.—
"[Sterne's] attitude toward tears always strikes one as objective: the attitude of a man, that is to say, who draws
more tears than he sheds."

Birkhead, Edith. "Sentiment and Sensibility in the Eigh- [307]
teenth Century Novel," *Essays and Studies of the English
Association,* XI (1925), 92-116.
Definitions of *sentiment, sentimental,* and *sensibility* as
they are revealed in the practice of the novelists. To
Sterne *sentimental* meant "a pleasant philandering with
emotion"; to Richardson it meant "sententious." See Allen
(301), Erämetsä (338), Curtis (705).

Birrell, Augustine. "Shandeism," *Nation and Athenaeum,* [308]
XLIV (1929), 754.
Informal comments on new editions of *A Sentimental
Journey,* edited by Virginia Woolf and Herbert Read, as
well as on the *Life and Times* of Cross.

———. "Sterne" in *The Collected Essays and Addresses.* Lon- [309]
don and Toronto: J. M. Dent and Sons, 1922. I, 184-188.
Discusses Sterne's "genius for pathos" and his equal
genius for turning plagiarism into genuine originality.

Buchan, John. *A History of English Literature.* New York: [310]
Thomas Nelson and Sons, 1927. Pp. 347-350.
"[Sterne] applied himself, not to make a general picture of life, but to find an uncharted region of human
nature where his freakish imagination could frolic un-
checked."

Burton, Richard. *Masters of the English Novel: A Study of* [311]
Principles and Personalities. New York: Henry Holt and
Company, 1909. Pp. 84-87.
Presents Sterne chiefly as an essayist in the guise of a

fiction maker.—"Sterne was eight years publishing the various parts of 'Tristram Shandy' . . . Bona fide novels are not thus written." Cf. Stevenson (418).

Calverton, V. F. *Sex Expression in Literature.* New York: [312]
Boni and Liveright, 1926. Pp. 147-152.
    Stressing Sterne's influence on the "religion of self" in France and Germany, Calverton calls him "the superb philander of his age . . . no puritan . . . In things sexual and coprolalic Sterne . . . enjoyed the teasing innuendo and allusion." See De Froe (342).

Cazamian, Louis. *The Development of English Humor, Parts*   [313]
I and II. Durham, North Carolina: Duke University Press, 1952. *Passim.*
    Comments on Sterne's relationship to the English humorists from the earliest times through the Renaissance. See also Cazamian's treatment of Sterne in *L'Humour anglais* (Paris: Didier, 1942 [Études d'Aujourd'hui]) and in Legouis (364).

Chandler, Frank W. *The Literature of Roguery.* (Reprint   [314]
from 1907 edition in Burt Franklin Bibliographical Series, IX) New York: Burt Franklin, 1958. I, 320-321.
    "Whatever picaresque influence Sterne may have felt from Rabelais, Béroalde de Verville, or Scarron, he makes all his own, and diverts the channels of roguery."

Church, Richard. *The Growth of the English Novel.* (Home   [315]
Study Books) London: Methuen & Company, 1957 [1951]. Pp. 88 ff.
    Perhaps "the first impressionist," Sterne introduced a method of working by sensory suggestion "which sooner or later must become controlled by sentiment." Two predominant characteristics of his work were "its dependence upon physical aspects and associations" and "its recoil from this dependence, in moods perhaps of disgust and fear." Cf. Texte (895).

Churchill, R. C. *English Literature of the XVIIIth Century.*   [316]
London: University Tutorial Press, 1953. Pp. 207-214.
    "[Sterne] was notoriously a borrower of other men's styles, but his chief characters were the product of his own imagination . . . [He was] if not a great humourist, 'a fellow of infinite jest.'"

Cohen, J. M. ["First of Modern Writers"], *Spectator*,   [317]
CLXXXVI (1951), 314.
    Review-article occasioned by the publication of
Sterne, edited by Douglas Grant (120). Sees Sterne as
"a perverse writer, forever concerned with the impression
he is making" and as "one of the most powerful forces
behind the whole Romantic movement."

Collins, Norman. "Laurence Sterne and His Fragment of   [318]
Life" in *The Facts of Fiction*. New York: E. P. Dutton
and Company, 1933. Pp. 70-81.
    A loosely constructed and not always well founded
essay treating Sterne as "not only revolutionary but reactionary" and "the founder of sentimental fiction," though
"not a true sentimentalist himself."

Connolly, Cyril. "Distress of Plenty" in *The Condemned*   [319]
Playground: Essays 1927-1944. London: Routledge
[1945]; New York: The Macmillan Company, 1946. Pp.
21-26.
    A reprint of a review-article published on the occasion
of the Shakespeare Head Edition of the *Works* in the *New
Statesman*, XXIX (June 25, 1927), 345-346.

————. "Sterne and Swift," *Atlantic Monthly*, CLXXV (1945),   [320]
94-96.
    Asserts that the intensity lacking in Sterne's emotion
is retrieved in style, for "there is hardly any diction in English so perverse, and yet so adequately under control."

"Creator of Sentimentalism," *Living Age*, CCLXV (1910),   [321]
700-702.
    Reviews Sichel's *Sterne* (253), praising its epigram-
matic style and asserting its superiority to Cross's "pon-
derous and prolix book."—"Sterne is unique, a creature of
contrast, a man who took nothing seriously, least of all
himself, though he always meant well and had genuine
paternal affection for his dowdy daughter."

Cross, Wilbur L. "Laurence Sterne" in *The Development of*   [322]
the English Novel. New York: The Macmillan Company,
1905. Pp. 69-76.
    A revision of the original 1899 edition, reprinted many
times thereafter. Treats Sterne's sources, his eccentricities
of style and method, his successes at characterization, and

his contribution to a structural reversion of the novel "to
what it was when left by the wits of the Renaissance."

————. "Laurence Sterne in the Twentieth Century," *Yale Re-*   [323]
view, N.S. XV (1925), 99-112.
   An informal essay on Sterne's contribution ("an art,
that nature makes") and his popularity and influence in
the twentieth century.

Daiches, David. *A Critical History of English Literature.*   [324]
New York: The Ronald Press, 1960. I, 731-737.
   A compact and perceptive treatment.—"[Sterne] is in
many ways—in his attitude to time, to the individual
consciousness, his use of shifts in perspective—the most
modern of eighteenth-century novelists."

"The Dashing Sterne," *TLS*, March 2, 1951, p. 132.   [325]
   A review-article based on Douglas Grant's *Sterne*
(120). Discusses the uniqueness and contemporaneity of
Sterne, who "established that association of ideas was
much more than a mere blemish on the face of reason
(such as Locke had suggested), which sound intellectual
habits could ward off . . . but belonged to the very ground-
work of personality." With delicacy of perception added
to a jester's personality, Sterne was admirably equipped
for his task. His essentially personal note makes him
closer to Proust than to Joyce, with whom he is often
compared.

De Froe, Arie. *See* [342].

Dermée, Paul. "Le Reverend Laurence Sterne," *Mercure de*   [326]
France, XVI (1913), 539-551.
   Reviews the bicentenary revival of interest in Sterne,
gives a brief account of his life, and sums up his significance and his influence, particularly on European literature.

Digeon, Aurélien. "Un inventeur et un destructeur: Sterne"   [327]
in *Le roman anglais au dix-huitieme siècle.* (Études d'Au-
jourd'hui) Paris: Didier, 1940. Ch. V.
   Sterne and the structure of the novel. See 192.

Dilworth, Ernest Nevin. "Sterne: Some Devices," *N&Q*,   [328]
CXCVII (1952), 165-166.

Comments on stylistic differences between *Tristram Shandy* and *A Sentimental Journey* that are particularly noticeable in tempo.

———. *The Unsentimental Journey of Laurence Sterne.* New [329]
York: King's Crown Press, 1948.
A vigorous and witty, though not completely convincing, argument that Sterne was a jester first, last, and always, and that he has been regarded as "prince of sentimentalists" only through perverse misapprehension of his purpose. See Putney, *PQ*, XIX (1940), 349-369 (659); cf. Dyson (332).—Reviewed by James A. Work in *PQ*, XXVIII (1949), 402-404; by Lodwick Hartley in *MLN*, LXIV (1949), 356; by Wayne Booth in *MP*, XLVI (1949), 280-282; by C. R. T. in *Queen's Quarterly*, LVI (1949), 296; in *TLS*, April 9, 1949, p. 232 (350); by D. P. Vidyarthi in *MLQ*, XI (1949), 112-113; by J. M. S. Tompkins in *RES*, I (1949), 364-366.

Drinkwater, John. "Laurence Sterne" in *The Outline of* [330]
Literature, revised by Horace Shipp. London: Newnes, 1950 [1930]. Pp. 320-322.
A routine and valueless discussion.

Dyson, A. E. "Sterne: The Novelist as Jester," *Critical* [331]
Quarterly, IV (1962), 309-320. Reprinted in *The Crazy Fabric: Essays in Irony*, London: Macmillan; New York: St. Martin's Press, 1965.
Comedy in Sterne tends "to become almost an act of faith in human nature . . . the presentation does much to reconcile us to people who at first sight appear to be only objects of fun. The propensity of ridicule to overreach itself . . . is exactly one of those things which Sterne's ridicule sets out to check." Though in *Tristram Shandy* we are confronted with complexity and eccentricity, we are "challenged to find behind it the simple decency of the human heart." This challenge defines the manner in which the novel is a moral work. Cf. Dilworth (329), Putney (660).

Dyson, H. V. D., and John Butt. "Laurence Sterne" in *Au-* [332]
gustans and Romantics, 1689-1830. (Introductions to English Literature, edited by Bonamy Dobrée, III) New York: Dover Publications; London: The Cresset Press, 1940. Pp. 64-65, 232.

Sterne's work, full of "impudence" and "emotional excess," achieves a unity through style.—"[Sterne] is our greatest master of extravaganza."

Edgar, Pelham. "The Contribution of Sterne" in *The Art of* [333] *the Novel from 1700 to the Present Time.* London and New York: Macmillan, 1933. Pp. 68-78.
Sterne is discussed as "the most evasive and volatile writer of his century."

Elton, Oliver. "Laurence Sterne" in *A Survey of English Literature, 1730-1780.* New York: Macmillan; London: Edward Arnold & Company, 1928, I, 217-231. [334]
Still a sound standard account.—"[Sterne] loosened for good and for all the conventions of the novel. . . . He showed the oddity, the cross-lights, of common scenes, of ordinary people, of small events."

Elwin, Whitwell. "Laurence Sterne" in *Some Eighteenth Century Men of Letters,* edited by Warwick Elwin. London: J. Murray, 1902. [335]
Reprints an essay originally in the *Quarterly Review* of March, 1854, containing a biographical sketch, now out of date, and a still valuable critical discussion.

Engel, Edward. "Laurence Sterne" in *A History of English Literature.* Translated from the German. Revised by Hamley Bent. New York: E. P. Dutton & Company, 1902. [336]
Counters argument that Sterne is "the highest incorporation of humour" . . . "We laugh at 'Tristram Shandy,' and forget him; we read him once, a good deal of his story with increasing impatience, much perhaps two or three times over; but it does not come home to our heart of hearts."

Engstrom, Alfred G. "The Single Tear: A Stereotype of Literary Sensibility," *PQ,* XLII (1963), 106-109. [337]
Tracing the use of the single tear for understating melancholy as far back as Homer, the author discusses the ways in which the device flourished in the eighteenth and nineteenth centuries in such writers as Sterne, Mackenzie, Hugo, Balzac, Gautier, Flaubert, and Melville, achieving a probable *terminus ad quem* in James Joyce. See 898.

Erämetsä, Erik. *A Study of the Word 'Sentimental' and of* [338] *Other Linguistic Characteristics of Eighteenth Century*

Sentimentalism in England. (Suomalaisen Tiedeakatem-
ian Toimituksia Annales Academie Sientiarum Fennicae,
Sarja-Ser. B. Nide—Tom. 74) Helsinki: Helsingin Liike-
kirjapaino Oy, 1951.
An exhaustive philological investigation into the background of the word and the development of its meaning,
with particular reference to Sterne (pp. 39-63). Sterne's
A Sentimental Journey (1768) brought about a big in-
crease in the use of 'sentimental' . . . [making it] *"the*
fashionable word of the day" (p. 20). Cf. Allen (301),
Birkhead (307), Curtis (705).

Forster, E. M. "Laurence Sterne" in *Aspects of the Novel.* [339]
New York: Harcourt, Brace & Company, 1927. Pp. 34-37,
146.
"[Virginia Woolf] and Sterne are both fantasists. They
start with a little object, take a flutter from it, and settle
on it again. They combine a humorous appreciation of the
muddle of life with a keen sense of its beauty." Cf. Jefferson (563).

Foster, J. R. "Laurence Sterne" in *The History of the Pre-* [340]
Romantic Novel in England. New York: Modern Language Association; London: Oxford University Press, 1949.
Pp. 130-138 and *passim.*
Contrasts Richardson and Sterne, one "first of all a
moralist" and the other "the wit and artist." As sentimentalists they could hardly be more unlike. To one
sensibility was "a timid modest maid"; to the other it was
an "unrestrained nymph." Sees *Tristram Shandy* as a
"bourgeois saga," painting a "Lilliputian world of domestic
trivia" that was the culmination of a tendency developing
in the sentimental novel from its inception. See Baker
(304).

Freedman, Ralph. *The Lyrical Novel: Studies in Herman* [341]
Hesse, André Gide, and Virginia Woolf. Princeton, N. J.:
Princeton University Press, 1963. Pp. 11-17, and *passim.*
The relationship of *Tristram Shandy* and *A Senti-
mental Journey* to the tradition of the "lyrical novel."

Froe, Arie de. *Laurence Sterne and His Novels Studied in the* [342]
Light of Modern Psychology. Groningen: P. Noordhoff,
1925.
Though this doctoral thesis brings together some sig-

nificant observations, it is limited in psychological background and application to McDougall's analysis of
instinct as found in his *Outline of Psychology* and it is
based on something less than the soundest elements of
psychoanalysis. Cf. Calverton (312), Towers (610).—Reviewed by Louis Cazamian in *RAA*, III (1926), 448-450;
by B. Fehr in *Beiblatt*, XXXVI (1925), 289-294. See also
Cross (156).

Garnett, Richard, and Edmund Gosse. "Laurence Sterne" in   [343]
English Literature, An Illustrated Record. New York:
Grosset and Dunlap, 1903. III, 316-322.
   Representing rather typical nineteenth-century attitudes, this discussion treats Sterne as a "fantastic sentimentalist and disingenuous idealist," an "ethical heretic"
in whom "the qualities of imagination were heightened,
and the susceptibilities permitted to become as feverish
and neurotic as possible." [Gosse]

Gerould, Gordon Hall. "The Sentimental Strain" in *The Pat-*   [344]
terns of English and American Fiction. Boston: Little,
Brown & Company, 1942. Pp. 103-111.
   Sterne is presented as "the first and greatest of writers
who deliberately cultivated sentimentalism in fiction."

Gosse, Edmund. "Bi-centenary of Laurence Sterne," *English*   [345]
Review, XVI (1914), 228-234; *Living Age,* CCLXXX
(1914), 611-615.
   An address delivered before the Author's Club, November 24, 1913. In Sterne the "faithful tender color of
modern life competed with the preposterous oddity of
burlesque erudition." His artistic growth was achieved
when he got away from the influence of Rabelais and
dropped his "uncouth saurian jokes" in favor of his own
"observations taken directly from human nature." As "the
best conversational writing in the English language" his
books have had pervasive modern influence. Cf. 343.

———. "The Charm of Sterne" in *Some Diversions of Men of*   [346]
Letters. New York: Charles Scribner's Sons, 1919. Pp. 93-
100. Reprinted in *Selected Essays,* First Series (The
Travellers' Library) London: W. Heinemann, 1928, pp.
59-70.
   Reprints address above.

Grabo, Carl H. *The Technique of the Novel.* New York: [347]
Charles Scribner's Sons, 1928. Pp. 291-295.
Discusses similarities in the "expressionism" of Sterne,
Mrs. Radcliffe, and Proust.

Grant, Douglas. "The Novel and Its Critical Terms," *Essays*   [348]
in Criticism, I (1951), 421-429.
Discusses a dilemma of modern criticism in regard to
the novel.—"It is . . . apparent that the modern novelist, so
brilliantly anticipated by Laurence Sterne, is freed by his
conception of character from . . . dependence on plot."

Gwynn, Stephen. "Sterne" in *The Masters of English Litera-*   [349]
ture. London: Macmillan and Company, 1938 [1925]. Pp.
225-230.
"[A tendency toward indecent allusion] is the central
defect in Sterne, and it cannot be too strongly insisted on
. . . prurience pervades everything . . . However, it has to
be said that Sterne offends against taste rather than
against morals."

"The Head and the Heart," *TLS,* April 9, 1949, p. 232.   [350]
A reply to Dilworth (329).—"Sterne. . .is one of the
least sentimental writers, for he never confused his heart
with his head. But there is no reason for thinking that he
faked what he felt . . . To represent [him] as a satirist is
to suppose in him a moral sense which he did not possess."

Heidler, Joseph Bunn. "The History of English Criticism of   [351]
Prose Fiction, 1700-1800," *University of Illinois Studies in*
Language and Literature, XIII (1928), 78-85.
Abstract of a University of Illinois dissertation treating
Sterne's critical ideas and concluding that "Sterne's con-
ception of the novel . . . cannot be attributed definitely to
any one source or group of sources." See 513.

Henriot, Emile. "Sterne" in *Courrier littéraire XVIIIᵉ siecle.*   [352]
Paris: La Renaissance du Livre, 1945. Vol. II.

Hnatko, Eugene. "Studies in the Prose Style of Laurence   [353]
Sterne," *DA,* XXIII (1963), 4685.
Abstract of a University of Syracuse dissertation. A
study of Sterne's style ranging from such "broad" elements
of language as irony and narrative point of view to minute
aspects of incidence of sound pattern, from the more tradi-

tional examination of the "trope" to the newer concern
with structure incidence, including an over-all attempt to
show the peculiar eighteenth-century aspects of the style.
See Stedmond (608).

Holland, Norman N. "The Laughter of Laurence Sterne,"   [354]
    Hudson Review, IX (1956), 422-430.
       A University of Virginia dissertation. Discusses
Sterne's "great liberalizing influence upon the theory of
novel writing."

Huffman, Charles H. *The Eighteenth Century Novel in*   [355]
    Theory and Practice. Dayton, Virginia: Ruebush-Kieffer,
    1920. Pp. 57-63.
       Contends that "the tags of sentimental or anti-senti-
mental cannot define Sterne's dual comic vision" centering
on the "hobby-horse," which he both ridicules and respects, ultimately presenting "the ridiculousness of both
hobby-horse and reality, the paradox of the little greatness
of man."

Humphrey, Robert. "Stream of Consciousness: Technique or   [356]
    Genre?" *PQ*, XXX (1951), 434-437.
       See below.

———. *Stream of Consciousness in the Modern Novel*. Berke-   [357]
    ley and Los Angeles: University of California Press, 1954.
    P. 127.
       Regards Sterne as the first novelist to exploit "this prin-
ciple of psychic functioning," but does not regard him as
belonging to the "stream-of-consciousness genre because
his concerns are not serious in representing psychic content for its own sake and as a mean of achieving essences
of characterization." Cf. Watkins (259) and Traugott
(611).

Jackson, Holbrook. "Laurence Sterne" in *Great English Nov-*   [358]
    elists. London: G. Richards; Philadelphia: George W.
    Jacobs and Co. [1908]. Pp. 108-130.
       A biographical-critical sketch presenting Sterne as "a
sentimental egoist with a certain and definite balance, an
insight into life, and a faculty for differentiating reality
from the myth of things." Insists that the "most curious
fact in the life of Laurence Sterne is that he was a parson."

Jefferson, D. W. *Laurence Sterne*. (Writers and Their Works,   [359]
No. 52) London, New York, Toronto: published for the
British Council and the National Book League by Long-
mans, Green & Company, 1954.
    A compact and discerning introduction to Sterne with
a useful bibliography.—"Sterne was long a sick man . . .
The gaiety of *Tristram Shandy* and also of *A Sentimental
Journey* takes on a different significance against this back-
ground."

Kettle, Arnold. *An Introduction to the English Novel*. Lon-   [360]
don: Hutchinson's University Library, 1951. Vol. I, pp.
81-86.
Reprinted in the Harper Torchbook Series/The Academy
Library, New York: Harper and Brothers, 1960.
    Excellent general treatment. *Tristram Shandy* is pre-
sented as "a great book [that] vastly and intricately extended the scope and possibilities of the English novel"
in spite of the fact that "the total effect is less than satisfy-
ing." Acknowledges indebtedness to D. W. Jefferson
(359) for basic discussion.

Knight, Grant C. "Sterne" in *The Novel in English*. New   [361]
York: Richard R. Smith, 1931. Pp. 63-71.
    A sound general treatment. Sterne removed "the novel
from the plane of the wiseacre, the realist, and the romance" to "regions made delightful with mixtures of non-
sense, wisdom, and sentimentality."

Leavis, F. R. *The Great Tradition*. Garden City, New York: [362]
Doubleday & Company, 1954. Pp. 10-11n.
    A provocative footnote. Countering the "confusion" of
such critics as Virginia Woolf and E. M. Forster in considering Defoe a great novelist, when "he made no preten-
sion to practising the novelist's art," Dr. Leavis charges
that the same kind of "use" was made of Sterne, "in whose
irresponsible (and nasty) trifling, regarded as in some way
extraordinarily significant and mature, was found a sanc-
tion for attributing value to other trifling." See 302, 540.

LeGallienne, Richard. "The Sentimental Mr. Sterne Gets His   [363]
Due," *Literary Digest International Book Review*, IV
(1926), 181-183.
    A review-article praising Cross's *Life* (211).—"The
everlasting humor of [Sterne] saves him . . . We must
accept him as he is or else close the book."

Legouis, Emile, and Louis Cazamian. "Sterne" in *A History*   [364]
  of English Literature. New York: The Macmillan Company, 1929. Pp. 880-886.
      One of the most astute of the brief commentaries.
  Finds in Sterne the "absolute victory of sentiment,"
  achieved through art and artifice and "a complete mastery
  of emotion by the devices employed"; hence his sentimentalism is "a new resource exploited by a severe and
  intellectual art," a source of enjoyment and an end in
  itself, proclaiming that sentimentalism will henceforth be
  liberated from ethics. [Cazamian]

Lockridge, Ernest H. "A View of the Sentimental Absurd: [365]
  Sterne and Camus," *Sewanee Review,* LXXII (1964), 652-
  667.
      The philosophy of the Absurd, as it is developed in
  Camus's *The Myth of Sisyphus,* is invoked to aid in an
  understanding of "Sterne's whole vision."

Lovett, Robert Morss. "Revival of Sterne," *New Republic,*   [366]
  XLV (1925), 55-56.
      Review-article on Cross's *Life* (211) and two recent
  editions of the novels.—"The twentieth century should
  recognize Sterne as a pioneer and example in exclusive-
  ness of material, in delicacy of workmanship, and above
  all in freedom of form."

———, and Helen Sard Hughes. "Laurence Sterne" in *The*   [367]
  History of the Novel in England. Boston: Houghton Mifflin Company, 1932. Pp. 85-91.
      A remarkably inadequate general critical appraisal,
  with no apparent comprehension of an underlying plan
  for *Tristram Shandy,* no treatment of the Lockean influences, or of the important themes.—"The novel form raised
  high by the careful workmanship of Richardson and Fielding, in the hands of Sterne was sacrificed to personal whim
  and deliberate eccentricity."

Maack, Rudolph. *Laurence Sterne im Lichte seiner Zeit.*   [368]
  (Brittanica. Herausgegeben vom Seminar für englische
  Sprache und Kultur an der Hansischen Universität, Heft
  10) Hamburg: Friederischen, de Gruyter & Company,
  1936.
      A careful and extensive treatment of Sterne as artist
  and thinker poised between the Neo-classical and Romantic periods. Contends that the artist made significant

breakthroughs from the old to the new without being totally conscious of what he had achieved. Cf. Booth (513), Boys (517), Brissenden (519), Emerson (536).— Reviewed by J. W. Beach in *JEGP*, XXXVI (1937), 594-596; by K. Arns in *LGRP*, LVIII (1937), 104-105; by W. Keller in *Zeitschrift für neusprachlichen Unterricht*, XXXVI (1937), 54; by O. Boerner in *Die neueren Sprachen*, XLV (1937), 378-379; by W. Mann in *Anglia Beiblatt*, L (1939), 202-206.

MacLean, Kenneth. *John Locke and English Literature of the Eighteenth Century.* New Haven: Yale University Press, 1936. *Passim.* [369]
    In a study of aspects of Locke's famous *Essay* that influenced certain English writers in subject matter and method, the treatment of Sterne is of particular interest. For limitations of the study, see review by R. S. C. below; cf. 424, 567.—Reviewed by Edith Morley in *YWES*, XVII (1936), 229-230; by R. S. C[rane] in *PQ*, XVI (1937), 180-181.

Mann, Elizabeth. "The Problem of Originality in English Literary Criticism, 1750-1800," *PQ*, XVIII (1939), 97-118. [370]
    A study of the problem of originality in criticism as "a significant preparation for the better understanding of such a 'singular' author as Sterne."

Maurois, André. "Portrait d'un original," *Nouvelles littéraires*, 25 May 1962, pp. 1, 8. [371]
    A review-article based on Fluchère (218). Like Cervantes, Voltaire, and sometimes Shakespeare, Sterne assumes the castigative function of the buffoon. The world and our existence are in his eyes vain and absurd pleasantries. But, to the contrary of Hamlet, Sterne, like Montaigne, reconstructs beyond humbled pride a humane ethic.

Mayoux, Jean-Jacques. "Laurence Sterne parmi nous," *Critique*, No. 177 (1962), 99-119. [372]
    A thoroughgoing analysis of Fluchère (218), with important dissenting opinions, together with perceptive comments on the literary relationship of Sterne with Rabelais and Diderot and with modern fiction.

McCullough, Bruce. "The Comic Novel: Laurence Sterne" in *Representative English Novelists: Defoe to Conrad.* New [373]

York and London: Harper and Brothers, 1946. Pp. 69-83.

By using a narrator belonging to the family circle and yet being able to attain a detachment from it, Sterne "achieved a more personal effect than any other novelist of his time had achieved." Competently summarizes the literary contributions and qualities and makes a comparison of Sterne and Proust.

McKillop, Alan Dugald. *English Literature from Dryden to* [374] *Burns.* (Appleton-Century Handbooks of Literature) New York-London: Appleton-Century-Crofts, 1948. Pp. 274-278.

Brief biographical-critical account with bibliography.

———. "Laurence Sterne" in *The Early Masters of English* [375] *Fiction.* Lawrence, Kansas: University of Kansas Press, 1956. Pp. 182-219.

An important expansion of the article in *Études Anglaises* (see below) with valuable additional comments; see also 148.

———. "The Reinterpretation of Laurence Sterne," *Études* [376] *Anglaises*, VII (1954), 36-47.

An article of first importance summing up contemporary scholarship and adding perceptive insights into the man, his methods, and subject matter, with an exceedingly valuable final paragraph concerning major eighteenth-century novelists "in terms of the adequacy they claim for their interpretation of life." See Rufus Putney's comment in *PQ*, XXXIV (1955), 313.

Montero-Bustamente, Raúl. "Una lectura de Sterne" in *La* [377] *ciudad de los libros.* Montevideo: Impresora L.I.G.U., 1944. Pp. 65-93.

Concerned chiefly with Sterne's personality and humor.

Moody, William Vaughn, and Robert Morss Lovett. *A His-* [378] *tory of English Literature.* New York: Charles Scribner's Sons, 1918 [1902]. Pp. 266-289.

Routine discussion of Sterne as a novelist, regarding *Tristram Shandy* as an "ill-regulated book" which was the product of "Sterne's ill-regulated existence."

More, Paul Elmer. "Laurence Sterne" in *Shelburne Essays.* [379] (Series 3) New York and London: G. P. Putnam's Sons, 1905. Pp. 177-212.

Occasioned by Cross's edition of the *Works* (100). Applauds the discovery of new material that aids in countering the "shameful" charges of Thackeray. Finds in *Tristram Shandy* "a philosophy, a new and distinct vision of the meaning of life, which makes Sterne something larger than a mere novelist." Emphasizes his place in the humanistic tradition of Rabelais and Cervantes.

Moulton, Charles Wells, *et al.* "Laurence Sterne" in *The Library of Literary Criticism of English and American Authors*. Buffalo, N.Y.: The Moulton Company, 1901-05. III, 501-517.   [380]
Useful excerpts from eighteenth- and nineteenth-century criticism.

Muir, Edwin. "Laurence Sterne," *AB*, LXXIII (1931), 1-5.   [381]
A graceful critical essay of importance. Sees Sterne's "operation [as] the operation of pure style . . . [a] style that creates the world contained in [his novels] . . . like Donne and Proust his aim is to find the intelligible and the spiritual in minute and curious manifestations of the physical . . . [He is] the most economical as the most leisurely of writers, the most perfect master of form as the novelist least concerned with it." Cf. Traugott (611).

———. "Laurence Sterne" in *Essays on Literature and Society*. London: The Hogarth Press, 1949. Pp. 49-56.   [382]
Reprints essay above with minor changes.

Murakami, Shikō. *Warai no bungaku* [Laughter in Literature]. Tokyo, 1955.   [383]
Sterne and Smollett as humorists.

Neill, S. Diana. "The Dynamic of Eccentricity" in *A Short History of the English Novel*. New York: The Macmillan Company; London: Jarrolds, 1951. Pp. 72-77.   [384]
Sterne as a rebel and an "enfant terrible" of fiction, whose work is congenial to the modern reader chiefly for "its puckish humour and individual charm."

Osgood, Charles G. "Laurence Sterne" in *The Voice of England*. New York and London: Harper and Brothers, 1935. Pp. 340-343.   [385]
A sensitive and delightful brief treatment.—"Sterne found the world sentimentalizing, and fed it more senti-

mentality; but he also laughed at it, and thus wiped away
its delicious tears."

Phelps, William Lyon. "The Advance of the English Novel,"   [386]
    AB, XLII (1915), 394-396.
        Unsympathetic treatment of Sterne as a man and as a
    writer.—"Literature lost little by [his] early disappearance
    . . . the very essence of [his] works is their incompleteness;
    and we have enough of both. . . . In sheer invention he
    was weak or lazy. . . . He was both irreverent and immoral.
    . . . Sterne's pathos . . . has always left me cold."

———. "Wilbur L. Cross's 'Laurence Sterne,'" *AB*, XXX   [387]
    (1909), 253-256.
        Review-article (see 211) indicating that the critic was
    not convinced by Cross's resuscitation of his subject's char-
    acter. Sterne was "a bad son, a bad husband, a sensualist,
    a plagiarist, and a liar." See reply by Newton (579).

Piper, William Bowman. "The Problem of the Self and the   [388]
    Other in the Novels of Sterne," *DA*, XIX (1959), 1762.
        Abstract of a University of Wisconsin dissertation.
    The study of self and the other is a matter of form, the
    basic principle of Sterne's art being split between the
    individual Tristram or Yorick and his surroundings
    treated in a different way in *Tristram Shandy* and the
    Journey. In the former, the hero is isolated "in a tense
    shifting conversational present . . . continuously trying to
    tell Sir, Madam, and other generalized social figures about
    his and his family's past. In the latter, Yorick in his study
    writes a selection of his social adventures in France. Finds
    a contrast between the "relentless I-you" present in the
    first novel and the fragmentary "I-they" past in the second.
    See Booth (514); also 584, 585.

Pons, Christian. "Laurence Sterne ou le génie de l'humour,"   [389]
    Cahiers du Sud, No. 367 (1962), 425-446.
        A review-essay on Fluchère (218) with emphasis on
    the rebirth of interest in Sterne in a century better able
    to appreciate his humor than was his own, with some
    "marginal commentaries" on Sterne's humor by the author.

Pope-Hennessy, Dame Una. "Lawrence [*sic*] Sterne," *Quarter-*   [390]
    ly Review, CCLXVI (1936), 87-101.
        Review-article occasioned by the publication of Cur-

tis's edition of the *Letters* (177), with a belated notice of *The Politicks* (213). Contends that the inclusion of the newly discovered letters and other material adds "practically nothing to our knowledge of Sterne," but does admit that "in America Sterne has been taken seriously."

Porter, Katherine Anne. "The Winged Skull," *The Nation*, [391] CLVII (July 17, 1943), 72-73.
A review-article based on Hartley's *This Is Lorence* (223) suggesting the difficulties of interpreting Sterne. Provides a first-rate statement of Sterne's primary appeal to the intelligent and sensitive reader.

Powys, Llewelyn. "Laurence Sterne," *AB*, LVIII (Sept., [392] 1923), 10-16.
An appreciation of Sterne as man and writer, pointing out as the particular virtue of *Tristram Shandy* "the wide, deep, generous humanism of its tone [that puts one] in a genial latitudinarian mood with all the universe." Sees the book as "sufficiently free from prurience."

Price, Martin. "Sterne: Art and Nature" in *To the Palace of* [393] *Wisdom*. Garden City, N.Y.: Doubleday and Company, 1964. Pp. 312-341.
In order to show the inherent absurdity of all schemes of ordering and ultimately to enact the confused state in which he finds man, Sterne assumes the manner of an egocentric and tyrannical author, at times affecting to lose control of the suggestion of his words, the movement of his memory, and the direction of his narrative. As an actor he remains detached from his role and in control of his audience. Insisting upon the fact of his performance, he allows the histrionic to become "the guarantee of sanity and the recovery of the natural."

Priestley, J. B. "Parson Yorick," *SRL*, II (1926), 569-570. [394]
Review of Cross's *Life* (211). Praises the biographer for vindicating Sterne from some of the graver charges against his character but contends that the novelist was not always sensitive in the "larger . . . concerns of life." Though Sterne was a "sensation-monger," his intellectual qualities should not be underestimated. He is described as "an amorous man destitute of virility and passion," "an elaborate pretender," "an artist first to last," "the literary sense personified," "one of the great Romantic influences." Cf. 139.

Putney, Rufus D. S. "Sensibility and the Novel." Unpublished   [395]
  Master's thesis, Washington University, 1932.
    See 659, 660.

Quiller-Couch, Arthur. "Laurence Sterne" in *Adventures in*   [396]
  Criticism. Cambridge: The University Press, 1924; New
  York: G. P. Putnam's Sons, 1925. [First ed. 1896]. Pp.
  95-102.
    Commenting on Whibley's introduction to his edition
  of *Tristram Shandy* (1894), contends that though "Sterne
  is indecent . . . [and] a convicted thief . . . he has genius
  enough to make it worth our while to listen without prejudice." See Whibley (431).

Rabizzani, Giovanni. *Lorenzo Sterne.* (Profili, No. 31)   [397]
  Genoa: A. F. Formiggini, 1914.
    A general introduction to Sterne for Italian readers,
  with bibliographical and critical notes.

Read, Herbert. *English Prose Style.* Boston: Beacon Press,   [398]
  1952. [Revision of original edition, London: Bell, 1928.]
    Sterne's "witty" paragraphing (pp. 57-58), "expression-
  ism" (pp. 163-164), eloquence (pp. 167-168).

——. "Sterne" in *The Sense of Glory.* New York: Harcourt,   [399]
  Brace & Company, 1930. Pp. 123-151.
    Reprints essay of first importance originally appearing
  in *TLS* on May 26, 1927, pp. 361-362. Counters charges
  of Sterne's impiety and lack of intellectual seriousness.
  See 101.

——. "Sterne" in *The Nature of Literature.* New York: [400]
  Horizon Press, 1951; also *Collected Essays in Literary*
  Criticism, London: Faber and Faber, Ltd., 1951. Pp. 247-
  264.
    Other reprints of the *TLS* essay above.

Reid, Ben. "The Sad Hilarity of Sterne," *VQR*, XXXII   [401]
  (1956), 107-130.
    ". . . the emotional strength of Sterne's comedy comes
  from its hidden roots in tragedy . . . the secret of its emotional force may be its origin in a vision we had best call
  tragic."

Ricks, Christopher. "The Novelist as Innovator: Laurence   [402]
  Sterne," *The Listener*, LXXIII (1965), 218-220.

A shortened version of a BBC Third Program.—
"Sterne's great innovation was that he wrote a novel about
writing a novel."

Robinson, Henry Crabb. *On Books and Their Writers,* edited   [403]
by Edith J. Morley. London: J. M. Dent & Sons, 1938.
II, 723.
A brief first-hand account of Thackeray's famous lecture on Sterne and Goldsmith.

Saintsbury, George. *The English Novel.* London: J. M. Dent   [404]
& Sons; New York: E. P. Dutton, 1913. Pp. 126-132.
An important commentary.—"[Sterne] showed how the
novel could present, in refreshed form, the *fatrasie,* the
pillar-to-post miscellany, of which Rabelais had perhaps
given the greatest example . . . and he showed the novel
of purpose in a form especially appealing to his contemporaries—the purpose being to exhibit, glorify, luxuriate in
the exhibition of sentiment or 'sensibility.'"

———. *The Peace of the Augustans.* London-New York-Toron-   [404]
to: Oxford University Press, 1946 [1916]. Pp. 14-16, 140-
145.
Discusses Sterne's "moral character" and his eccentricity.—"Sterne is inviting enough to anyone who does not
allow himself to be frightened off, either by moral taint or
by . . . artistic or inartistic tricks."

———. "Sterne's Life," *Living Age,* CCLXXVIII (1913), 480-   [405]
484.
A bi-centenary appreciation of the superlative "uniqueness" of Sterne reprinted from the *Bookman* (London).

Sampson, George. "Sterne and the Novel of His Times" in   [406]
The Concise Cambridge History of English Literature.
Cambridge: The University Press; New York: The Macmillan Company, 1941. Pp. 509-512.
Argues that the little that is known about Sterne's life
is "not very reputable" and finds his "sensibility" or "sentimentalism" to be "his most offensive quality," at the same
time conceding to him "an original and originating power
in literature," an unmatched subtlety in style and form,
making him "a liberator—even the first of the 'expression-
ists.'"

Sanders, J. W. *The Profession of English Letters.* London: [407]
    Routledge and K. Paul, 1964. Pp. 148-151.
       "In the novels of Sterne . . . there is implicit . . . an
    overriding satisfaction in playing up to the part of a public
    entertainer."

Schlötke, Charlotte. "Entwicklungsstufen des humoristisch-   [408]
    satyrischen Romans in England und Frankreich, Rabelais
    —Swift—Sterne," *Geist der Zeit,* XVI (1938), 166-175.
       Discusses Sterne as one of the three landmarks in the
    development of European humorous-satirical fiction for
    three centuries.

Schmidt-Hidding, Wolfgang. *Sieben Meister des literari-*   [409]
    schen Humors in England und Amerika. Heidelberg:
    Quelle & Meyer, 1959.
       Essays on Chaucer, Shakespeare, Fielding, Sterne,
    Lamb, Dickens, and Clemens.

Schöne, Annemarie. "Laurence Sterne—unter dem Aspekt der   [410]
    Nonsense-Dichtung," *Neophilologus* (Gröningen), XL
    (1956), 51-62.
       Considers Sterne in the tradition of English nonsense
    poetry that had its full flowering in the nineteenth century
    in Edward Lear and Lewis Carroll.

Seccombe, Thomas. "Laurence Sterne" in *The Age of John-*   [411]
    son. London: G. Bell & Sons, 1932 [1899]. Pp. 179-188.
       Still a sound, though limited, treatment.—". . . in the
    role of the nondescript no novel has ever surpassed *The
    Life and Opinions of Tristram Shandy, Gent.* . . . Sterne
    must rank with Fielding and Dickens in the van of En-
    glish humorists."

Sherman, Stuart Pratt. "Laurence Sterne: A Graceless Man of   [412]
    God" in *Critical Woodcuts.* New York-London: Charles
    Scribner's Sons, 1926. Pp. 284-295.
       An impressionistic essay based on Cross's biography
    (211) and originally published in *NYHTB.*

Shoup, Louise. "The Use of the Social Gathering as a Struc-   [413]
    tural Device in the Novels of Richardson, Smollett, and
    Sterne" in *Stanford University Abstracts of Dissertations,*
    1950, pp. 139-141.

Stedmond, J. M. "Laurence Sterne and the Technique of   [414]
Prose Fiction: A Critical Analysis." Unpublished Ph.D.
dissertation, Aberdeen University, 1953.
   See 605-608 inclusive.

Steinbrecht, Fritz. *Der Humor bei Laurence Sterne.* Halle,   [415]
1921.
   Summarized in *Jahrbuch d. phil. Fakultät* Halle-Wit-
tenberg, I (1921), 9-12.

"Sterne." *Spectator*, CXI (1913), 904-905. Reprinted in *Liv-*   [416]
ing Age, CCLXXX (1914), 121-124.
   A bicentenary appreciation.—"He gave his country
what the natural man instinctively finds the most acceptable literary form—prose that is an idealisation of the
conversational manner. . . [He] laughed pomposity and
formality out of face with enthusiastic support of all good
fellows."

"Sterne as the Father of Modern Impressionism," *Current*   [417]
Literature, XLIX (1910), 443-444.
   An article based on Sichel's biography (253), echoing
Sichel's contention that his subject was "our first great
literary impressionist" and that "sensationalism" is a truer
name for Sterne's manner than "sentimentality."

Stevenson, Lionel. *The English Novel, A Panorama.* Boston: [418]
Houghton-Mifflin Company, 1960. Pp. 124-132.
   A highly incisive and perceptive general account, treating *Tristram Shandy* as "a gigantic personal essay" fascinating for the personality that it reveals poised between
the "cynic wearing a mask of sympathy and a sentimentalist wearing a mask of cynicism," and attributing to Sterne
a unique contribution to the technique of the novel as a
precursor of the modern use of the "science of psychology"
in fiction.

Tave, Stuart M. *The Amiable Humorist: A Study in the*   [419]
Comic Theory and Criticism of the Eighteenth and Early
Nineteenth Century. Chicago: Chicago University Press,
1960. Pp. 148-151, 171-177, 222-227, 233-235, and *passim.*
   Contains a discussion of Sterne in relation to a concept
of comedy concerned with amiable, if slightly eccentric,
men of good will.

———. "Corbyn Harris: Falstaff, Humor, and Comic Theory in   [420]
the Eighteenth Century," *MP*, L (1952), 102-115.
Background for Sterne's humorous characterizations.

Thompson, Lawrence. A Comic Principle in Sterne-Meredith-   [421]
Joyce. British Institute, University of Oslo, 1954. [Mimeo-
graphed]
Transcript of a series of lectures. Sterne, Meredith,
and Joyce have such an artistic kinship that the reading of
each helps one to understand the other two. Each uses a
comic formula to arrive at an ultimately serious effect.
Each uses comic, mock-heroic, and even satirical conventions as a means of unmasking certain affectations of vanity and hypocrisy. Each defines a positive set of ideas in
terms of its opposite.

Todhunter, John. *An Essay in Search of a Subject.* [London: [422]
Printed by R. Folkard and Son (?1904)].
A paper read before "The Sette of Odd Volumes,"
May 3, 1904, commenting on Sterne.

Tronskaia, M. L. "Sterne the Moralist," *National Learned*   [423]
Notes (Leningrad), XIII (1948), 338-359. [In Russian]

Tuveson, Ernest. "Locke and Sterne" in *Reason and the*   [424]
Imagination, Studies in the History of Ideas, 1600-1800,
edited by J. A. Mazzeo. New York: Columbia University
Press; London: Routledge and Kegan Paul, 1962. Pp. 255-
277.
Locke was neither scientist nor philosopher but a reformer in a great movement of Western thought. It was
as the center of a great liberating force from a smothering
intellectual heritage of stultifying logic that he appealed
to Sterne, whose images "present with great exactitude
the intellectual world of his time." Sterne, like Locke,
attacks the traditional view of the independence of the
mind, realizing that "the body thinks" and is an integral
part of "one garment" with the mind. Cf. MacLean (369).

Vaughan, C. E. "Sterne and the Novel of His Times" in *The*   [425]
Cambridge History of English Literature. New York: G.
P. Putnam's Sons; Cambridge: The University Press, 1913.
X, 51-74.
"[Sterne] revolutionized the whole scope and purpose
of the novel . . . [using it] to give free utterance to his

own way of looking at life, his own moral and intellectual individuality."—This essay considers the special qualities of Sterne's humor in character (with emphasis on the influence of Cervantes) and in situation. It holds the author responsible for his "pruriency" and casts doubts on his "sincerity" in the extremes of sentimentalism.

Vogelreich, Erna. *Laurence Sternes Verhältnis zum Publikum* [426] *und der Ausdruck dieses Verhältnisses im Stil.* Marburg: Hermann Bauer, 1938.

A dissertation of the Phillipps-Universität at Marburg. A socio-psychological approach to Sterne, considering his ambivalence (*Doppelseitigkeit*) toward his audience as revealed in his prose style and in the structure of his fiction, as well as Sterne's historical place in the "liberation" of the artist.

Wagenknecht, Edward Charles. "The Triumph of Sensibility: [427] Laurence Sterne" in *Cavalcade of the English Novel from Elizabeth to George VI.* New York: Henry Holt & Company, 1943. Pp. 78-87.

A valuable brief critical treatment.—"If [Sterne's] psychology is crude his art is consummate." He creates a mad world, but "out of chaos a cosmos emerges, a universe in which everything is intimately connected with everything else."

Walsh, William S. "Mr. Sichel's Laurence Sterne," *New York* [428] *Times Saturday Review,* XV (1910), 518.

Mentions Sichel's (253) preciosity of style as being "not out of keeping in a biography of one who himself was a juggler with words," points out Sichel's alleged "discovery" of the relationship of Mrs. Sterne to Mrs. Montagu, and agrees with the biographer that instead of being the "foul satyr" of Thackeray, Sterne was "merely the whimsical, irresponsible, mischievous faun."

Watt, Ian. "Realism and the Later Tradition: A Note" in *The* [429] *Rise of the Novel: Studies in Defoe, Richardson, and Fielding.* Berkeley and Los Angeles: University of California Press, 1957. Pp. 290-296.

An illuminating and stimulating criticism. Argues that Sterne found a way to reconcile "Richardson's realism of presentation with Fielding's realism of assessment."

Weygandt, Cornelius. "Yorick Out-of-Doors" in *Tuesdays at*   [430]
Ten. Philadelphia: University of Pennsylvania Press,
1928. Pp. 76-86.
Examines Sterne's interest in nature—particularly ani-
mal life—only to conclude that his "records of people are
important, as his writings on the farm and things out-of-
doors generally are not." A negligible contribution.

Whibley, Charles. "Laurence Sterne" in *Studies in Frankness.*   [431]
London: Constable, 1910. Pp. 81-114.
Treats Sterne as "a prince among literary tramps" who
accomplished "a picaresque of the intellect." Cf. Quiller-
Couch (396).

Williams, Harold. "Laurence Sterne: Sentimentalist," *West-*   [432]
minster Review, CLXXIV (October, 1910), 399-409.
Comparing Sterne with Charles Lamb and Robert
Louis Stevenson, the writer treats Sterne as "a romantic
sentimentalist of the mind . . . in an age of prose, reason,
and logic."

Williamson, George. "The Rhetorical Pattern of Neo-Classical   [433]
Wit," *MP*, XXXIII (1935), 55-81.
Background for the study of Sterne's prose style. See
also Williamson's *The Senecan Amble* (London: Faber
and Faber, 1951), *passim.* Cf. Stedmond (608).

Wolff, S. L. "Laurence Sterne," *The Nation*, LXXXIX (1909),   [434]
346-349.
A review-article occasioned by Cross's *Life* (211).
Contends that no final judgment on Sterne can ever be
passed, for a matter of temperament is involved. The
novelist's lasting appeal is due to "that 'bit of chaos' that
each of us carries about."

Woolf, Virginia. "Sterne," *TLS*, August 13, 1909, pp. 289-290.   [435]
Reprinted in *Granite and Rainbow*, London: Hogarth
Press, 1958, pp. 167-175.
A review-article occasioned by Cross's *Life* (211).
Sterne's life combines "extraordinary flightiness and oddity
[with] the infinite painstaking and self-consciousness of
the artist." His fame depends partly upon his inimitable
style, but "rests most safely upon the extraordinary zest
with which he lived, and with the joy with which his mind
worked ceaselessly upon the world."

Wright, Walter Francis. "Sensibility in English Prose Fic-   [436]
tion, 1760-1814," *University of Illinois Studies in Lan-*
guage and Literature, XXII, Nos. 3-4 (1937). Pp. 25-29.
    A University of Illinois dissertation attempting to treat
"the full significance of sensibility" in the novelists of the
period indicated. Treats Sterne briefly, arguing that
"though [his] works and his conduct, superficially viewed,
may seem eccentric and whimsical, they were really the
consistent expression of a profound faith . . . shared by
many others of his generation."

See also 510, 519, 572, 579, 583, 588, 595, 660.

B. *Tristram Shandy*

Antal, Frederick. "The Moral Purpose of Hogarth's Art,"   [501]
Journal of the Warburg and Courtauld Institutes, XV
(1952), 193.
    The influence of Hogarth on Sterne's sketch of Trim.
See Brissenden (519).

Baird, Theodore. "The Time-Scheme of *Tristram Shandy* and   [502]
a Source," *PMLA,* LI (1936), 803-820.
    Argues that "far from being a wild and whimsical work
[*Tristram Shandy*] is an exactly executed historical novel,"
with a plan derived from Locke's remarks on duration.
Suggests source for historical materials included. Some
of the basic assumptions are subject to question. Cf. Watkins (259), Lehman (569), Mendilow (574), Stanzel
(604).

Balderston, Katherine, ed. *Thraliana, The Diary of Mrs. Hes-*   [503]
ter Lynch Thrale (Later Mrs. Piozzi), 1776-1809. Oxford:
Clarendon Press, 1951. I, 23-24.
    Mrs. Thrale's discovery of "the very novel [*The Life*
and Memoirs of Mr. Ephraim Tristram Bates] from which
Sterne took his first Idea." See Bensly (507) and Hughes
(558).

Barnett, George L. "Corporal Trim's Hat," *N&Q,* CC, N.S. II   [504]
(1955), 403-404.
    A reminiscence of *Tristram Shandy,* V, vii, in Dickens's
Old Curiosity Shop.

————. "Gay, Swift, and 'Tristram Shandy,'" *N&Q,* CLXXXV   [505]
(1943), 346-347.

An evidence of the contemporary popularity of *Tristram Shandy* in a rhymed receipt appearing in the *Gentleman's Magazine* in 1760. See 803.

Bayley, A. R. "Sterne and 'Dr. Slop'" (Burton of York),   [506]
N&Q, 11th ser., VI (1912), 375-376.
Dr. Burton's dates established from tablet on wall of Holy Trinity, Micklegate, York.

Bensly, Edward. "An Alleged Source of 'Tristram Shandy,'"   [507]
N&Q, CLIX (1930), 27, 84.
Concerning *The Life and Memoirs of Mr. Ephraim Tristram Bates* (1756). See Helen Sard Hughes's article in *JEGP*, XVII, 1918, 227-251 (558).

———. "Clothes and Their Influence," *N&Q*, 11th ser., I   [508]
(1910), 152.
Cites a passage from *Tristram Shandy*, Vol. VI, Ch. 23. See also, *N&Q*, p. 76.

———. "A Debt of Sterne's," *TLS*, November 1, 1928, p. 806.   [509]
Suggests Ephraim Chamber's *Cyclopedia: or, an Universal Dictionary of Arts and Sciences* (1728) as the source of much of the science of fortification in *Tristram Shandy* rather than numerous books on the subject cited by Cross and others. See Deedes (531) and Stedmond (607).

Binz-Winiger, Elisabeth. *Erziehungsfragen in den Romanen*   [510]
von Richardson, Fielding, Smollett, Goldsmith und Sterne.
Weida i. Thür.: Thomas & Hubert, 1926.
University of Basel dissertation. Concludes that Sterne added nothing to the area of the child in the novel either pedagogically or psychologically, but that he possessed the gift that no poet of his century had—that of penetrating into the phantasy-world of the child and reproducing it in the mirror of his own unique art of the vignette.

Birrell, Augustine. "That Fantastic Old Great Man," *Nation*   [511]
and Athenaeum, XXXVIII (1926), 678.
Sterne's indebtedness to Robert Burton. Occasioned by the publication of the *Nonesuch Burton*.

Booth, Wayne C. "Did Sterne Complete *Tristram Shandy?*"   [512]
MP, XLVIII (1951), 172-183.

Volume 9 "represented the completion of a plan, however rough, which was present in [Sterne's] mind from
the beginning." See below and Mendilow (574).

———. *The Rhetoric of Fiction.* Chicago: University of Chi-   [513]
cago Press, 1961. Pp. 221-240, 430-432.
A brilliant chapter on *Tristram Shandy* discusses the
way in which the "dramatized narrator" provides the
secret of coherence, cites influential traditions, explores
the principle of unity and the good and bad effects of the
"Shandean commentary." Valuable bibliography of works
"held together by the self-conscious portrait of the commentator," examples of satires using unreliable and self-
conscious narration, as well as examples of imitations of
Tristram Shandy and of other works influenced by Sterne.
Cf. Rolle (595).—Reviewed by A. D. McKillop, *MP,* IX
(1963), 297, *q.v.*

———. "The Self-Conscious Narrator in Comic Fiction before   [514]
Tristram Shandy," *PMLA,* LXVII (1952), 163-185.
Argues that *Tristram Shandy,* though seemingly chaotic, has a unity achieved and developed through devices
already established by other English writers. See above.

———. "*Tristram Shandy* and Its Precursors: The Self-Con-   [515]
scious Narrator." Unpublished Ph.D. dissertation, University of Chicago, 1950.
See all three of the items above.

Bowen, Elizabeth. *English Novelists.* (Britain in Pictures)   [516]
London: William Collins, 1942. P. 20.
"*Tristram Shandy* . . . is dementedly natural in its
course, surrealist in its association of images. One does
not attempt to 'follow' [it]; one consigns oneself, dizzily,
to it."

Boys, Richard C. "*Tristram Shandy* and the Conventional   [517]
Novel," *Papers of the Michigan Academy of Science, Arts,
and Letters,* XXXVII (1951), 423-436.
Points out the difficulty of determining Sterne's true
place in the development of the English novel, rejecting as
"a gross oversimplification" any contention that Sterne
turned to a new form, breaking down the structure of the
novel out of a dissatisfaction with the novels of Fielding
and Smollett. Cf. Maack (368), Booth (513), Emerson
(536).

Brewster, William T. "Tristram Shandy" in *Encyclopedia*   [518]
Americana. New York, Chicago, Washington: Americana
Corporation, 1960 [1918], XXVII, 78-79.
   Describes novel as "practically without story or plot,"
chiefly "quiddity, digression, eccentricity, and interlude."
Replaced by Hartley (554).

Brissenden, R. F. "Sterne and Painting" in *Of Books and Hu-*   [519]
mankind: Essays and Poems Presented to Bonamy Do-
brée, edited by John Butt. London: Routledge and Kegan
Paul, 1964. Pp. 93-108.
   Discusses the significant relationship between Sterne's
interest in painting and his qualities as a writer, investi-
gating the ways in which his technique as a novelist bene-
fited from his experience as an amateur artist, as well as
his treatment of various eighteenth-century theoretical
studies of painting as an index to the philosophical bases
of his satire. Finally reveals the remarkable similarity between his ideas and those of William Hogarth.—"Joseph
Burke has pronounced Hogarth 'the supreme master of
the satiric rococo' . . . in literature there is no one to
whom it could be applied more aptly than Sterne." See
Antal (500), Fluchère's chapter, "Le peintre et l'écrivain"
(218), and Maack (368).

Brogan, Howard O. "Fiction and Philosophy in the Educa-   [520]
tion of Tom Jones, Tristram Shandy, and Richard Fever-
el," *CE,* XIV (1952), 144-149.
   Discusses the educational theories underlying the
novels. Cf. Binz-Winiger (510).

Brown, Huntington. *Rabelais in English Literature.* Cam-   [521]
bridge, Mass.: Harvard University Press, 1933. Pp. 188-
206 and *passim.*
   ". . . the example of both Rabelais the realist and
Rabelais the eccentric is apparent [in *Tristram Shandy*]
at every turn." See 607.

Burckhardt, Sigurd. "Tristram Shandy's Law of Gravity,"   [522]
ELH, XXVIII (1961), 70-88.
   Rejecting both Lockean psychology and rhetorical
analysis as revealing fully "the law by which the Shandean world moves," the author proposes gravity (in
Sterne's definition "a mysterious carriage of the body to
cover defects of the mind" and in simpler statement,

"things fall") as the law of the novel and suggests that
Sterne's "irony," like Swift's, embodies the "final joke . . .
that he is not joking."

Calder-Marshall, Arthur. "Laurence Sterne" in *The English*   [523]
Novelists: A Survey of the Novel by Twenty Contempo-
rary Novelists, edited by Derek Verschoyle. London:
Chatto & Windus, 1936. Pp. 81-95.
    Finds *Tristram Shandy* "technically a hotch-potch"
without unity of mood and exhibiting more caprice than
plan, half novel–half familiar essay by a "lazy," non-pro-
fessional, egotistical, sentimental writer.

Carver, Wayne. "The Worlds of Tom [Jones] and Tristram,"   [524]
WHR, XII (1958), 67-74.
    This discussion makes perhaps too severe a contrast
between the "common-sense, work-a-day world" of *Tom*
Jones and the "frangible" world of *Tristram Shandy,*
where the reader's response is laughter mingled with apprehension—a fear of being "abandoned in the unpruned
brakes of the mind."

Cash, Arthur Hill. "The Lockean Psychology of *Tristram*   [525]
Shandy," *ELH,* XXII (1955), 125-135.
    A comprehensive reappraisal, contending that though
Locke's associationism served Sterne well, it is not the
organizing device of *Tristram Shandy.* Cf. MacLean
(369), Towers (610), Traugott (611).

Caskey, J. Homer. "Two Notes on Uncle Toby," *MLN,* XLII   [526]
(1927), 321-323.
    Possible borrowings from Edward Moore.

Chwalewik, Witwold. "O 'Tristramie Shandy' Sterné a,"   [527]
Kwartalnik Neofilologiozny, z 3 (1957), 212-229.

———. *"Tristram Shandy* i sternizm," *Blok-Notes Mickiewicza,*   [528]
No 1 (1959), 101-105. Illus.

Cook, Albert Spaulding. "Reflexive Attitudes: Sterne, Gogol,   [529]
Gide," *Criticism,* II (1960), 164-74. Reprinted in *The*
Meaning of Fiction. Detroit: Wayne State University
Press, 1960. Pp. 24-37.
    A discussion of "reflexivity," the artifice of the author's
speaking of his make-believe as make-believe, in *Tristram*

Shandy.—". . . in its own peculiar way it demonstrates the queer reality of appearance by reflexively calling itself an artifice at every step." See Booth (513).

Davis, Robert Gorham. "The Sense of the Real in English Fiction," *Comp. Lit.*, III (1951), 211-212.   [530]
    In their existential interrelationship, the mental and physical particularities and eccentricities of "originals" are observed in *Tristram Shandy* with equal attention.

Deedes, [Prebendary] Cecil. "Gobesius: Sheeter," *N&Q*, 10th Ser., V (1906), 115.   [531]
    Identifies two of the writers on mechanics and military engineering in *Tristram Shandy*, II, iii. See Bensly, "A Debt" (509) and Stedmond (607).

Dibelius, Wilhelm. "Laurence Sterne" in *Englische Roman-kunst. Die Technik des englischen Romans im achtzehnten und zu Anfang des neunzehnten Jahrhunderts.* (Palaestra, 92) Berlin u. Leipzig: Mayer & Müller, 1922. Pp. 237-281.   [532]
    Regards *Tristram Shandy* as less a novel than a philosophical treatise or a lyric poem, or rather a *mixtum compositum* of these and many other sundry ingredients.

Drew, Elizabeth. *The Novel: A Modern Guide to Fifteen English Masterpieces.* New York: Dell Publishing Co., 1963. Pp. 75-94.   [533]
    One of the best brief critical treatments.—". . . the sexual tinge [in Tristram Shandy] is so pervasive because in a sense the whole book is about the paradoxical creativeness and helplessness of man . . ."

Eaves, T. C. Duncan. "George Romney: His *Tristram Shandy* Paintings and Trip to Lancaster," *HLQ*, VII (1944), 321-326.   [534]
    Information concerning Romney's now lost paintings illustrating *Tristram Shandy*. See 11a.

Eddy, William A. "Tom Brown and *Tristram Shandy*," *MLN*, XLIV (1929), 379-381.   [535]
    Traces the "irrelevant interruption" in *Tristram Shandy*, Chapter 1, to Tom Brown; also cites indebtedness of "The Dwarf" in *A Sentimental Journey* to Brown's translation of Scarron's *Le roman comique*. See Stedmond (607).

Criticism

Emerson, Everett H. "An Apology for *Tristram Shandy*" in **[536]**
Louisiana State University Studies, Humanities Series, No.
5, 1954, pp. 1-10.
    Attempts to answer the question as to whether Sterne
was a destroyer of the novel form or an extender of it,
concluding with the latter view and arguing that Sterne
"saw the world as if it were put together without rhyme
or reason and, happily, regarded the result as humorous."
See Maack (368), Booth (513), Boys (517).

Eskin, Stanley G. "*Tristram Shandy* and *Oedipus Rex*: Reflec- **[537]**
tions on Comedy and Tragedy," *CE*, XXIV (1963), 271-
277.
    "The incongruities more commonly associated with
comedy are paralleled and reinforced in *Tristram Shandy*
in the incongruity between man and his destiny, but this
in turn brings *Tristram Shandy* close to a tragedy like
Oedipus Rex which is centrally concerned with that very
incongruity."—See rebuttal by James Schroeter, *ibid.*, 565-
566, and reply by Eskin, p. 566.

Falls, Cyril. "Tristram Shandy, Gent," *Illustrated London* **[538]**
News, CCXXIV (1954), 520.
    An appreciation written by the Chichele Professor of
the History of War at Oxford.

Farrell, William J. "Nature Versus Art as Comic Pattern in **[539]**
Tristram Shandy," *ELH*, XXX (1963), 16-35.
    Demonstrates how not only on the level of style and
action (that is, in his character's use of the figures, ges-
tures, and *topoi* of traditional rhetoric) but even in the
structure of the novel itself (the "collapsed art" of *Tristram Shandy* parodying the shapeless "true account" technique of most eighteenth-century fiction), Sterne creates
a comic conflict of artifice and nature mocking the fact-
minded reader and the detail-bound writer as well as the
naive and pedantic character in the novel. Cf. Traugott
(611).

Fluchère, Henri. *Laurence Sterne, de l'homme à l'oeuvre: Bi-* **[540]**
ographie critique et essai d'interprétation de Tristram
Shandy. (Bibliotheque des idées) Paris: Gallimard, 1961.
    Analyzes *Tristram Shandy* exhaustively in terms of
structure, themes, style, together with a consideration of
special problems of time and causality. Purpose is to

demonstrate that far from simply engaging in "nasty trifling," Sterne's intent is to present life in all its complexity
and strangeness, arriving at a kind of *pantagruélisme* based
not on a Rousseauistic belief in natural goodness as much
as on a simple faith that life in its totality is good if it is
truly·apprehended through the comic mode of Shandyism.
See 218, 362, 541.

————. *Laurence Sterne: From Tristram to Yorick, An Inter-*   [541]
pretation of "Tristram Shandy." Translated and abridged
by Barbara Bray. Oxford: Oxford University Press, 1965.
   Omits the biographical section of the original edition
and replaces the extensive bibliography with a selected
short list. See 218, 540.

Frye, Northrop. *Anatomy of Criticism: Four Essays.* Prince-   [542]
ton: Princeton University Press, 1957. Pp. 303-308.
   An adaptation of "The Four Forms of Prose Fiction"
below.

————. "The Four Forms of Prose Fiction," *Hudson Review,*   [543]
II (1950), 582-595.
   Suggesting that, in form, fiction manifests four strands
binding it together—novel, confession, anatomy, and romance—the article maintains that *Tristram Shandy,* though
at the beginning a novel, eventually acquires all the fea-
tures that belong to an "anatomy." See also Frye's *Anat-*
omy of Criticism, pp. 303-308 above. Cf. Booth (513),
Jefferson (562), Stedmond (605).

————. "Towards Defining an Age of Sensibility," *ELH,*   [544]
XXIII (1956), 144-152.
   Sterne brings the sense of literature as a process to an
exquisite perfection.

Geismar, Maxwell. "Child Is Born," *New Republic,* CXXXV   [545]
(November 12, 1956), 21-22.
   A brief appreciation of *Tristram Shandy,* summed up
as "an idiosyncratic ode to an epoch which has just discovered reason, the machine and the infinite possibilities,
so it seemed, of man's worldly prospects." See 146.

Gordon, George. "Sterne's *Tristram Shandy*" in *Companion-*   [546]
able Books. (Series I) London: Chatto & Windus, 1927.
Pp. 29-44.

A talk on Sterne made over the B.B.C.—". . . it is this partnership of effort [between reader and author] which makes *Tristram Shandy* the exciting book that it is."

Graham, W. H. "Sterne's *Tristram Shandy*," *Contemporary* [547] *Review*, CLXXIII (1948), 43-47.
A routine and inconsequential essay dealing chiefly with Sterne's skill in the characterization of Mr. Shandy, Uncle Toby, and Corporal Trim.

Greenberg, Bernard L. "Laurence Sterne and Plutarch," [548] *N&Q*, V (1958), 443.
Plutarch's "Alexander" and *Tristram Shandy*, IV, xi. See Stedmond (607).

———. "Laurence Sterne and *Chambers' Cyclopaedia*," *MLN*, [549] LXIX (1954), 560-62.
Shows Sterne's indebtedness chiefly in Vols. II and III of *Tristram Shandy*. See Bensly (509), Deedes (531), and Stedmond (607).

Greene, Graham. "Fielding and Sterne" in *From Anne to Vic-* [550] *toria*, edited by Bonamy Dobrée. New York: Charles Scribner's Sons, 1937. Pp. 279-289.
An important modern novelist expresses a reactionary opinion.—"*Tristram Shandy* exists, a lovely sterile eccentricity, the last word in literary egotism . . . the man Sterne is unbearable. . . ." Fielding gave the novel moral seriousness and form; Sterne gave it "graceful play with emotions . . . amusing little indecencies." Cf. Jefferson (563).

Griffin, Robert J. "Tristram Shandy and Language," *CE*, [551] XXIII (November, 1961), 108-112.
Supplements Traugott (611) in considering the ways in which Tristram responds to Locke's ideas on language —the problem of human communication as reflected in the uses, abuses, and imperfections of words.—"Sterne was not overly dismayed by Locke's treatment of [linguistic] communication . . . proof is . . . available in the constant confident play on or with words."

Hall, Joan Joffe. "The Hobbyhorsical World of 'Tristram [552] Shandy,'" *MLQ*, XXIV (1963), 131-143.
An examination of two kinds of hobby horses in Sterne

—first, the obsessions that cause the comic failure of com-
munications among the Shandy characters and, second,
the progression by digression and the curious relationship
entered into by narrator and reader which constitute
Tristram's own hobby horse—one controlling the behavior
of the characters and the other, the structure of the narrative. See Towers (610).

Hardy, Barbara. "A Mistake in 'Tristram Shandy,'" *N&Q*,   [553]
IX (1962), 261.
    Argues that "Sterne is wrong in telling us that the ac-
count of Uncle Toby's history has come between the ring-
ing of the bell and the rapping at the door." See *Tristram
Shandy*, Vol. 2, Ch. 8, and Baird (502).

Hartley, Lodwick. "Tristram Shandy" in *Encyclopedia Ameri-*   [554]
cana. New York: The Americana Corporation, 1964.
XXVII, 129.
    Replaces Brewster (518).

Hewlett, Maurice. "Alter Egos" in *Extemporary Essays*. Ox-   [555]
ford: Oxford University Press, 1922. Pp. 191-194.
    A brief essay on Sterne and his assumption of the char-
acter of Yorick.—"Here . . . is an *alter ego* which is much
more than a stalking horse. Here is an alias." Cf. Booth,
513.

Hicks, John H. "The Critical History of *Tristram Shandy*,"   [556]
Boston University Studies in English, II (1956), 65-84.
    A brief review of the criticism from the eighteenth cen-
tury to the present day. Sees the critical history of the
novel as "a testimony to the irrepressibleness of the humor
of genius . . . also [as] an account of the gradual recognition of craftsmanship [that is] able, finally, to reconcile a
long struggle between an English propensity for virile
forthrightness . . . and . . . a traditional English fastidious-
ness about moral propriety." See Parish (582), Howes
(803).

Hine, Reginald L. "Captain Robert Hinde," *TLS*, May 21,   [557]
1931, p. 408.
    Another candidate for the original of Uncle Toby.

Hughes, Helen Sard. "A Precursor of *Tristram Shandy*,"   [558]
JEGP, XVII (1918), 227-251.
    Discusses *Life and Memoirs of Mr. Ephriam Tristram*

Bates, Commonly Called Corporal Bates (1756), suggesting that there are "parallels in matter and method" with *Tristram Shandy*. See Balderston (503), Bensly (507), and Howes (803), p. 81.

Humphreys, A. L. "Eighteenth-Century Physician Upon Pre- [559] destination," *N&Q*, 11th ser., XI (1915), 192-194.
  Answers query in *ibid.*, p. 67, by identifying physician mentioned in *Tristram Shandy*, Vol. III, Ch. 20, as Dr. William Coward.

Jackson, William A. "The Curse of Ernulphus," *Harvard Li- [560] brary Bulletin*, XIV (1960), 392-394.
  Sterne's responsibility for the immortality of Ernulph, Bishop of Rochester (1114-1124) as author of an anathema that he probably did not write.

James, Overton Philip. "The Relation of *Tristram Shandy* to [561] the Life of Sterne," *DA*, XXIII (1963), 3888.
  A Vanderbilt University dissertation. Concludes that although *Tristram Shandy* is primarily and preponderantly a work of fiction, it ultimately reveals and is a most important part of the life of Sterne—man, minister, and novelist.

Jefferson, D. W. "*Tristram Shandy* and the Tradition of [562] Learned Wit," *Essays in Criticism*, I (1951), 225-248.
  Countering Forster's charge of "muddling" (340) and Greene's of "whimsicality" (550), argues that *Tristram Shandy* has form and thematic pattern in an established tradition of wit "essentially similar to that based on scholastic ideas," deriving in part from Rabelais and found in considerable quantity in Augustan comic and satirical writing (*Tale of a Tub, The Art of Sinking in Poetry, Memoirs of Scriblerus*). Cf. Booth (513), Frye (543), Stedmond (605). See also 359.

———. " 'Tristram Shandy' and Its Tradition" in *From Dryden* [563] *to Johnson*, edited by Boris Ford. (The Pelican Guide to English Literature, No. 4) Harmondsworth, Middlesex: Penguins Books, 1957.
  Adapted from essay of similar title in *Essays in Criticism*, I (1951), 225-248, above.

Kleinstück, Johannes. "Zur Form und Methode des *Tristram* [564] *Shandy*," *Archiv*, CXCIV (1957), 122-137.

Sterne in the role of author formulating, concealing, and apparently abandoning his narrative plans, together with the tactics he employed of conscious digression, yielding to genuine or simulated impulse, and pretended frustration at the great variety of material to be mastered. Considers also the function of the reader as an active part of the creative process. See comment of A. D. McKillop, *PQ*, XXXVII (1958), 353.

Kolb, Gwin J. "A Note on 'Tristram Shandy': Some New   [565]
Sources," *N&Q*, CXCVI (1951), 226-227.
New sources suggested are John Wilkins's *Mathematical Magick*, Bacon's "Of death," Pope's *Dunciad*, and (with less assurance) Steele's *Englishman*. See Stedmond (607).

Kroeger, Frederick P. "Uncle Toby's Pipe and Whistle,"   [566]
Papers of the Michigan Academy of Science, Arts, and Letters, XLVII (1962), 669-685.
A detailed consideration of the ways in which Sterne employs the pipe and the whistling of *Lillabullero* to develop Toby's character.

Laird, John. "Shandean Philosophy" in *Philosophical Incur-*   [567]
sions into English Literature. Cambridge: The University Press, 1946. Pp. 74-91.
Shandean philosophy was "an elaborate application of Locke's methods," for the largest part accurately applied and sometimes even constructively improved upon. See 369, 424.

Landa, Louis. "The Shandean Homunculus: The Background   [568]
of Sterne's 'Little Gentleman'" in *Restoration and Eighteenth-Century Literature*, edited by Carroll Camden. (Rice University Semicentennial Publications) Chicago: The University of Chicago Press, 1963. Pp. 49-68.
Demonstrates that the homunculus was widely known before Sterne, vigorously debated among embryologists who took sides as "ovists" and "animalculists," and readily available for the kind of witty treatment that Sterne supplied. Cites Sir John Hill's *Lucina sine Concubitu* (1750) as a possibility for giving a cue to Sterne.

Lehman, B. H. "Of Time, Personality, and the Author. A   [569]
Study of *Tristram Shandy*: Comedy" in *Studies in the*

Comic (University of California Publications in English, Vol. VIII, No. 2, 1941). Pp. 233-250.

Sterne's "rendering of reality without moral . . . pre-occupation" is explained and vindicated. Argues that the form that the novel took was an appropriate vehicle for such a view. Important comments on Sterne's treatment of time. Cf. Baird (502), Mendilow (574).

Lisowski, Jerzy. "Nad 'Tristramen Shandy' uwagi niekom-   [570]
pletne acz nieurolnie w stylu Sterné a utrzymane," *Twórczosć*, No. 4 (1959), 76-85.

Remarks on *Tristram Shandy* made in an approxima-tion of Sterne's style.

Macaffee, C. H. G. "The Obstetrical Aspects of 'Tristram   [571]
Shandy,'" *Ulster Medical Journal*, XIX (May 1, 1950), 12-22.

Shows that Sterne has given an accurate picture of the obstetrical practices of his time, as well as of the revolu-tion then in process and of the discussion that it aroused.

Millar, J. H. *The Mid-Eighteenth Century*. New York: Char-   [572]
les Scribner's Sons, 1902. Pp. 165-168.

Routine early twentieth-century comment on *Tristram Shandy*: its pathos is "intolerably false," its style is a "monument of artificiality," the "indomitable self-con-sciousness" of the author is repellent; but his apparent "want of purpose" and his humorous, and thus sympa-thetic, portrayal of certain human types are saving graces.

Mann, Thomas. *The Theme of the Joseph Novels*. Washing-   [573]
ton, D.C.: U.S. Government Printing Office, 1942. Pp. 15ff.

In an address delivered in the Library of Congress on November 17, 1942, Mann discusses the ways in which he profited from the reading of *Tristram Shandy* while writ-ing the Joseph novels. See Seidlin (893).

Mendilow, A. A. *Time and the Novel*. London: Peter Nevill,   [574]
1952. Pp. 158-199 and *passim*.

Discusses the nature of Sterne's "revolt" from the struc-tural tradition of the novel of his time, especially in the time factor.—"In his treatment of structure, Sterne antici-pated so many modern experiments that the study of this single book could almost serve as a summary of all the problems involved in the consideration of the time factors and values of the novel." See Baird (502), Lehman (569).

Meyer, Herman. *Das Zitat in der Erzählkunst zur Geschichte*   [575]
und Poetik des Europäischen Romans. Stuttgart: Metzler,
1961.
    Contains chapter on plagiarism in *Tristram Shandy.*
See Stedmond (607).—Reviewed by L. H. C. Thomas,
MLR, LVII (1962), 77-78.

————. "Zitat und Plagiat in *Tristram Shandy*" in *Amor Lib-*   [576]
rorum, Bibliographic and Other Essays, a Tribute to Abra-
ham Horodisch on His Sixtieth Birthday. Amsterdam:
Erasmus Antiquariaat, 1958. Pp. 293-304.
    Sterne's use of quotation and plagiarism as "hetero-
geneous matter" deliberately inserted "to keep up that just
balance betwixt wisdom and folly, without which a book
would not hold together a single year." See above.

Myers, Walter. "O, the Hobby-Horse," *VQR,* XIX (1943),   [577]
268-277.
    A light essay on the mild paradox of Uncle Toby's
"militaristic obsessions and his virtues of unparalleled
modesty, innocence, patience, sympathy, and general
goodness of heart."

Nakamura, Sumio. "Sterne as Puppet Operator," *Studies in*   [578]
English Literature (Tokyo), XXXVI (1959), 145-175. [In
Japanese]

Newton. A. Edward. "A 'Divine' and His Works" in *The*   [579]
Greatest Book in the World and Other Papers. Boston:
Little, Brown and Company, 1925. Pp. 194-215.
    Chiefly a defense of *Tristram Shandy* against the
charge of Professor William Lyon Phelps that it is "infernally dull." See Phelps (387).

Parish, Charles. "The Nature of Mr. Tristram Shandy, Au-   [580]
thor," *Boston University Studies in English,* V (Summer,
1961), 74-90.
    Tristram Shandy, of whose mind the novel is a history,
plays a three-fold part: as a minor character seen by
others as a child, as narrator who tells about himself as a
child and about others in the story, and as author, who is
concerned with ideas of himself as narrator. See 582.

————. "A Table of Contents for *Tristram Shandy,*" *CE,* XXII   [581]
(1960), 143-150.
    The first purpose of this useful guide is "to provide . . .

a handy key to the happenings and ideas in the novel";
a second is "to demonstrate the consistency in the pres-
ence and role of the author-narrator Tristram." An ancil-
lary purpose is to refute Cross's statement that "Sterne
never got beyond [Tristram's] birth, baptism, and breech-
ing." See Cross, *YR*, XV (1926), 104.

———. "Twentieth-Century Criticism of Form in *Tristram*   [582]
Shandy," *DA*, XX (1960), 2806-07 [N.M.].
The eighteenth century regarded the novel only part
by part, declining to consider it a seriously coherent work.
The nineteenth century began to consider the larger plan
of the novel: character construction and dramatic relationships as dependent upon the whole conception, digressions as form (Coleridge). These views were not pervasive. The twentieth-century trend in serious criticism has
been to seek coherence in the underlying Lockean psychology, the relationship between Sterne and Tristram,
and the relationship between narrative and digression.
Conclusion is that "the form of *Tristram Shandy* takes its
meaning, receives its justification from the character
Tristram, just as Tristram becomes finally and completely
understood and identified not from the events of his life
but from the book whose very structure reflects his mind
and character." See Booth (513), Hicks (556).

Paul, Herbert W. "Sterne" in *Men and Letters*. London and   [583]
New York: John Lane, 1901. Pp. 67-89.
Treats *Tristram Shandy* as "one of the most elaborate
of human compositions . . . [with] not a sentence in it but
Sterne knew well how it came there. . . . Of all English
humourists, except Shakespeare, Sterne is still the greatest
force."

Piper, William Bowman. "Tristram Shandy's Digressive Ar-   [584]
tistry," *Studies in English Literature*, I, iii (Summer,
1961), 65-76.
The controlled artistry of the digressions, fulfilling
Sterne's different communicative obligations—to explain,
to instruct, to amuse. See 388.

———. "Tristram Shandy's Tragicomical Testimony," *Criti-*   [585]
cism, III (1961), 171-185.
Using Ian Watt's idea that a novel is like trial evidence
and its readers like jurymen, the author examines Tris-

tram's testimony before a partially built-in and often sus-
picious mixed jury consisting of Sir, Madam, and the
others. Tristram holds the pose as a dutiful Shandy heir
and a dedicated memorialist throughout the book, which
by "reason and suggestion" constituting a "novelistic certainty" ends with the narrator's death as a childless man.
The comedy is maintained by holding Tristram before a
mixed audience to whom he recounts the main concerns
of his life, "not in the dreadful terms of decay and desola-
tion but in the risqué and titillating terms of suspected
sexual impotence." See Watt (429) and Booth (513).

Priestley, J. B. "The Brothers Shandy" in *The English Comic*   [586]
Characters. New York: Dodd, Mead and Company, 1925.
Pp. 128-157.
    Although both characters are "triumphant" creations,
Uncle Toby is more "firmly seated, as a figure, in our
imagination" than is Walter Shandy.

————. "Three Novelists" in *English Humour*. (The English   [587]
Heritage Series) London-New York-Toronto: Longmans,
Green and Company, 1933. Pp. 125-130.
    Sees *Tristram Shandy* as one of the most "strictly
humorous" novels in the language, "one gigantic whim
or . . . nest of whims," a "humorous vision of this life"
seemingly "outside time."

Pritchett, V. S. ["Sterne's Temperament"] "Books in General,"   [588]
New Statesman and Nation, XLI (1951), 41.
    Occasioned by the publication of *Sterne*, edited by
Douglas Grant (120). A brilliant essay on the "madness"
of Sterne, whose "discovery of soliloquising man, the life
lived in fantasy, is the source of what is called the 'great
character' in the English novel, a kind which only Russian
fiction, with its own feeling for 'madness' in the 19th century, has enjoyed."

————. "Tristram Shandy" in *Books in General*. New York: [589]
Harcourt, Brace & Co. [1953]. Pp. 173-178.
    Adaptation of essay in *New Statesman and Nation*,
above.

Rauter, Herbert. "Eine Anleihe Sternes bei George Herbert,"   [590]
Anglia, LXXX (1963), 290-294.
    Argues that Strophe 40 of Herbert's "The Church-

porch" corresponds almost exactly to Walter Shandy's cry,
"Everything in this world, said my father, is big with jest—
and has wit in it, and instruction, too,—if we can but find
it out." Contends that a recognition of this borrowing influences the interpretation of *Tristram Shandy*, V, 32.

Rawson, C. J. "'Tristram Shandy' and 'Candide,'" *N&Q*, [591]
CCIII, N.S. V (1958), 226.
   Possible echoes of *Candide* in *Tristram Shandy* II, xix,
and VI, xi.

———. "Two Notes on Sterne," *N&Q*, CCII, N.S. IV (1957), [592]
255-256.
   On the traditional model for Uncle Toby (Captain
Robert Hinde) and on Obadiah Walker's *Of Education*
(1673). See 612.

Read, Herbert. "The Writer and His Region" in *The Tenth* [593]
Muse. London: Routledge and Kegan Paul, 1957; New
York: Horizon Press, 1958. Pp. 66-74.
   "*Tristram Shandy* is a book wholly rooted . . . in the
ethos of a particular countryside, and yet it is universal."

Ridgeway, Ann. "Two Authors in Search of a Reader," *James* [594]
Joyce Quarterly, I, 4 (Summer, 1964), 41-51.
   A discussion of the ways in which *Tristram Shandy*
and *Ulysses* achieve similar effects by employing incidents
and styles atypical of their age. Cf. 421.

Rolle, Dietrich. *Fielding und Sterne: Untersuchungen über* [595]
die Funktion des Erzählers. Münster: Verlag Aschen-
dorff, 1963.
   In a thoroughgoing investigation of the role of the
narrator ("Erzähler")—not to be confused with the author
("Verfasser")—this study expands and modifies conclusions of Booth (513). Considers Fielding the founder of
the "authorial" novel and contends that Sterne follows the
trail blazed by *Tom Jones*, which is more of "a novel
about novel writing" than *Tristram Shandy*, which shows
that novels cannot be written.—Reviewed by George
Worth, *JEGP*, LXIV (1965), 176-177.

Russell, H. K. "Tristram Shandy and the Technique of the [596]
Novel," *SP*, XLII (1945), 581-593; also in *Studies in Lan-*
guage and Literature, edited by George R. Coffman (The

University of North Carolina Sesquicentennial Publications) Chapel Hill: University of North Carolina Press, 1945. Pp. 203-215.

Sterne's technique was a criticism of the style in vogue and "an exploitation of devices better suited to the novel of character."

Sallé, Jean Claude. "A Source of Sterne's Conception of Time," *RES*, new ser., VI (1955), 180-182.   [597]
Suggests *Spectator*, No. 94, 18 June 1711, as a source rather than a direct borrowing from Locke.

Sander, Volkmar. "Handlungsstränge and Handlungsgefüge in Laurence Sternes 'Tristram Shandy'" in *Eine Untersuchung über additive Verknüpfungsformen*. Frankfurt, 1957.   [598]
Plot lines and plot construction in *Tristram Shandy*.

Shackford, John B. "Sterne's Use of Catachresis in *Tristram Shandy*," *Iowa English Yearbook*, No. 6 (Fall, 1961), 74-79.   [599]
Sterne's use of two types of catachrestic aposiopesis to avoid printing prurient words: (1) a directed variety, in which connotative words surrounding the omission force one to insert the most bawdy possibility; and (2) an undirected kind, in which the reader is at liberty to insert any bawdy word that he wishes.

Shklovsky, Victor. *Tristram Shendi Sternes i Teorija Romana*. Petrograd, 1921. Also in *O Teorii prozy*. Moscow, 1925.   [600]
See Harper (862) for summary and analysis.

Simons, Jan Walter. "Die Frage der Romanstruktur in Laurence Sternes *Tristram Shandy*." Unpublished dissertation. Freiburg, 1960.   [601]

Sinko, Zofia. "The Decomposition of Realism in the Novels of Laurence Sterne," *Comptes Rendu de la Societé des Sciences et des Lettres de Wroclaw*, V (1951).   [602]

Speaight, George. "Battles and Raree Shows," *N&Q*, CCI, N.S. III (1956), 133-134.   [603]
Supplements Stedmond (609).

Stanzel, Franz. "*Tom Jones* und *Tristram Shandy*," *English Miscellany*, V (1954), 107-148.   [604]

A comparison of the two novels in regard to narrative control, medium, use of the narrator, and time structure. See Baird (502), Booth (513), Rolle (595).

Stedmond, J. M. "Genre and *Tristram Shandy*," *PQ*, [605]
XXXVIII (1959), 37-51.
Sterne's relation to the tradition of "learned wit," "philosophic rhetoric," and "Menippean satire," with particular comment on the novelist's relation to Rabelais, Burton, and Swift, as well as to contemporary novelists on whom he drew when he made his mixture of genres. See Booth (513), Frye (543), Jefferson (562), Traugott (611); also 414.

——. "Satire and *Tristram Shandy*," *Studies in English Lit-* [606]
erature, I, iii (Summer, 1961), 53-63.
Examines the relationship of *Tristram Shandy* to the tradition of *Scriblerus*, *A Tale of a Tub*, and the "Dunciad." The novel is "one more engagement in the perpetual war between wits and dunces" in which the mechanical means of communication are becoming ever more and more efficient—while at the same time the articulateness, the ability to communicate, is steadily declining." Cf. Frye (543) and Jefferson (562); also 414.

——. "Sterne as a Plagiarist," *ES*, XLI (1960), 308-312. [607]
Summary, with sources, of verbatim borrowings in *Tristram Shandy* and *A Sentimental Journey*. Cf. Bensly (509), Brown (521), Eddy (535), Greenberg (548), Kolb (565), Turnbull (613), Stout (609a), Williams (617).

——. "Style and 'Tristram Shandy,'" *MLQ*, XX (1959), 243- [608]
251.
Sterne's adoption of well-established stylistic modes of the seventeenth century: the anti-Ciceronian style of Bacon and Burton, the Rabelaisian "orchestration of ideas," and the Cervantic "perspectivistic" attitude.—"In attempting to keep himself and the reader aware of the compromises necessary in all forms of verbal art, Sterne inevitably subjected his artistic medium, language, to critical scrutiny. Paradoxically, in so doing, he was, in fact, adopting well-established conventions of the previous century." See 353, 414, 433.

——. "Uncle Toby's 'Campaigns' and Raree-Shows." *N&Q*, [609]
CCI, N.S. III (1956), 28-29.

Possible connection between passages in *Tristram
Shandy* and "mock battlefield" in "travelling 'raree
shows.'" Cf. Speaight (603).

Stout, Gardner B., Jr. "Some Borrowings in Sterne from   [609a]
Rabelais and Cervantes," *ELN*, III (1965), 111-117.
Hitherto unnoticed paraphrases or echoes chiefly in
Tristram Shandy. See Stedmond (607).

Towers, A. R. "Sterne's Cock and Bull Story." *ELH*, XXIV   [610]
(1957), 12-29.
The "sexual comedy of Tristram Shandy as revealed
in such incidents as those involving Tristram's nose, mis-
naming, and the accident of the sash window"—the
"comedy of inadequacy"; in Uncle Toby's substitution of
fortifications for women, the normal object of his sexual
desires—the "comedy of displacement"; and in Walter
Shandy's sexual frustrations as finally symbolized in the
"cock and bull story"—the "comedy of frustration." Counters Cash's contention that *Tristram Shandy* contains "no
hint of the unconscious mind in the Freudian sense." Cf.
De Froe (342); also 525, 552.

Traugott, John L. *Tristram Shandy's World: Sterne's Philo-*   [611]
sophical Rhetoric. Berkeley and Los Angeles: University
of California Press, 1954.
The first section treats Sterne's exploitation of Locke's
ideas, challenging Cross's conclusion that *Tristram Shandy*
is "organized throughout on Locke's doctrine of the Association of Ideas" and taking issue with MacLean (369)
at several points. The second part, concerned with the
rhetorical structure of the novel, contends that the whole
conduct of the book is under the control of Tristram as
"facetious rhetor" and suggests the link between the rhetorical art of Sterne as novelist and preacher. See particularly the reviews of MacLean, Booth, and Dearing,
below.—Reviewed by K. MacLean in *PQ*, XXXIV (1955),
314; by Wayne C. Booth in *MP*, LIII (1955), 138-141; by
Bruce Dearing in *CE*, XVII (1956), 242-243; by Ernest
Dilworth in *JEGP*, LIV (1955), 424-426; by Alan D. Mc-
Killop in *SR*, LXIII (1955), 687-690; in *TLS*, July 29,
1955, p. 430; by D. R. Elloway in *Essays in Criticism*, VI
(1956), 326-334; by S. H. Monk in *MLN*, LXXI (1956),
48-50; by D. W. Jefferson in *RES*, n.s., VIII (1957), 320-
322.

Turnbull, John M. "The Prototype of Walter Shandy's Tris- [612]
trapaedia," *RES*, II (1926), 212-215.
Obadiah Walker's *Of Education Especially of Young
Gentlemen* (1673) cited as source. See 592.

Urbahn, Therese. "Die Geste in Sternes *Tristram Shandy*," [613]
Britannica, XIII (1936), 171-187.
A rich but incomplete collection of the instances in
Tristram Shandy in which Sterne makes use of the *Geste*.

Van Ghent, Dorothy. "On *Tristram Shandy*" in *The English* [614]
Novel, Form and Function. New York: Rinehart & Co.,
1953. Pp. 83-98.
One of the most penetrating of text-book treatments.
Discusses Sterne's importance in introducing a new structural principle employing "the operative character of consciousness as such," thus creating a world in the form of a
mind conceived in the figure of "one of Leibnitz's monads,
those elemental units of energy that have 'mirrors but no
windows,'.... the mirroring capacity of which makes it
a microcosm of the universe." Sterne's method has no
parallel until Proust and Joyce.

Watson, Wilfred. "The Fifth Commandment: Some Allusions [615]
to Sir Robert Filmer's Writing in *Tristram Shandy*,"
MLN, LXII (1947), 234-240.
The question of authority and obedience to authority
in *Tristram Shandy* as related to Filmer.

Weales, Gerald. "Tristram Shandy's Anti-book" in *Twelve* [616]
Original Essays on Great English Novels, edited by
Charles Shapiro. Detroit, Mich.: Wayne State University
Press, 1960. Pp. 43-47.
Digression is basic to form and intention, a comic
method in itself, and Sterne's instrument for "achieving
order by making disorder." The book is unified by an
attitude rather than by a plan. See 147.

Williams, Franklin B., Jr. "Robert Tofte -an Oxford Man," [617]
RES, new ser., VI (1955), 177-179.
A borrowing from Tofte, via Burton's *Anatomy of
Melancholy*, in *Tristram Shandy*. See Stedmond (607).

Wolfe, Thomas. *The Letters*, edited by Elizabeth Nowell. [618]
New York: Charles Scribner's Sons, 1956. Pp. 256, 586,
643.

An important American novelist's opinion of *Tristram Shandy* as more difficult than Joyce's *Ulysses* but "indubitably" great because of its spontaneous qualities.

See also Putney (660).

C. *A Sentimental Journey*

"Affable Hawk" [Desmond MacCarthy]. ["The Sentimental   [650]
Journey" (*sic*)] under "Books in General," *New Statesman*, XXI (1923), 620.
　　Random remarks on the novel in reference to Sterne's
travels to France during wartime and in reference to the
factual elements in the book.

Bensly, Edward. "Anecdote of Laurence Sterne," *N&Q*, 12th   [651]
ser., VIII (1921), 215.
　　Commenting on item in *ibid.*, p. 129, suggests that the
anecdote anticipates a passage in *A Sentimental Journey*,
III. See reply, *ibid.*, IX (1921), 55.

Cash, Arthur Hill. "Sterne's Comedy of Moral Sentiments: A   [652]
Revaluation of the *Journey*," *DA*, XXII (1962), 4013-4014.
　　A Columbia University dissertation. Supports view of
Sterne as a humorist initiated by Jean Paul Richter and
followed by Coleridge, Edmond Scherer, and Sir Herbert
Read: namely, that Sterne sees as laughable the clash of
man's fleshly lusts with his high ideals. Sees the *Journey*
as a "comedy of common moral problems" with Sterne's
ethical rationalism (as found in the sermons) as its underlying assumption. Cf. Cash (750) and Czerny (851).

———. *Sterne's Comedy of Moral Sentiments: The Ethical*   [652a]
Dimension of the "Journey." (A MHRA Monograph: Du-
quesne Studies Phil. Ser., 6). Introduction by Herbert
Read. Pittsburgh: Duquesne University Press, 1966.
　　A revision of 652 above.

Legnani, Emilio Sioli. "L'avventura milanese di Sterne con la   [653]
'Marquesina di F*** fu 'fabbricata di pianta,'" *English
Miscellany*, VI (1955), 247-257.
　　Concerns the identity of the lady of Sterne's Milanese
adventure.

MacLean, Kenneth. "Imagination and Sympathy: Sterne and   [654]
Adam Smith." *JHI*, X (1949), 399-410.

Uses Smith's doctrine of sympathy in his *Theory of Moral Sentiments* to assist in explaining the rhapsodies of the *Journal* and the pathetic vignettes of the *Journey*. Demonstrates that sympathy like Yorick's has no moral consequences and provides "welcome support for the view that *A Sentimental Journey* is a comedy through which the equivocal figure of Yorick wanders, seldom at the right time doing the right thing, often saying or thinking the wrong."—Reviewed by Putney, *PQ*, XXIX (1950), 300. See Dilworth (329), Putney (659).

Mander, Gerald P. "The Shorn Lamb." Correspondence in [654a]
    TLS, July 17, 1937, p. 528.
    The possible original of the famous phrase in the French inscription on a card from the pack of a "Juvenile Card Game," *circa* 1750.

Milic, Louis T. "Sterne and Smollett's *Travels*." *N&Q*, CCI, [655]
    N.S. III (1956), 80-81.
    Contends that *A Sentimental Journey* parodies the *Travels* throughout. Cf. 658.

Murakami, Shikō. "On *A Sentimental Journey*," *Studies in* [656]
    English Literature (Tokyo), XV (1934-1935), 345-359. [In Japanese]
    See 383.

Palmer, A. Smythe. "Swift's Starling," *N&Q*, 9th ser., X [657]
    (1902), 325.
    Mary Cholmondeley's *Red Pottage* opens with a line assigning Sterne's starling in *A Sentimental Journey* to Swift. Another inaccurate allusion (a thrush for the starling) in Mrs. B. M. Croker's *The Cat's-Paw* is cited by Walter Jerrold, *ibid.*, p. 451.

Pons, Emile. "Le 'Voyage' genre littéraire au XVIIIe siècle," [658]
    Bulletin de la Faculté des Lettres de Strasbourg, IV (1926), 201-207.
    Suggests that *A Sentimental Journey* should be studied in relation to the *genre* of travel accounts as it developed in England, with particular reference to Smollett's *Travels Through France and Italy* and Arthur Young's *Travels in France*. Cf. 655, 665.

Putney, Rufus D. S. "The Evolution of *A Sentimental Jour-* [659]
    ney," *PQ*, XIX (1940), 349-369.

A defense of Sterne against the charge of excessive sentimentality, regarding the *Journey* as a "hoax." See below.

————. "Laurence Sterne, Apostle of Laughter" in *The Age of Johnson: Essays Presented to Chauncey Brewster Tinker.* New Haven: Yale University Press, 1949. Pp. 159-170. Reprinted in *Eighteenth-Century English Literature: Modern Essays in Criticism,* edited by James. L. Clifford. New York: Oxford University Press, 1959. Pp. 274-284.   [660]

An essay of first importance extending the attitude toward Sterne expressed in the essay above to the interpretation of his whole literary production. Contends that a misunderstanding of *A Sentimental Journey* is chiefly responsible for giving Sterne a reputation of "lachrymose sensibility" and insists that to call Sterne a sentimentalist in the usual sense of the term is to ignore his "hard core of comic irony." Cf. Dilworth (329), Dyson (331).

Quennell, Peter. ["*A Sentimental Journey*"] under "Books in General," *New Statesman and Nation,* XVIII (1939), 523-524.   [661]

See 246.

Stout, Gardner Dominick, Jr. "Laurence Sterne: *A Sentimental Journey through France and Italy* by Mr. Yorick. Edited with an Introduction and Notes. In Two Volumes," *DA,* XXIV (1963), 305.   [662]

A Stanford University dissertation. Introduction contains a critical interpretation of *A Sentimental Journey* as a comic "Pilgrim's Progress" for an "Age of Sensibility," an analysis of the textual authority of the first edition, and a study of extant MSS, with special reference to the Morgan Library MS. See below.

————. "Sterne's Borrowings from Bishop Joseph Hall's *Quo Vadis,*" *ELN,* II (1965), 196-200.   [662a]

Yorick's comments in the preface to *A Sentimental Journey* on the disadvantages of travel are largely borrowed from Bishop Hall.

————. "Yorick's *Sentimental Journey*: A Comic 'Pilgrim's Progress' for the Man of Feeling," *ELH,* XXX (1963), 395-412.   [663]

Argues that both the "sentimental" and the comic

"handles" of the novel can be reconciled as comprehensive aspects of a unified comic vision of human existence. See 622 above and McKillop's *Early Masters* (375).

Ulanov, Barry. "Sterne and Fielding: The Allegory of Irony," in *Sources and Resources: The Literary Traditions of Christian Humanism.* Westminster, Md.: Newman Press, 1960. Pp. 206-227.   [664]
Sterne's first sermon, an "Inquiry after Happiness" as it reflects on the interpretation of *A Sentimental Journey,* with particular attention to ironic method.

Vrooman, Alan H. "The Origin and Development of the *Sentimental Journey* as a Work of Travel Literature and of Sensibility." Unpublished Ph.D. dissertation, Princeton University, 1940. (Ann Arbor: University Microfilm, 1952.)   [665]
See Pons (658), Putney (659).

Woolf, Virginia. "A Sentimental Journey," *TLS,* Dec. 7, 1922, p. 808.   [666]
A review of *A Sentimental Journey* in Abbey Classics (155). See below and 159.

———. "The 'Sentimental Journey.'" *The Common Reader: Second Series.* London: Leonard and Virginia Woolf at the Hogarth Press, 1932. Pp. 78-85.   [667]
Reprints the introduction to the World's Classics edition (159).—"[Sterne] was travelling in France, indeed, but the road was often through his own mind, and his chief adventures were . . . the emotions of his own heart," the assertion of the goodness of which becomes the novel's chief fault. The novel does develop something fundamentally philosophic—the "philosophy of pleasure." See 829.

See also 301, 307, 308, 318, 328, 329, 338, 341, 388, 395.

D. The Letters

Bond, Richmond P. "Eighteenth Century Correspondence: A Survey," *SP,* XXXIII (1936), 575.   [700]
Comments on the Curtis edition of the *Letters* (177).

Cash, Arthur Hill. "Some New Sterne Letters," *TLS,* April 8, 1965, p. 284.   [701]

From the Hertfordshire County Records Office, a short note and two letters from Sterne to Dr. Henry Egerton, written in the critical winter of 1762, together with three letters of a traveling companion, Richard Phelps. See Monkman (710).

Clark, Edwin. "Sterne's Letters are a Mystery," *TBR*, January [702] 15, 1928, pp. 1, 25.
Occasioned by the publication of R. Brimley Johnson's edition of the letters (176). Discusses problems of forgeries raised by Curtis (177) and neither adequately considered by Johnson nor countered by Shaw (712).

Curtis, Lewis Perry. "Forged Letters of Laurence Sterne," [703] *PMLA*, L (1935), 1076-1106.
Examines forty-seven doubtful letters, demonstrating why they cannot be attributed to Sterne. See 177.

———. "New Light on Sterne," *MLN*, LXXVI (1961), 498-501. [704]
Letters acquired by the Bodleian in 1957, five from the Reverend Thomas Newton to the Reverend John Dealtary, referring to the early volumes of *Tristram Shandy,* and one from Sterne to Dealtary—the earliest known letter of the novelist.

———. "Sterne and 'Sentimental,'" *TLS*, June 23, 1927, p. 440. [705]
Raises question of the authenticity of four letters written to Mrs. Sterne (Elizabeth Lumley) in 1740. Reply by M. R. B. Shaw, *ibid.,* July 21, 1927, p. 504 (712). See Allen (301) and Clark (702).

Fluchère, Henri. "Laurence Sterne et William Combe: vol, [706] plagiat, imitation?" *RAA*, VIII (1931), 313-328.
Cites reasons for believing and doubting the authenticity of the *Second Journal to Eliza,* edited by M. R. B. Shaw (179), concluding that Miss Shaw's reasoning is far from convincing.

———. "Sterne épistolier," *RAA*, XIII (1936), 297-310. [707]
Occasioned by Curtis's edition of the *Letters* (177). Discusses aspects of Sterne's character and art revealed in his correspondence.—"Il est moderne . . . et proche de nous, qu'il revendique la totalité des risques qu'il court à exposer ainsi sous le pronom *Je.*"

Irving, William H. *The Providence of Wit in the English Let-*   [708]
ter *Writers.* Durham, North Carolina: Duke University
Press, 1955. Pp. 268-270 and *passim.*
    Stresses the "charming tone of informality" and the
"sentimentality" of the letters, giving somewhat short
shrift to Sterne as a major letter writer in his century.

Milic, Louis T. "A Sterne Letter Re-Dated," *N&Q*, CCI, N.S.   [709]
III (1956), 212-213.
    Offers evidence for redating Letter No. 158, p. 269 in
Curtis (177).

Monkman, Kenneth. "Some New Sterne Letters," *TLS*, May   [710]
. 6, 1965, p. 356.
    How Sterne met Dr. Henry Egerton. See Cash (701).

Shaw, Margaret R. B. "Letters of Laurence Sterne," *TLS*,   [711]
June 6, 1935, p. 364.
    Challenges reviewer of Curtis's edition of the *Letters*
in *TLS*, March 21, 1935, p. 173, as well as Curtis himself,
especially on the matter of Lydia Medalle's alterations of
the letters.

———. "Sterne's 'Letters to His Wife,'" *TLS*, July 21, 1927, p.   [712]
504.
    Replying to Curtis (705), argues chiefly on internal
evidence that the letters involved were written in 1740
and are not forgeries. See Clark (702).

Shepperson, Archibald B. "Yorick as Ministering Angel,"   [713]
VQR, XXX (1954), 54-66.
    Five letters that Sterne wrote in 1763 in Toulouse on
the occasion of the death of an English acquaintance.

Tupper, James W. "Sterne as a Letter-Writer," *Dial*, LIII   [714]
(1912), 51-52.
    An article based on Melville's *Life and Letters* (172).
Contends that the letters are more valuable as biographical material than as literature, for in them there is "no distinguished style, no real humor, no convincingly genuine
feeling throughout."—See 232.

Wasserman, Earl R. "Unedited Letters by Sterne, Hume, and   [715]
Rousseau," *MLN*, LXVI (1951), 73-80.
    A reprint of texts of letters in *European Magazine*
(1825-1826) hitherto unnoticed.

Wild, John. *Unpublished Letters from the Collection of John*   [716]
    Wild, selected and edited by R. N. Carew Hunt. London:
    P. Allen and Co., 1930.
        Includes letter to Dodsley, No. 37 in Curtis (117).

See also 16, 171-179.

E. The Sermons

Cash, Arthur H. "The Sermon in *Tristram Shandy*," *ELH*,   [750]
    XXXI (1961), 395-417.
        Demonstrates the ways in which *The Abuses of Con-
        science Considered*—published first as a pamphlet in 1750,
        second in *Tristram Shandy*, and third in the last volume of
        the sermons that Sterne himself saw through the press—
        is typical of Sterne's ethics as a whole. Cf. 644.

Hammond, Lansing Van der Heyden. *Laurence Sterne's*   [751]
    "Sermons of Mr. Yorick." (Yale Studies in English, Vol.
    108) New Haven: Yale University Press, 1948.
        First detailed study of the sermons with the objective
        of determining the extent of the borrowings and of estab-
        lishing Sterne's theological position. Absolves Sterne of
        "having attempted conscious literary deception" and of
        heresy, while admitting that he had more interest in
        philanthropy and virtues kindred to it than to doctrinal
        Christianity. Finds most of the verbatim copying in the
        posthumously published sermons (Vols. V-VII) and
        argues that many of the discourses were composed prior
        to 1751. Valuable appendix demonstrating Sterne's use
        of his sources. Cf. 664, 750.—Reviewed by Margaret Gren-
        nan in *MLN*, LXIV (1949), 141; by James A. Work in
        JEGP, XLVIII (1949), 154-156; by Edith Morley in
        YWES, XXIX (1948), 222-223; by J. M. S. Tompkins in
        RES, I (1949), 364-366.

Voitle, Robert. *Samuel Johnson the Moralist.* Cambridge: [752]
    Harvard University Press, 1961. P. 130.
        Comments on Sermon VII in Vol. I, "Vindication of
        Human Nature," to the effect that "on such optimistic esti-
        mates of humanity . . . was based the cult of feeling."

See also 664.

V

Literary Reputation

Brown, Herbert R. "Richardson and Sterne in the *Massachu-*   [800]
setts Magazine," New England Quarterly, V (1932), 65-82.
    Sterne was ecstatically praised as the "high priest
of the cult of sensibility" during the existence of the magazine (1789-96), though he was at times charged with
"gross laxity." Against this latter charge, however, he was
not without champions. Also notes influences. Cf. Coad
(818) and McDowell (826).

Cornu, Donald. "Shandy in America," *N&Q,* CXCVI (1951),   [801]
273-274.
    Evidence of "recent" and appreciative reading of *Tris-*
tram Shandy in letters of Captain Lewis Ourry, serving
in America from 1756-65.

Davis, Richard Beale. *Intellectual Life in Jefferson's Virginia,*   [801a]
1790-1830. Chapel Hill: University of North Carolina
Press, 1964. Pp. 81, 103, 109, 294, 373, 405.
    Incidental references to the popularity of Sterne in the
period indicated.

Findeisen, Helmut. "Lorenzo-Kult in Seifersdorf," *Zeitschrift*   [802]
für Anglistik und Amerikanistik (East Berlin), VI (1958),
51-53.
    Monuments in Seifersdorfer Tal northeast of Dresden
showing the impression made there by Sterne and Edward Young.

Hewett-Thayer, Harvey W. See Thayer, Harvey Waterman.

Howes, Alan B. *Yorick and the Critics: Sterne's Reputation in*   [803]
England, 1760-1868. (Yale Studies in English, Vol. 139)
New Haven: Yale University Press, 1958.

A thoroughgoing and a highly valuable study of the
reputation within the limits indicated. Deals with the immediate reaction to the serial publication of the novel,
the development of the novel into a "classic," the matter of
"beauties" and Bowdlerization, the question of sources
and plagiarism, the "rediscovery" of *Tristram Shandy,* the
Victorian dilemma.—Reviewed by A. D. McKillop, *PQ,*
XXXVIII (1959), 349; by D. W. Jefferson in *MLR,* LIV
(1959), 598-599; in *TLS,* January 16, 1959, p. 30; by Lee
Morgan in *Books Abroad,* XXXIII (1959), 352.

Thayer, Harvey Waterman. *Laurence Sterne in Germany: A*   [804]
*Contribution to the Study of the Literary Relations of
England and Germany in the Eighteenth Century.* New
York: The Macmillan Company, 1905.
A Columbia University dissertation. Based largely on
German periodical literature of the eighteenth century,
this study contends that Sterne's fame in Germany was due
almost solely to *A Sentimental Journey.*—"The story of
Laurence Sterne in Germany is an individual example of
sweeping popularity, servile admiration, extensive limita-
tion, and concomitant opposition." Valuable bibliography.
—See review of Thomas Stockman Baker, *MLN,* XXII
(1907), 89-94.

See also 505, 556, 582, 818a, 828, 837, 843, 851, 853, 878,
882, 886, 887.

VI

Literary Influences,
Affinities, and Imitations

A. British and American

Beaty, Frederick L. "Ae Spark o' Nature's Fire," *ELN*, I [810]
(1964), 203-207.
    Although *Tristram Shandy* is the source of the famous
stanza in the "Epistle to J. Lapraik," the stanza is best
understood as a rejection of Pope's view of the ancients in
Part I of the *Essay on Criticism* in favor of Addison's
view on "great natural geniuses" in the *Spectator*. See
Maxwell (824).

Behrmann, Friedrich. *Laurence Sterne und sein Einfluss auf* [811]
die englische Prosa des achtzehnten Jahrhunderts.
Lachen: A. Kessler, 1936.
    A University of Zurich dissertation. After surveying
the judgment of Sterne in the eighteenth century (the de-
tractors, the admirers, the reasons for Sterne's success),
the author analyzes Sterne's manner of writing, treating in
detail the imitations in separate publications and in
periodicals. An appendix considers the question of the
Second Journal to Eliza and provides an index of imitations. See Shaw (179), Howes (803), Shepperson (834),
Tompkins (837).

———. "Samuel Paterson and Sterne," *N&Q*, CLXV (1933), [812]
247.
    Paterson's defense against the charge of the *Critical
Review* that he had imitated *A Sentimental Journey*.

Bensly, Edward. "Dickens and Sterne," *N&Q*, 9th ser., V   [813]
(1900), 185-186.
A comparison of two passages in *Tristram Shandy* and
Pickwick Papers.

Blackstone, B. *Virginia Woolf: A Commentary.* London: Ho-   [814]
garth Press; New York: Harcourt, Brace and Company,
1949. Pp. 246 and *passim.*
Sterne's appeal to and his influence on Mrs. Woolf.
Cf. 817, 829.

Boll, Ernest. "*At Mrs. Lippincote's* and *Tristram Shandy,*"   [815]
MLN, LXV (1950), 119-121.
An echo of Sterne in a novel of Elizabeth Taylor.

Brown, Herbert R. *The Sentimental Novel in America,*   [816]
1789-1860. Durham: Duke University Press, 1940. Pp.
74-99.
Influence of Sterne on American writers and readers.
Cf. McDowell (826).

Brown, Robert Curtis. "Laurence Sterne and Virginia Woolf: [817]
A Study in Literary Continuity," *UKCR*, XXVI (1959),
153-159.
Both novelists modeled structure on the "operative
character of consciousness," believing that "the only true
reality exists in the inner flow of thought," to be sought in
"the moment of being," that each moment presents a new
viewpoint altering existence, and that life exists fully in
"what is thought small." Both created characters who tried
to impose an artificial pattern on existence. Cf. 814, 829.

Coad, Oral Sumner. *William Dunlap: A Study of His Life*   [818]
and Works and His Place in Contemporary Culture. New
York: The Dunlap Society, 1917.
The most extensive treatment of Sterne's influence on
the early American dramatist, William Dunlap (1766-
1839) in such plays as *The Father; or, American Shandy-
ism,* a sentimental comedy, and *Sterne's Maria; or, The
Vintage,* an opera with music by Pelisier. This material is
essentially summarized by Arthur Hobson Quinn in *The
History of the American Drama from the Beginning to the
Civil War,* rev. ed., New York, 1943, pp. 74-76.
See Brown (800).

Fradin, Joseph I. "Edward Bulwer-Lytton and Lawrence [*sic*] Sterne, *History of Ideas News Letter*, II (1956), 74-76.
    A note on Sterne's influence on Bulwer-Lytton, completely ignoring Franz Heinrich (820). [819]

Gross, Seymour L. "Laurence Sterne and Eliot's 'Prufrock:' An Object Lesson in Explication," *CE*, XIX (1957), 72-73.
    Similarity between a line in "Prufrock" and a supposed passage in a letter of Sterne, the latter of which—as I. B. Cauthen, Jr., points out in *CE*, XIX (1957), 157—was not by Sterne at all but by W. B. C. Watkins, who composed it as the epigraph to the chapter on Sterne in his *Perilous Balance* (259), p. 99. [819a]

Heinrich, Franz. *Laurence Sterne und Edward Bulwer (Lord Lytton)*. Buttstädt: Fr. Kühn, 1904.
    A Leipzig University dissertation. A study of the influence of Sterne on Bulwer-Lytton's experiment in eighteenth-century humor published anonymously in *Blackwood's Magazine*: namely, *The Caxtons* (1849), *My Novel* (1850), and *What Will He Do With It* (1858). Cf. 819. [820]

Hirn, Yrjö. *Den gamla postvagnen och några av dess passagerare*. Helsingfors, 1926.
    A study of Sterne and George Borrow. [821]

Horn, Andreas. *Byron's "Don Juan" and the Eighteenth-Century Novel*. (Schweizer Anglistische Arbeiten, 51) Bern: Francke, 1962.
    Contains a chapter relating Byron's "subjectivism" to Sterne's. [822]

Loofbourow, John. *Thackeray and the Form of Fiction*. Princeton: Princeton University Press, 1964. Pp. 10, 14, 16, 78, 79, 125.
    Incidental comments on the influence of Sterne on the form of Thackeray's fiction. [822a]

Ludwig, Albert. "Zwei Kleinigkeiten zu Dickens. 1. Zu Dickens und Sterne," *Archiv*, CLVI (1929), 235-236.
    Similarities between Mr. Jarndyce in *Bleak House* and Sterne's friend, John Hall-Stevenson, in their eccentric reaction to the East Wind. [823]

Maxwell, J. C. "Burns: An Echo of *Tristram Shandy*," *N&Q*,   [824]
VIII (1961), 302.
   Possible echo in "Epistle to J. Lapraik," stanza 13.
See Beaty (810).

Mayo, Robert D. "The Imitators of Sterne" in *The English*   [825]
Novel in the Magazines, 1740-1815. Evanston: Northwest-
ern University Press, 1962. Pp. 336-346.
   Chronicles the long parade of Shandean imitations in
the miscellanies that "for more than forty years is one of
the dreariest chapters in magazine history."

McDowell, Tremaine. "Sensibility in the Eighteenth-Century   [826]
American Novel," *SP*, XXIV (1927), 383-402.
   Influence of Sterne on such early American novelists
as Mrs. Sarah Morton, Mrs. Susannah Rowson, and Mrs.
Hannah Webster Foster. Cf. Brown (816).

Melchiori, Georgio. *The Tightrope Walkers: Studies of Man-*   [827]
nerism in Modern English Literature. London: Routledge
& Paul; New York: The Macmillan Company, 1956.
Pp. 41-45 and *passim*.
   In discussing the influence of Sterne on Joyce, the author demonstrates the considerable number of "points of
contact" between *Tristram Shandy* and *Ulysses* in concepts, structure, and materials. Cf. Rubin (832).

Monk, Samuel Holt. "Laurence Sterne at Princeton," *Prince-*   [828]
ton University Library Chronicle, X (1949), 137-139.
   The letter book of correspondence between Samuel
Stanhope Smith, seventh president of Princeton, and his
cousins Samuel and Susan Shippen Blair as "a charming
and surprising record of the impact of Sterne on a cultivated and sophisticated group in late eighteenth-century
America."

"Mrs. Woolf and Sterne," *TLS*, January 10, 1929, p. 25.   [829]
   Occasioned by Mrs. Woolf's edition of *A Sentimental*
Journey in World's Classics (159). Mrs. Woolf's introduction reflects affinities between herself and Sterne. See 814,
817.

   CCXXXVIII (1932), 761-763.
   Corrects André Fontainas's elaboration on Edgar Allan
Poe's attribution of the authorship of the *Koran* to Sterne

in "Mallarmé et Victor Hugo," *ibid.*, CCXXXVIII (1932), 71. Cf. Tompkins (963).

Pearce, Roy Harvey. "Sterne and Sensibility in American [831]
Diaries," *MLN*, LIX (1944), 403-407.
    Imitation of Sterne particularly in the four short travel
diaries, 1777-1779, of William Ellery. Other evidences of
sensibility (not Shandean) in other diaries.

Rubin, Louis D., Jr. "Joyce and Sterne: A Study in Affinity," [832]
Hopkins Review, III (1950), 14-22.
    Sterne and Joyce shared a common interest in a tech-
nique "known variously as the association of ideas and the
stream of consciousness," as well as a similar approach to
temporal duration. More fundamentally they held the
basic view of life as a tragi-comic situation. Cf. 827.

Russell, John. *Henry Green: Nine Novels and an Unpacked* [833]
Bag. New Brunswick, N.J.: Rutger's University Press,
1960. P. 251.
    Relates Green's humor to that of Sterne and Lewis
Carroll.

Shepperson, Archibald Bolling. "The Offspring of Tristram [834]
Shandy" in *The Novel in Motley: A History of the Bur-*
lesque Novel in English. Cambridge, Mass.: Harvard University Press, 1936. Pp. 39-60.
    Burlesquers and imitators chiefly picked up Sterne's
"cheap devices of eccentric typography, plagiarism, and
indecency. . . . Except in a few instances . . . the burlesques missed fire and the imitations were uninspired."
Cf. Behrmann (811), Tompkins (837).

Stidson, Russell Osborne. " 'The Doctor' and 'Tristram [835]
Shandy,'" *Dial*, LVIII (1915), 293.
    Similarities between Southey's miscellany and Sterne's
novel. Though in material used, "the two books resemble
one another unmistakably," . . . "the vigorous and stable
views of life" in the former are not found in the latter.

Thompson, Harold William. *A Scottish Man of Feeling: Hen-* [836]
ry Mackenzie. London and New York: Oxford University
Press, 1931. Pp. 102-104 and *passim.*
    Though Mackenzie borrows from Sterne, he "feels that
this writer has betrayed his friends. Wit of this kind will
not do if you are to be a sincere sentimentalist."

Tompkins, J. M. S. *The Popular Novel in England, 1770-*   [837]
    1800. London: Constable, 1932; Lincoln, Nebraska: Uni-
    versity of Nebraska Press, 1961 [Reprint]. Pp. 50-54.
        The imitations of Sterne.—"Sterne's great revelation to
    his age was the significance of the small and of the fleet-
    ing; and he excels in capturing the evanescent colour of
    a momentarily perfect but unconfirmed intimacy, a fellow-
    ship built on a breath and dissolved with a breath, but
    nevertheless, as he felt and persuaded his age to feel, of
    infinite value." See Behrmann (811), Shepperson (834).

V. R. " 'Esmond': An Allusion," *N&Q*, CLXXII (1937), 189.   [838]
        A possible reference to Sterne's famous valet, La
    Fleur, in Thackeray's novel.

Wasserman, Earl R. "Byron and Sterne," *MLN*, LXX (1955),   [839]
    25.
        Sees direct evidence of influence of "Slawkenbergius's
    Tale" on *Don Juan.* See also Baker (304), Brown (800).

B. Continental

Aglianò, Sebastiano. "Gli Anni di Lorenzo Sterne," *Belfagor,*   [840]
    VII (1952), 106-108.
        An error in the computation of Sterne's life-span in re-
    lation to the Italian translation of the inscription on
    Sterne's tomb by "two masons," involving Ugo Foscolo
    and others. See 856.

Alciatore, Jules C. "Stendhal, Sterne et Chamfort," *MLN,*   [841]
    LXXV (1960), 582-585.
        An epigraph in Stendhal attributed to Sterne is prob-
    ably by Chamfort.

Baldwin, Charles Sears. "The Literary Influence of Sterne in   [842]
    France," *PMLA*, XVII (1902), 221-236.
        Minimizes Sterne's influence in France. See 843.

Barton, Francis Brown. *Étude sur l'Influence de Laurence*   [843]
    Sterne en France au dix-huitième Siècle. Paris: Hachette
    et Cie., 1911.
        University of Paris dissertation. The first exhaustive
    study of influence and imitations. Cf. 842.

————. "Laurence Sterne and Charles Nodier, *MP*, XIV   [844]
(1916), 217-228.
    The influence of Sterne seems most apparent when
Nodier writes for his own amusement or "when he wished
to let fly a dart at *Messieurs les savants.*" Cf. Baldwin
(842).

————. "Laurence Sterne and Théophile Gautier," *MP*, XVI   [845]
(1918), 205-212.
    Sterne's influence is important in Gautier only in those
works that are "hors-d'oeuvres—nothing more." Cf. Baldwin (842).

Binni, Walter. "Sterne e Foscolo," *Lo Spettatore Italiano*, July   [846]
1, 1948, pp. 105-107.
    See 856.

Booth, Wayne C. "Thomas Mann and Eighteenth Century   [847]
Comic Fiction," *Furioso*, VI, No. 1 (1951), 25-36.
    A bright and salutary satire on literary source-hunting,
arguing that Sterne is not only "the fountainhead of all
modern literature" but also the "culminating receptacle of
all previous development." Cf. 894.

Brix, Hans. *Tristram Shandy—Citater in 'Levned og Men-*   [848]
inger.' Copenhagen: Gyldendal, 1938.
    See also *Undersögelser i den aeldre danske*, IV (1938),
159-161.—Sterne and the autobiography of Johannes Ewals
(1743-1781), the greatest Danish lyric poet.

Corbellini, Mario. "La versione foscoliana de Viaggio di   [849]
Sterne," *Ulisse*, IX (1955), 567-571.
    A *Sentimental Journey* as translated by Ugo Foscolo.
See 856, 857.

Cru, Robert Loyalty. *Diderot as a Disciple of English*   [850]
Thought. New York: Columbia University Press, 1913.
Pp. 97, 373-89, 451.
    Sterne's influence on Diderot. Cf. Baldwin (842) and
Fredman (858).

Czerny, Johann. *Sterne, Hippel und Jean Paul.* (Forschungen   [851]
zur neueren Literaturgeschichte. Herausgegeben von Dr.
Franz Muncker, Professor an der Universität München,
XXVII) Berlin: Alexander Duncker, 1904.

An attempt to determine the exact relationship of Jean
Paul [Richter] to two of his favorite literary figures and
thus to prepare the way for a philological treatment of the
poet. Chapters on the reputation of Sterne and on his influence in England and Germany. See 652-890.—Reviewed
by R. M. Werner in *Deutsche Literaturzeitung*, XXV
(1904), 286 ff; by P. Landau in *Studien zur vergleichen-
den Literaturgeschichte*, VI (1906), 283; and by J. Firm-
ery in *Revue Germanique*, IV (1908), 58 ff.

De Robertis, Guiseppe. "Foscolo-Sterne-Didimo," *Paragone*,   [852]
II (December, 1951), 3-7.
    See 856.

Devonshire, M. G. *The English Novel in France, 1830-1870.*   [853]
London: University of London Press, 1929. Pp. 90-92.
    Translations of Sterne in France and their audience.
Cf. 10.

Doernenburg, Emil. "W. Raabe und Laurence Sterne," *Mit-   [854]
teilungen für die Gesellschaft der Freunde Wilhelm
Raabes*, XXIX (1939), 10-18.
    The concept of *Eigenheiten* [singularity] in Sterne,
Goethe, and Wilhelm Raabe (*pseud.* Jakob Corvinus),
poet and novelist, 1831-1910. Cf. Klingemann (866).

Erämetsä, Erik. "Über den englischen Einfluss auf den deut-   [855]
schen Wortvorrat des 18. Jahrhunderts," *Neuphilologische
Mitteilungen*, LIX (1958), 34-40.
    Based on words in novels by Fielding, Richardson,
Mackenzie, Sterne, and Goldsmith.

Fasano, Pino. "L' 'Amicizia' Foscolo-Sterne e la Traduzione   [856]
Didimea del *Sentimental Journey*," *English Miscellany*,
XIV (1963), 115-169.
    Critics tend to explain Foscolo's 1820 translation of *A
Sentimental Journey* by talking of a "modern" Foscolo,
a Sterne-Foscolo, ignoring the facts of the "friendship" between the two writers that can be traced for twenty years,
beginning with parallels between Sterne's "poor Maria"
and the episode in Foscolo's *Ultimi Lettre di Jacopo Orti*,
Part One (c.1798) dealing with Lauretta. See 849, 852,
857, 877.

Foligno, Cesare. "Sterne and Foscolo," *N&Q*, CLXXI [857]
(1936), 29.
Concerns Foscolo's translation of *A Sentimental Journey* in Pisa, 1813. See 856.

Fredman, Alice G. *Diderot and Sterne*. New York: King's [858]
Crown Press, 1955.
This study has two purposes: (1) to demonstrate how
both Sterne and Diderot were attempting to break away
from certain aspects of the neo-classical manner and how
they in doing so arrived at modes of literary expression
foreshadowing Romanticism; (2) to defend Diderot from
a charge of plagiarism. See also *DA*, XIV (1954), 108-
109, and cf. 842, 850, 873, 875.—Reviewed by Lodwick
Hartley in *SAQ*, LIV (1955), 564-565; in *TLS*, July 8,
1955, p. 382; by A. D. McKillop in *PQ*, XXXV (1956),
327-329; by Richard T. Arndt in *History of Ideas News
Letter*, II (1956), 39-42; by H. Brugmans in *Neophilol-
ogus*, XL (1956), 152; by Herbert Dieckmann in *MLN*,
LXXI (1956), 615-617; by James Doolittle in *Romanic
Review*, XLVII (1956), 145-146; by Rodney E. Harris in
Comp. Lit., VIII (1956), 268-269; by J. R. Smiley in
JEGP, LV (1956), 330-331; by R. Nicklaus in *MLR*, LIII
(1957), 115; by J. C. Sallé in *RES*, N.S., VIII (1957), 98-
99. See Warning (899a).

Glaesener, Henri. "Laurence Sterne et Xavier de Maistre," [859]
Revue de Littérature Comparée, VII (1927), 459-479.
Examines the influence of *A Sentimental Journey* on
Abbé Xavier de Maistre's *Voyage autour de ma chambre*
and *Expédition nocturne*. See Baldwin (842) and Barton
(843).

Green, Frederick Charles. *Minuet: A Critical Survey of* [860]
*French and English Literary Ideas in the Eighteenth Cen-
tury*. London: J. M. Dent; New York: E. P. Dutton, 1935.
Pp. 457, 459-463.
Praises Diderot to the disparagement of Sterne. See
Barton (843).

Hallamore, Gertrude Joyce. *Das Bild Laurence Sternes in* [861]
Deutschland von der Aufklärung bis zur Romantik. (Ger-
manische Studien, Heft 172) Berlin: Verlag Dr. Emil
Ebering, 1936.
A University of Munich dissertation. Treats Sterne's
part in and influence upon German intellectual history

during two generations of writers. See Ransmeier (886)
and Vacano (897).–Reviewed by W. Baungart in *Zeitschrift für deutsche Phil.*, LXIV (1939), 119.

Harper, Kenneth E. "A Russian Critic and *Tristram Shandy*,"   [862]
MP, LII (1954), 92-99.
A study of *Tristram Shandy* by Victor Shklovsky, St.
Petersburg, 1921. See 600, 894.

Hayes, Joseph C. *Laurence Sterne and Jean Paul [Richter].*   [863]
New York: Privately printed?, 1939.
An abridgement of a New York University dissertation.
Bibliographical footnotes. See 851.

Hearn, Lafcadio. *A History of English Literature*, edited by   [864]
R. Tanabe and T. Ochiai. Tokyo: The Hokuseido Press,
1938. Pp. 390-397.
The relationship of Sterne to French literature.

Jones, C. F. "The French Sources of Sterne." Unpublished   [865]
dissertation, University of London, 1931.

Klingemann, Gisbert. *Goethes Verhältnis zu Laurence Sterne.*   [866]
Marburg: J. Hamel, 1929.
A Philipps-Universität dissertation. Discusses Goethe's
use of *Eigenheiten* in the structure of the novel in the
Wanderjahre and his association of the concept expressly
with Sterne. Goethe differs from Sterne in that the concept is not a source of humor and that it is ultimately
given a mythical and mystical explanation. See Doernenburg (854) and Price (881).

Kupper, Helmut. *Jean Pauls "Wuz."* Halle (Saale): M. Niemeyer. 1928.   [867]
The relationship of Sterne and Jean Paul [Richter].
See 851.–Reviewed by H. Ahrbeck in *Zeitschrift für
deutsche Phil.*, XLIX (1930), 196 ff.; by L. Mis in *Revue
Germanique*, XXI (1930), 59 ff.

Kyrieleis, Richard. *Moritz August v. Thümmels Roman "Reise*   [868]
in d. mittäglichen Provinzen von Frankreich." (Beiträge
zur deutschen Literaturwissenschaft) Marburg, 1908.
Sterne's influence on Thümmel. See Thayer (804) and
Price (881) for summary.

L. C.-M. "Sterne in Italy," *Athenaeum,* 1 October 1920, p.   [869]
451.
A review of Rabizzani's posthumous *Sterne in Italia*
(885).

Lang, D. M. "Sterne and Radischev: An Episode in Russian   [870]
Sentimentalism," *Revue de Littérature Comparée,* XXI
(1947), 254-260.
Influence of *A Sentimental Journey* on Alexander
Radishchev's *Journey from St. Petersburg to Moscow,*
1790.

Lange, Victor. "Erzählformen im Roman des achtzehnten   [871]
Jahrhunderts," *Anglia,* LXXVI (1958), 142 ff.
The relationship of Goethe's *Werther* to Sterne. See
903.

Lohman, F. Louise W. M. Buisman-de Savornin. *Laurence*   [872]
Sterne en der Nederlandse schrijvers van c. 1780-c.1840.
Wageningen, 1939.
The influence and reputation of Sterne in Holland.

Loy J. Robert. *Diderot's Determined Fatalist.* New York: [873]
King's Crown Press, 1950. Pp. 32-50.
The most extensive exoneration of Diderot from the
charge of the deleterious influence of Sterne in *Jacques le*
Fataliste. See 858.

Lussky, Alfred E. *Tieck's Romantic Irony with Special Em-*   [874]
phasis upon the Influence of Cervantes, Sterne, and Goe-
the. Chapel Hill: University of North Carolina Press,
1932.
Shows similarity of ironic methods and devices in Cervantes, Sterne, and Goethe, and the influence of these
writers on Tieck.

Majut, J. "Some Literary Affiliations of Georg Büchner with   [874a]
England," *MLR,* L (1955), 35-36.
Sterne and Büchner.

Mayoux, Jean-Jacques. "Diderot and the Technique of Mod-   [875]
ern Literature," *MLR,* XXXI (1936), 524.
"Sterne was to a great extent Diderot's model in
Jacques; but the waywardness of narrative and caprice of
digression which is with Sterne a portrait of the mind . . .

is with Diderot a portrait of life, as it appears: a substantial and significant difference." Cf. 858.

McCormick, C. A. "Foscolo's Two Theories of Translation [876] and the Version of the 'Sentimental Journey,'" *AUMLA*, XVIII (1962), 198-209.
   See 846, 856, 877.

Messeri, Anna Laura. "La prima traduzione italiana del [877] 'Viaggio Sentimentale' di Sterne," *Revista di Letteratura Moderne*, V (1954), 102-103.
   See 846, 856, 876.

Michelson, Peter. *Laurence Sterne und der deutsche Roman* [878] *des achtzehnten Jahrhunderts.* (Palaestra, Band 232) Göttingen: Vandenhoeck & Ruprecht, 1962.
   An exhaustive study of Sterne's influence on the German novel, beginning with a consideration of the form of Sterne's novels, the German translations, and the imitations, proceeding to a discussion of Sterne's influence on J. G. Schummel's "Sentimental Journey through Germany," on Friedrich von Blankenburg's theory of the novel, on C. M. Wieland's treatment of the eccentric character, on M. A. von Thümmel's treatment of the travels of a hypochondriac, T. G. Von Hippel's view of the world as chaos, and, finally, the cleavage in Jean Paul [Richter]. Cf. 851.—Reviewed by Paul Goetsch in *Die neueren Sprachen*, XI (1962), 386-387; by Horst Heldmann in *Germanisch-Romanische Monatsschrift*, XLIV (1963), 224-227; by Roy Paschal in *German Life and Letters*, n.s., XVI (1963), 149-150; by Guy Stern in *JEGP*, LXII (1963), 858-860; by Reinhold Grimm in *RLC*, XXXVIII (1964), 161-163; by Eberhard Reichmann in *Monatshefte*, LVI (1965), 135-137.

Partridge, Eric. "Deux Dettes Anglaises de Gautier" in *A* [879] *Critical Medley.* Paris: H. Champion, 1926.
   The influence of Thomson and Sterne on Théophile Gautier. Cf. 845.

Pinger, W. R. Richard. "Laurence Sterne and Goethe," *Uni-* [880] *versity of California Publications in Modern Philology*, X (1920-1925), 1-65.
   Materials (including a paper read by Professor Pinger to the Pacific Coast Division of the American Philological

Association in 1901) compiled and edited by Lawrence M. Price (881), cataloguing Goethe's references and allusions to Sterne and demonstrating how Goethe made Sterne "a companion," imitating his whimsical manner of expression "most charmingly" in his more intimate personal correspondence, showing his delight at being free from the conventional shackles of logic and pedantry. Cf. 866.

Price, Lawrence Marsden. *English>German Literary Influences: Bibliography and Survey.* (University of California Publications in Modern Philology, IX) Berkeley: University of California Press, 1919. Pp. 316-333 and *passim.*   [881]
    A survey of Sterne's influence and reputation, with important comments on studies by Vacano (897), Czerny (851), Thayer (804), Kyrieleis (868), *et al.*

———. "Sterne" in *The Reception of English Literature in Germany.* Berkeley: University of California Press, 1932. Pp. 232-247.   [882]
    An important revision of the earlier survey. Bibliography of first importance.

———. "Sterne and the Sentimental Novel," in *English Literature in Germany.* (University of California Publications in Modern Philology, XXXVII) Berkeley: University of California Press, 1953. Pp. 193-206.   [883]
    The final version of Price's monumental study. Repeats essentially the survey of Sterne in the 1932 edition. Revised bibliography.

———. "The Pilgrim Journeys of Bunyan and Heinrich Jung-Stilling," *Comp. Lit.,* XII (1960), 14-18.   [884]
    Stilling's acknowledged indebtedness to Sterne.

Rabizzani, Giovanni. *Sterne in Italia, Riflessi Nostrani dell'-Umorismo Sentimentale.* With a preface by Odoardo Gori. Rome: A. F. Formiggini [1920].   [885]
    The first section treats Sterne in Italy as he was known through the translation of Ugo Foscolo. The second deals with Sterne's influence on the Romanticists: Guerrazi, Bini, Leopardi, Pananti e Giusti, Ferri di S. Costante, Lorenzo Borsini, Guiseppe Torelli, Carlo Varese. See 869.

Ransmeier, J. C. "Heines 'Reisebilder' und Laurence Sterne," *Archiv,* CXVIII (1907), 289-317.   [886]
    See Hallamore (861) and Vacano (897).

Reeve, Franklin Dolier. "Through Hell on a Hobby-Horse, [887]
Notes on Gogol and Sterne," *Symposium*, XIII (1959), 73-
87.
Reviews popularity and influence of Sterne in Russia
with special reference to Gogol.—"[Gogol] and Sterne are
concerned with the immediate, the traditional, the percep-
tible, the fanciful, and not so much with actual and in-
ternal machinations."

Rosati, Salvatore. "Laurence Sterne" in *Enciclopedia Italiana*. [888]
Rome: Instituto della Enciclopedia Italiano, 1949. Vol.
XXXII, 721-723.
Contains brief discussion of Sterne's influence in Italy.
Bibliography.

Rudy, Peter. "Young Tolstoy and Laurence Sterne," *DA*, [889]
XVII (1957), 1756.
A Columbia University dissertation. Sterne was a
"favorite author" of the young Tolstoy, who was influenced particularly by *A Sentimental Journey* and the *Sermons*.

Schmitz, Werner. *Die Empfindsamkeit Jean Pauls*. (Beiträge [890]
zur neueren Literaturgeschichte, XV) Heidelberg: C.
Winter, 1930.
The relationship of Sterne and Jean Paul [Richter].
Cf. 652, 851.—Reviewed by E. Berend in *Deutsche Litera-
turzeitung*, XIII (1931), 1070-1072; by G. Bianquis in
Revue Germanique, XXII (1931), 331.

Schneider, Ferdinand Joseph. "Studien zu Th. G. von Hip- [892]
pels 'Lebensläufen'" u. "Über den Humor L. Sternes und
Th. G. von Hippels," *Euphorion*, XXII (1915), 678-702.
Summarized in Price, *Reception* (882), p. 241.

Seidlin, Oskar. "Ironische Brüderschaft: Thomas Manns *Der* [893]
Ernährer und Laurence Sternes *Tristram Shandy*," *Orbis
litterarum*, XIII (1958), 44-63.
See below.

———. "Laurence Sterne's *Tristram Shandy* and Thomas [893a]
Mann's *Joseph the Provider*," *MLQ*, VIII (1947), 101-118.
Reprinted in Seidlin, *Essays in German and Comparative
Literature*. (Studies in Comparative Literature) Chapel
Hill: University of North Carolina, 1961. Pp. 182-202.

See above and cf. Jonas Lesser, *Thomas Mann in der Epoche seiner Vollendung* (München: K. Desch [1952]), p. 323; also 847.

Shklovsky, Victor. *"Eugene Onegin": Pushkin and Sterne.* [894]
(Studies in Pushkin's Poetry, No. 3) Berlin: Epocha, 1923.
[In Russian]
See Harper (862).

Texte, Joseph. *Jean-Jacques Rousseau and the Cosmopolitan* [895]
Spirit in Literature. Trans. by J. W. Matthews. New
York: Stechert, 1929 [1895]. Pp. 277-291.
Sterne's influence in France in a reprint of a classic
critical work.

Thayer, Harvey Waterman. "Thümmel's *Reise* and Laurence [896]
Sterne," *MLN*, XXIV (1909), 6-8.
One of the most important German imitations of *A
Sentimental Journey.* Cf. 878.

Vacano, Stefan. *Heine und Sterne.* Berlin: F. Fontane & [897]
Company, 1907.
For summary, see Hallamore (861) and cf. brief treatment of Heine's admiration and feeling of kinship for
Sterne in Laura Hofrichter's *Heinrich Heine*, trans. by Bar-
ker Fairley (Oxford: The Clarendon Press, 1963), pp. 78-
79.—Reviewed by F. Baldensperger in *Revue Germanique*,
III (1907), 617; by M. Koch in *Deutsche Literaturzeitung*
(1908), 100; by F. Kratz in *Anglia Beiblatt*, XX (1909),
46-48; by R. F. Arnold in *Literarisches Echo*, XII (1910),
670-671.

van Tieghem, Paul. "Quelques aspects de la sensibilité pré- [898]
romantique dans le roman européen au XVIIIe siècle,"
Edda, XXVII (1927), 172 ff.
Sterne's influence as promoter of "disinterested tears."
Cf. 337.

Varese, Claudio. *Linguaggio Sterniano e Linguaggio Fosco-* [899]
liano. (Biblioteca del Leonardo, 38) Florence, 1947.

Warning, Reiner. "Fiktion und Wirklichkeit in Sternes Tris- [899a]
tram Shandy und Diderots Jacques le Fataliste" in
Nachahmung und Illusion, edited by H. R. Jauß. München
Eidos Verlag, 1964.
Cf. Fredman (858).

Wedel, Erwin. "L. N. Tolstojs Übersetzung von L. Sternes   [900]
    *A Sentimental Journey through France and Italy," Die
    Welt der Slaven*, V (1960), 425-451.
        See 889.

Weintraub, W. "Alexander Fredro and His Anti-Romantic   [901]
    Memoirs," *American Slavic Review*, XII (1953), 535-548.
        Fredro's model is *Tristram Shandy*.

Wellek, René, and Austin Warren. *Theory of Literature.*   [902]
    New York: Harcourt, Brace and Company, 1942. Pp. 212-
    213.
        A significant brief discussion of the influence of Sterne
    as the "founder" of a line of novels in the "romantic-ironic"
    mode of epic narration particularly on Jean Paul Richter
    and Tieck in Germany, and Veltman and Gogol in Russia.

Wundt, M. *Goethes Wilhelm Meister*. Berlin u. Leipzig,   [903]
    1913. Pp. 493-507.
        The relationship of Sterne and Goethe. For summary,
    see Price (881). Cf. Lang (871).

For other comment on literary influences and relations, see
    341, 342, 351, 354, 372, 408, 421, 500, 519, 521, 573.

VII

Miscellaneous

Bensly, Edward. " 'The Glorious Uncertainty of the Law:'   [950]
    Sterne and Maclin," *N&Q*, CLVII (1929), 294-295.
      The possibly coincidental use of similar phrases by
Sterne and Maclin.

――. "Inaccurate Allusions to Sterne, Thackeray, and Dick-   [951]
    ens," *N&Q*, 9th ser., X (1902), 5.
      Inaccuracies in an article by T. S. Escott in the *Sketch*
of February 19, 1902.

"Digression on Wit," *Golden Book*, II (1925), 12.   [952]
    Quotations from *The Koran*. See 963.

Esdaile, Katherine A. *Life and Works of Louis François*   [953]
    Roubiliac. London: Oxford University Press, 1928. P. 110.
      The portrait bust of Sterne.

Greenwood, Sir George. "Sterne and the Verb *to Lay*," *TLS*,   [954]
    July 6, 1922.
      See comment of R. Pierpont, *ibid.*, July 13.

Hartley, Lodwick. "From Crazy Castle to the House of   [955]
    Usher," *Studies in Short Fiction*, II (1965), 256-261.
      Sterne, John Hall-Stevenson, and Edgar Allan Poe—a
possible literary relationship.

"How Great Men Really Looked," *Life*, XXXIII (Decem-   [956]
    ber 22, 1952), 74.
      Sterne's death mask.

"Little Course in Lovemaking," *Golden Book,* XIV (1931),   [957]
131.
    "The Remise Door, Calais," from *A Sentimental Journey,* reprinted.

"Poo-Poo of Nations," *Golden Book,* XX (1934), 352.   [958]
    Quotes from *Tristram Shandy,* IV, Ch. 21.

"Portrait," *SRL,* V (1929), 1067.   [959]
    Illustration for Mary M. Colum's "The Changing Novel," *ibid.,* pp. 1070-1071.

"Portrait by Joseph Nollekens," *Connoisseur,* LXV (March,   [960]
1923), 135.

Thompson, Karl F. "The Authorship of Yorick's 'Sentimental   [961]
Journey Continued,'" *N&Q,* CXCV (1950), 318-319.
    Argues that John Hall-Stevenson may not have been the author.

"Toleration or Persecution," *Golden Book,* I (1925), 600.   [962]
    Passage on Voltaire's *Toleration,* quoted from spurious *The Koran of the Life, Character and Sentiments of TRIA JUNCTA IN UNO, M.N.A., or Master of No Arts, or Posthumous Works of a Late Celebrated Genius,* not Sterne (as assumed) but Richard Griffith.

Tompkins, J. M. S. "Triglyph and Tristram," *TLS,* July 11,   [963]
1929, p. 558.
    Speculates that Richard Griffith's *Posthumous Works of a Late Celebrated Author* (also known as *The Koran*), though spurious, may contain some echoes of Sterne's conversation. See 830.

Xylographer [pseud.]. "Sterne: Parody," *N&Q,* 9th ser., XII   [964]
(1903), 447.
    Query about the authorship of "Fragments in the manner of Sterne" (1797).

*Appendix**

Coleridge, Samuel Taylor. "Lecture IX. On the Distinctions   [1000]
of the Witty, the Droll, the Odd, and the Humorous" in
Works, edited by William G. T. Shedd. New York, 1871.
IV, 275 ff.
A highly important brief analysis of the metaphysical
basis of humor, with comments on Sterne.

Hazlitt, William. "On the English Novelists" in *English*   [1001]
Comic Writers. (*The Complete Works,* edited by P. P.
Howe) London: J. M. Dent & Sons, 1931. VI, 120-121.
A one-paragraph critical comment of first importance.
Numerous other editions.

Scherer, Edmond. "Laurence Sterne, or the Humorist" in   [1002]
Essays on English Literature, translated by George Saintsbury. New York, 1891. Pp. 150 ff.
Another classic discussion of the nature of humor in
general and Sterne in particular.

Scott, Sir Walter. "Sterne" in *Lives of the Novelists.* With an   [1003]
introduction by Austin Dobson. London, New York, and
Toronto: H. Frowde, Oxford University Press [1906].
A modern reprint of a pioneering biographical sketch.

Thackeray, William Makepeace. "Sterne and Goldsmith" in   [1004]
The English Humorists. (*The Complete Works,* edited
by W. P. Trent and J. B. Henneman) New York: Thomas
Y. Crowell [1904], XXIII, 208-247.
The well-known attack on Sterne as man and writer,
typical of the "Victorian" attitude.

* Basic critical items mentioned in the Essay but not included in the Bibliography.

Traill, H. D. *Sterne.* (English Men of Letters) London, 1882.   [1005]
    Although the biographical material is no longer useful,
the critical comments retain much of their value.

Walckenaer, Charles Athanase. "Laurence Sterne" in *Bio-*   [1006]
    graphie Universelle. Paris, 1825. XL, 229-232.
    An early nineteenth-century attempt to construct a
brief biographical sketch from primary materials.

Addenda

Addenda

Editions

The Life and Opinions of Tristram Shandy, Gentleman. [1100]
Edited by Graham Petrie. Introduction by Christopher
Ricks. (The Penguin English Library.) Baltimore: Pen-
guin Books, Inc., [1967.].
See Ricks (402)

A Sentimental Journey through France and Italy. Edited by [1101]
Graham Petrie. Introduction by A. Alvarez. (The Penguin English Library.) Baltimore: Penguin Books, Inc.,
[1967.].
See Alvarez (1104), reprinted as the introduction to
this edition.

A Sentimental Journey through France and Italy by Mr. Yor-. [1102]
ick. Edited by Gardner B. Stout, Jr. Berkeley: University
of California Press, 1967.
The definitive edition. Valuable introduction, annotation, and appendices. See discussion above, pp. 42 and
154-155. Cf. Milic (1144) and Vrooman (665).

Books and Articles: Critical, Biographical, and Miscellaneous

Alter, Robert. "*Tristram Shandy* and the Game of Love," [1103]
American Scholar, XXXVII (1968), 316-323.
Sterne's sexual comedy is "the indispensable means
[for him] to say what he has to say." Opposing Locke,
Sterne rehabilitates wit, making it the basis of communication in *Tristram Shandy* and of his whole peculiar narrative
method. Wit is chiefly sexual because "sexuality energizes
the imagination, [and] invites it to free and rapid play."

Alvarez, A. "The Delinquent Aesthetic," *Hudson Review,* [1104]
XIX (1966), 590-600.

Sees Sterne's work as "evolving a style of pure talk, of controlled inconsequentiality, irrelevance and continual interruption," like the "modern 'cool' style with its controlled and detached delinquency."

Anderson, Howard. "Sterne's Letters: Consciousness and Sympathy" in *The Familiar Letter in the Eighteenth Century*, edited by Howard Anderson, Philip B. Daghlian, and Irvin Ehrenpreis. Lawrence: University of Kansas Press, 1966. Pp. 130-134. [1105]

Relates Sterne's fictive techniques (verbal associationism, allusiveness, witty indecision, dramatic casting) to his letters, comparing the effect of the best of these with that of the unfictionalized *Journal to Eliza*. Cf. Fluchère (707).

———. "*Tristram Shandy*: A History of the Human Mind," *DA*, XXVI (1965), 351. [1106]

A University of Minnesota dissertation.—Like his Renaissance and Augustan forebears, Sterne emphasizes the irrational in human nature, differing from earlier writers in accepting the illogical character of thought as universal and "natural" and insisting on the comprehension and the use of the irrational in achieving the understanding and sympathy necessary for human society to exist. Thus he achieves a moral purpose. In his moral and social values, as in many of his literary techniques, he is close to the Renaissance comic tradition.

———. "A Version of Pastoral: Class and Society in *Tristram Shandy*," *Studies in English Literature*, VII (1967), 508-529. [1107]

Attempts an Empsonian interpretation, contending that with apparently artless techniques Sterne achieves aims at once comic and serious. By placing "both his narrator and the milieu of his novel outside of ordinary contemporary society—making his narrator a clown (a country man and a jester) and his milieu the rural past—Sterne provides himself with a point of vantage which reveals some of the limitations of modern society."

Arntzen, H. *Satirischer Stil: zur Satire Robert Musils im "Mann ohne Eigenschaften."* Bonn: H. Bouvier, 1960. [1108]

Possible influence of Sterne, among others, on Robert Musil's novel.

Boyce, George K. "Modern Language Manuscripts in the Mor- [1109]
gan Library," *PMLA*, LXVII (1952), 21-22.
Sterne manuscripts, with special reference to that of *A
Sentimental Journey*, considered to be in a hand other than
that of the novelist. Cf. T. J. Brown (5).

Brandi-Dohrn, B. *Der Einfluss Laurence Sternes auf Jean* [1110]
Paul. Studie zum Problem des literarischen Einflusses.
Munich dissertation, 1964.
Cf. 851, 863, 867, 878.

Carr, John Dixon. *The Demoniacs*. New York: Harper & [1111]
Row, 1962; Bantam ed., 1964.
An historical mystery novel in which Sterne appears as
a minor comic figure.

Cash, Arthur H. "Who Was Sterne's Mother?" *N & Q*, XIV [1112]
(1967), 162-169.
A thoroughgoing re-examination of the case of the identity of Agnes Sterne, concluding that, since there is no
really satisfactory solution to the puzzle of evidence,
Sterne's own statement that she was the daughter of a poor
sutler must be accepted.

Chatterjee, Ambarnarth. "Dramatic Technique in *Tristram* [1113]
Shandy," *Indian Journal of English Studies* (Calcutta),
VI (1965), 33-43.
Discusses Sterne's use of theatrical metaphor, his dramatic presentation of ideas and feelings, and his extensive
employment of gesture.—"By . . . adroitly exploiting some
of the devices of dramatic technique, Sterne brings to his
scenes the vividness of actuality, invests his ideas with
the effect of the spoken word, and thus succeeds in draw-
ing his readers more intimately into the world of his creation." Cf. Hafter (1121), Hartley (1124).

Craven, Kenneth. "Laurence Sterne and Russia: Four Case [1114]
Studies." Columbia University dissertation, 1967.
The influence of Sterne on Radischev, Karamazin,
Pushkin, and Tolstoy. Emphasis on the importance of
what Sterne contributed to the content and style of the
novel in addition to what he contributed in sentimentalism
and form. See 862, 870, 889, 894, 900, 902.

Cruttwell, Patrick. "Makers and Persons," *Hudson Review*, [1115]
XII (1959-60), 487-507.

Contains some rather obvious remarks on Sterne's use
of Tristram and Yorick as masks—the one "Bohemian,
Rabelaisian, complacently incompetent at the ordinary
business of living"; the other, "the sentimental parson,
knowing himself doomed to an early death, the cultivator
of the tearful smile."

Damf, Martha Savannah. *"Tristram Shandy*: A Dramatic   [1116]
Adaptation," Master's thesis, Vanderbilt University, 1966.
An attempt to explore the dramatic potentialities of the
novel by extracting a script for the stage from it. Cf.
Chatterjee (1113).

Donovan, Robert Alan. *The Shaping Vision: Imagination in*   [1117]
the English Novel from Defoe to Dickens. Ithaca: Cornell
University Press, 1966.
Contains chapter on *Tristram Shandy*, examining
Sterne's language and irony.

Fletcher, John. "Beckett and the Fictional Tradition," *Caliban*   [1118]
(Annales pub. par la Faculté des Lettres et Sciences Hu-
maines de Toulouse), N. S. I, i (1965), 147-158.
Samuel Beckett's indebtedness to the eighteenth-century tradition, especially to Sterne in the use of irony, the
"self-conscious" narrator, and the picaresque elements. Cf.
Kenner (1138).

Goodin, George, "The Comic as a Critique of Reason: *Tris-*   [1119]
tram Shandy," *CE*, XXIX (1967), 206-223.
"The form of the comic forces it to be critical of reason
. . . the subject matter of a comic scene may also be the
operations of reason. If this is the case with many comic
scenes in a work [as in *Tristram Shandy*], and if the choral
comment is largely concerned with mental operations, the
work itself may be seen as a critique of reason."

Grebenickova, Ruzena. "Sterne módszere a Dosztojevszkij   [1120]
elötti orosz regényben," *Helikon*, XI (1965), 394-399.
Sterne's method in the Russian novel before Dostoyev-
ski.

Hafter, Ronald. "Garrick and *Tristram Shandy*," *Studies in*   [1121]
English Literature, VII (1967), 475-479.
Explores the influence of Garrick's challenge to the
formalism of the "old" school of acting on the formation of
Sterne's prose style, as well as Sterne's use of Garrick's au-

thority in defending "his own seemingly idiosyncratic style." Cf. Chatterjee (1113), Hartley (1124).

Hamilton, Harlan W. "William Combe and *The Original* [1122] *Letters of the Late Reverend Mr. Laurence Sterne* (1788)," *PMLA*, LXXXII (1967), 420-429.
  Argues for William Combe's authorship of "most of the contents" of these letters on the basis of the fact that thirty-three of them were printed first in the *Daily Universal Register* when Combe was most active in that publication. Discusses at length Combe's probable method of fabrication by weaving bits and pieces of Sterne's own writing into the fabric of the book; and concludes that "the letters, as we have them, whether authentic, imitative, or mixed, set forth facts about Sterne and Combe which biographers must treat with cautious respect."

Hartley, Lodwick. "The Eustace-Sterne Correspondence: [1123] A Note on Sterne's Reputation in America," *ELN*, V (1968), 175-183.
  A background and textual study of a famous exchange of letters between the novelist and a North Carolina physician.

———. "Laurence Sterne and the Eighteenth-Century Stage," [1124] *Papers on Language and Literature*, IV (1968), 144-157.
  Argues against an exaggeration of the influence of the stage on Sterne's fictional style, pointing to other influence and observing that eighteenth-century attempts to dramatize Sterne's novels tend to emphasize their nondramaturgic qualities. Cf. Chatterjee (1113), Hafter (1121).

Hnatko, Eugene. "*Tristram Shandy's* Wit," *JEGP*, LXIV [1125] (1965), 47-64.
  Analyzes basic elements of Sterne's wit as (1) a deliberate compounding of a conventional means of representing a mode of reality with reality itself (as in the handling of time); (2) an extensive use of what to neoclassic critics would have been heterogeneous terms engaged in similitude—by means of the extension of a metaphor into further points of correspondence and the repetition of dominant metaphors; (3) a peculiar irony growing out of an adopted "blind spot"; and (4) a displacement of emphasis on some aspect of discourse. See 353.

Hohoff, Curt. *Schnittpunkte. Gesammelte Aufsätze.* Stutt- [1126]
gart: Deutsche, Verlags-Anstalt, 1963.
   Includes essay on Sterne. Reviewed by P. K. Kurz in
Stimmen der Zeit, CLXXIV (1964), 77-78.

Holman, C. Hugh. "The Loneliness at the Core," *The New* [1127]
Republic, CXIII (October 10, 1955), 16-17. Reprinted in
The Idea of an American Novel, edited by Louis D. Rubin,
Jr., and John Rees Moore. New York: Thomas Y. Crowell
Co., 1961. Pp. 348-351.
   A comparison between *Look Homeward, Angel* and
Tristram Shandy, contending that essentially both books
are family novels whose authors "were oppressed by the
tragic sense of human insularity."

Holtz, William. "The Journey and the Picture: The Art of [1128]
Sterne and Hogarth," *BNYPL,* LXXI (1967), 25-38.
   "A pictorialist theory of literature and a literary theory
of painting" brought Sterne and Hogarth together. "Given
the objective mode of their art, they in some measure
achieved a complementary mode in the objective realm."

———. "Literary Pictorialism and *Tristram Shandy,*" DA, XXV [1129]
(1965), 7269-7270.
   A University of Michigan dissertation—Discusses the
tradition of literary pictorialism and its vigorous flowering
in neoclassical England as a background for understanding
the bizarre and whimsical in Sterne. See above and below.

———. "Pictures for Parson Yorick: Laurence Sterne's Visit [1130]
of 1760," *Eighteenth-Century Studies,* I (1968), 169-184.
   Concerns the relationship among Sterne, Hogarth, and
Reynolds, involving their theories of art. See 218, 368,
500, 519.

———. "Sterne, Reynolds, and Hogarth: Biographical In- [1131]
ferences from a Borrowing," *Art Bulletin,* XLVIII (March,
1966), 82-84.
   See Brissenden (519) for an identification of the same
borrowing with a different emphasis.

———. "Time's Chariot and *Tristram Shandy,*" *Michigan* [1132]
Quarterly Review, V (Summer, 1966), 179-203.
   "In a very real sense [Sterne's] effort in *Tristram*
Shandy was to achieve the effects of simultaneity and co-
existence that Lessing would reserve for pictorial art. . . ."

[He] opened a new dimension in literature: the imitation of that ever-changing but essentially static inner identity which all men feel but which can be expressed only by devices that transcend the temporal nature of language and of narrative." See 569 and above.

———. "Yorick and the Rotary Club," *Yale University Library Gazette*, XL (1966), 28-30.   [1133]
A curious imitation of Sterne in J. R. Perkins's *A Thin Volume*. The author is an Iowa prison warden and a Rotarian who "translates Sterne's humanitarianism into an enlightened business ethic."

Isaacs, Neils D. "The Autoerotic Metaphor in Joyce, Sterne, Lawrence, Stephens, and Whitman," *Literature and Psychology*, XV (Winter, 1965), 92-106.   [1134]
In *Tristram Shandy*, Book V, Chapter 15, Sterne describes an autoerotic interlude in terms of practicing on a violin. Cf. Alter (1103).

James, Overton Philip. *The Relation of Tristram Shandy to the Life of Sterne*. (Studies in English Literature, XXII). The Hague: Mouton & Co., 1966.   [1135]
A revised version of a Vanderbilt University dissertation, examining the old question of the extent to which *Tristram Shandy* is autobiographical. See 561.

Jennings, Edward Morton. "Reader-Narrative Relationships in *Tom Jones, Tristram Shandy*, and *Humphrey Clinker*." *DA*, XXVI (1965), 3303-3304.   [1136]
University of Wisconsin dissertation—Discusses the "narrative distance" in the three novels.

Johnson, Maurice. "A Comic Homunculus before *Tristram Shandy*," *The Library Chronicle*, XXXI (1965), 83-90.   [1137]
The History of the Human Heart: or, The Adventures of a Young Gentleman (1749), a rare anonymous piece in the Singer-Mendenhall Collection of English fiction in the Rare Book Collection of the University of Pennsylvania, is cited as another forerunner of Sterne's use of the animalculist view of the homunculus's adventurous travels in search of "a proper Nidus" in the womb. Similarities to *Tristram Shandy* are even more striking than those in Hill's *Lucina sine Concubitu* (1750) pointed out by Landa. See 568.

Kenner, Hugh. *Flaubert, Joyce and Beckett.* Boston: Beacon   [1138]
Press, 1962. Pp. 48-49.
Relates Sterne to the above group of "stoic comedians."
See Stedmond (1161), p. 133 and *n* for reference to
similar treatment by Marshall McLuhan in *The Gutenberg Galaxy* (Toronto: University of Toronto Press, 1962,
p. 252), and Christopher Ricks, *The Listener,* December 17, 1964, p. 964. Cf. Fletcher (1118).

Klukoff, Philip J. "Two Smollett Attributions in the 'Critical   [1139]
Review': 'The Reverie' and 'Tristram Shandy,'" *N & Q,*
XIII (1966), 465-466.
Smollett's presumed review of *Tristram Shandy* in the
Critical Review is used to make an assumption as to the
authorship of *The Reverie.*

Lutwack, Leonard. "Mixed and Uniform Prose Styles in the   [1140]
Novel," *The Journal of Aesthetic and Art Criticism,*
XVIII (1960), 350-357.
Reprinted in Stevick (1165).—Sees *Tristram Shandy*
and *Moby Dick* as "early attempts to depart from conventional style for first-person narration by exploiting the idio-
syncrasies of the narrator's language."

MacLean, Kenneth. "The Imagination in *Tristram Shandy,*"   [1141]
Explorations; Studies in Culture and Communication,
edited by E. S. Carpenter (Toronto), III (August, 1954),
59-64.
Sterne's anticipation of Coleridge's definition. Cf. 654.

Mayoux, Jean-Jacques. "At the Source of Symbolism," *Criti-*   [1142]
cism, I (1959), 279-297.
Diderot's view of individual organization came from
Tristram Shandy. See 875.

McGlynn, Paul D. "Laurence Sterne's Religion: The Ser-   [1143]
mons and Novels." Rice University dissertation, 1967.
Argues that Sterne's Latitudinarian Anglicanism, as
manifested in his sermons, is a major influence on the characterization, themes, and structures of his novels. Cf.
Hammond (751).

Milic, Louis T. "An Annotated Critical Edition of Sterne's   [1144]
Sentimental Journey." Unpublished Master's thesis, Co-
lumbia University, 1950.
See 655; also Stout (1102) and Vrooman (665).

Miller, David M. "The Reader-Characters in *Tristram* [1145]
Shandy," *Louisiana History*, VII, 2 (Spring, 1966), 13-16.
 The implied author is balanced by several implied
readers, or rather conversers, whose various attitudes draw
replies from Tristram contributing to the satire of the novel
and its *double-entendres*. Cf. Wagoner (1172).

Moglen, Helene S. "The Philosophical Irony of Laurence [1146]
Sterne," *DA*, XXVII (1966), 184A-185A.
 A Yale University dissertation.—A study of the ironic
method and meaning of *Tristram Shandy* made expressive
of one another through the mediating consciousness of the
fictive narrator.

Monkman, Kenneth, and James Diggle. "Yorick and His [1147]
Flock: A New Sterne Letter," *TLS*, March 14, 1968, p. 276.
 A long letter written from Sutton on March 14, 1758, to
Robert Sturdy (?) in which Sterne defends himself from
gossip concerning his extramarital sexual relations. Cf.
Kuist (227).

Moore, Isabel. *Talks in a Library with Laurence Hutton.* [1148]
New York and London: G. P. Putnam's Sons, 1905. Pp.
210-211.
 Discusses the assumption that a death mask in the Laurence Hutton collection in the Princeton University Library may be that of Sterne. See 956.

New, Melvyn. "*Tristram Shandy* as a Prose Satire," Vander- [1149]
bilt University dissertation, 1966.
 Argues that the primary organization of *Tristram
Shandy* is metaphorical, the satire moving from an opening
in birth and creation to a conclusion in dissolution and
death. A satiric pattern is everywhere operative, control-
ing the form and function of the work.

Park, William. "Change in the Criticism of the Novel after [1150]
1760," *PQ*, XLVI (1967), 34-41.
 The part played by the appearance of *Tristram Shandy*
in changing the criticism of the novel as a *genre*.

Paulson, Ronald. "Sterne: The Subversion" and "Yorick: [1151]
From Self-Revelation to Self-Analysis" in *Satire and the
Novel in Eighteenth-Century England.* (New Haven
and London: Yale University Press, 1967), pp. 248-265.
 "[Sterne's] particular effect is . . . the romantic irony of

complicating the reader's reaction through satire followed by acceptance." The novelist "picked up one strand of the anti-romantic tradition," achieving "the ultimate expression of a-literature" in the century by "subverting the conventions of Richardson, Swift, and Fielding."

Petrakis, Byron. "Sterne and the Tradition of Christian Folly." [1152] University of Florida dissertation, 1968.

An examination of Sterne's fiction in the light of the Pauline tradition of Christian folly (1 Cor. 1.18-25, 3.18-19, 4.10, and Rom. 1.22). Beginning with a study of the development of the tradition from the Church Fathers to Sterne's day, the thesis focuses on Tristram's turning blame into praise of Yorick's Christian folly in *Tristram Shandy* in much the same way as Erasmus's Stultitia turns blame into praise of the Pauline fool for Christ in *The Praise of Folly*.

Piper, William Bowman. *Laurence Sterne.* (Twayne English [1153] Authors Series, No. 26). New York: Twayne, 1966.
Exhaustive analysis of the fiction, tracing the equivocal qualities in *Tristram Shandy* of the narrator's discourse from their roots in "the essential social unsuitability of his life story," and demonstrating that *A Sentimental Journey* is a kind of empirical fiction with the use of universal benevolence as a central concern.—Reviewed by John Carroll, *University of Toronto Quarterly*, XXXVII (1968), 212-215. See 388, 584, 585.

Reid, Ben L. "Sterne and the Absurd Homunculus," *VQR*, [1154] XLIII (1967), 71-95.
Regards *Tristram Shandy* as "an Anatomy of Hilarity" in which the pose of Shandeism functions as "a bolus of laughter . . . calculated to cleanse and sweeten a bitter concoction." With the life of man conceived as a journey serving as a "co-ordinating metaphor," Sterne concerns himself with "the standard ludicrousness of the Homunculus who is man, inadequate to the event which is life, perpetually too small for his costume," ultimately achieving the catharsis of great comedy that gives us "the purgative spectacle of dignity addressed to fate." Cf. 401, 568.

Resink, G. J. "Tristram, Max en Jim," *De Nieuwe Stem*, XX [1155] (1965), 247-256.

Rexroth, Kenneth. "Classics Revisited-LVIII: *Tristram Shan-* [1156]
dy," *Saturday Review*, (January 20, 1968), p. 15.
    "The message of Tristram Shandy . . . is the constantly
reiterated theme of his now unread sermons which were
unique in a time when the pulpit in England was not distinguished for the clergy's identification with the sufferings
and the absurdities of the lives of the humble." Cf. 750,
751.

Rudy, Peter. "Young Lev Tolstoj's Acquaintance with Sterne's [1157]
Sermons and Griffith's *The Koran*," *Slavic and Eastern
Journal*, IV (XVIII), 2 (Summer, 1960), 119-126.
    Not only did Tolstoy admire *Tristram Shandy* and *A
Sentimental Journey* but he also drew on other items in the
1818 edition of Sterne's collected works, quoting on occasion from the *Sermons* and from *The Koran*—then attributed to Sterne. See Rudy (889).

Simon, Ernest. "A Tradition of the Comic Novel: Sorrel, [1158]
Scarron, Furetière, Sterne, Diderot," *DA*, XXIV (1964),
3732.
    A Columbia University dissertation.—Considers realism
and the comic spirit in five French novels and *Tristram
Shandy*.

Singleton, Marvin. "Trismegistic Tenor and Vehicle in [1159]
Sterne's *Tristram Shandy*," *Papers on Language and Literature*, IV (1968), 158-169.
    The background and influence of Hermetism in Sterne's
novel.

Starkie, Walter F. "Miguel de Cervantes and the English [1160]
Novel," *Essays by Divers Hands Being the Transactions
of the Royal Society of Literature*, XXXIV (1966), 159-179.
    Discusses the influence of Cervantes on Sterne as well
as on other English novelists. See Stout (609a).

Stedmond, John M. *The Comic Art of Laurence Sterne:* [1161]
Convention and Innovation in Tristram Shandy *and* A Sentimental Journey. Toronto: University of Toronto Press,
1967.
    A discussion of context and meaning, genre, style,
satire, and the comic view, with an appendix on plagiarism
and originality. Uses material that previously had ap-

peared in articles in various journals. See 605, 606, 607, 608, and review by R. Paulson, *Studies in English Literature*, VII (1967), 551.

Stephen, Leslie. "Sterne" in *Hours in a Library*, III. London: [1162] John Murray, 1926.

Originally published in 1879, this volume has had numerous reprints. The essay on Sterne is still valuable, though much of its importance in the twentieth century resides in the stimulus that it has provided for the refutation of some of its salient conclusions. See above pp. 17, 103, Watkins (259), and Read (399).

Stevick, Philip. "Fictional Chapters and Open Ends," *Journal* [1163] *of General Education*, XVII (1966), 261-273.

Sterne (pp. 265-266) is included as a part of a general discussion.—Since the raw materials of experience are so intractable to Tristram that the normal conventions of chapter construction violate the novelist's mimetic obligations, the actual transference of such material to the page produces chapters colliding with the reader's expectation. This collision is comic.

———. "The Theory of Fictional Chapters," *Western Humanities Review*, XX (Winter, 1966), 231-234. [1164]

Sterne is considered along with Defoe, Richardson, and Fielding in the display of a range of possibilities in chapter divisions only slightly modified by later novelists.

———, ed. *The Theory of the Novel*. New York: The Free [1165] Press, 1967.

Reprints portions of essays and chapters of Lutwack (1140), Mendilow (574), and Stevick (1164). References to *Tristram Shandy passim*.

Stobie, Margaret. "Walter Shandy: Generative Grammarian," [1166] *Humanities Association Bulletin* (Canada), XVII, i (1966), 13-19.

In the discussion of the *Tristrapoedia* [*sic*], Sterne astonishingly foreshadows the modern conception of the generative nature of language—"the scientific awareness, the idea of the machine, the terms, the role of the child, the capacities of the native speaker, the wealth of examples."

Tennyson, G. B. "The true Shekinah is man," *American* [1167]
Notes and Queries, III, iv (December, 1964), 58.
 In the quotation from St. Chrysostom, borrowed by
Thomas Carlyle by way of *Tristram Shandy,* V, i, the word
used by Chrysostom is not *shekinah* but εἰϰων.

Theobald, D. W. "Philosophy and Imagination: An Eigh- [1168]
teenth-Century Example," *Personalist,* XLVII (1966), 315-
327.
 Tristram Shandy as an illustration of the fringe area
where philosophy and literature interact. Sterne's use of
rhetoric touches upon the central difficulty of ideas and
symbols. Ideas for Sterne are phenomenological in that
he suggests a theory of human consciousness as a total
awareness of diversity in the world through an emotive
apprehension of it. Rationalism is a state of perpetual dis-
appointment with experience. Sterne demonstrates that
the criticism of philosophy by the comic imagination is
possible and effective.

Traugott, John, ed. *Laurence Sterne: A Collection of Critical* [1169]
Essays. (Twentieth Century Views) Englewood Cliffs:
Prentice-Hall, Inc., 1968.
 A collection of essays, most of them reprints of articles
or sections of books by B. H. Lehman, Viktor Shklovsky,
A. A. Mendilow, Jean-Jacques Mayoux, A. D. McKillop,
John Traugott, D. W. Jefferson, and W. B. C. Watkins.
The Mayoux and Shklovsky items are especially translated
for the collection. For another translation of Shklovsky,
see *Russian Formalist Criticism: Four Essays,* edited by
Lee T. Lemon and Marion J. Reis (Lincoln, Nebraska:
University of Nebraska Press, 1965). See also 259, 372,
375, 562, 569, 600, 611, 862.

———. Review of Henri Fluchère's *Laurence Sterne: From* [1170]
Tristram to Yorick, translated and abridged by Barbara
Bray. *English Language Notes,* IV (1967), 297-302.
 Though Fluchère's study is the most comprehensive
that we have and is "keen by fits and starts, it is the victim
of an unfortunate conjunction of English Shandeism, that
comic vision of the world as a reticule of cross accidents,
and the French *thèse de doctorat ès lettres,* that triumph
of the *esprit analytique* which would reduce all the world
to a set of clear headings." Thus the book sees Sterne
ultimately in "bits and pieces" rather than as a whole.

"What is obvious about Sterne," says Traugott pressing his own thesis, "is that he is a sentimentalist. . . . Sterne loves style, and he would say that if a reader can be made to love it, too, how can he not love mankind, that collection of styles?" See 218 and 611.

Trowbridge, Ronald Lee. "The Echoes of Swift and Sterne [1171] in the Works of Thomas Carlyle," *DA*, XXVIII (1967), 2223A.
  A University of Michigan dissertation.—Employing numerous examples of "echoes" in corroboration, this dissertation suggests that the German influence on Carlyle, especially that of Jean Paul Richter, has tended to be overestimated to the neglect of the pervasive influence of Swift and Sterne.

Wagoner, Mary S. "Satire of the Reader in *Tristram Shandy*," [1172] *Texas Studies in Literature and Language*, VIII (1966), 337-344.
  Sterne's subject matter is conversation, the premise being that Tristram is talking "with a reader"—upon whom the author clearly has "ulterior designs" to lure him "into laughing at a parody of the conversation to which he has been party." The reader is addressed some 350 times in the novel. If he participates (that is, by reading), he subjects himself "to Sterne's control and with that to nipping satire." Cf. Booth (514), Piper (584), Miller (1145).

Warning, Rainer. *Illusion und Wirklichkeit in Tristram* [1173] *Shandy und Jacques le Fataliste*. München: Fink, 1965.
  Rev. by Ernest Simon, *MP*, LXIV (1967), 354-357. See 899a.

Watson, Wilfred. "Sterne's Satire on Mechanism: A Study of [1174] *Tristram Shandy*." University of Toronto dissertation, 1951.
  Argues that *Tristram Shandy* can be read as a satirical account of the interaction of Cartesian science and natural philosophy that results in Tristram's materialistic and naturalistic temper.

Watt, Ian. "The Comic Syntax of *Tristram Shandy*" in *Studies* [1175] *in Criticism and Aesthetics, 1660-1800: Essays in Honor of Samuel Holt Monk*, edited by Howard Anderson and John S. Shea. Minneapolis: University of Minnesota Press, 1967. Pp. 315-331.

Discusses Sterne's discovery of a principle of order "which resides not so much in linear development in time as in a kind of timeless consistency of texture . . . [a] primary autonomy . . . which controls every narrative element, from the phrase to the paragraph, the chapter, and the book." Sees the unity of *Tristram Shandy* in an "essentially complex but consistent comic mode of speech." Cf. Traugott (611).

Wendell, Charles Warner. "Narrative Style in Rabelais and   [1176]
Sterne," *DA*, XXV (1965), 4711-4712.
    A Yale University dissertation.—Similarities abound on the technical level, but Rabelais' spatial externalization, requiring sequential progression, is minimized in Sterne as the life of the mental world emphasizes the world of time. Sterne's characterization is fuller than Rabelais' and his technique and tone are more refined. Cf. Wickler (1177).

Wickler, Franz-Joseph. *Rabelais und Sterne*. Bonn, 1963.   [1177]
    A dissertation of the Rheinische Friedrich-Wilhelms-Universität.—Re-examines the relationship of Rabelais and Sterne, discussing Sterne's knowledge of Rabelais, comparing their prose styles and their methods of achieving the comic, and contrasting their temperaments. The conclusion is that, though Rabelais made a definite impression on Sterne's style (*Sprachstil*), he was unable to influence his mentality (*Mentalität*); and that consequently Sterne like others must fall under Rabelais' "Pantagrueline Prognostication" of 1533: "Angleterre, Escosse, les Estrelins, seront assez mauvais Pantagruelistes." Cf. Wendell (1176).

Wulling, Emerson G. *Sterne on Shandyism. Remarks by*   [1178]
Laurence Sterne on His Rhetorical Practice: A Patchwork
Essay. LaCrosse, Wisconsin: Sumac Press, 1949.
    See catalogue of the Huntington Library.

Index of Names

Index of Names

(References are to page numbers)